Decomposing Figures

CYNTHIA CHASE

Decomposing Figures

Rhetorical Readings in the Romantic Tradition

The Johns Hopkins University Press

Baltimore and London

This book has been brought to publication with the generous
assistance of the Andrew W. Mellon Foundation.

The Johns Hopkins University Press
701 West 40th Street
Baltimore, Maryland 21211
The Johns Hopkins Press Ltd., London

The paper used in this publication meets the minimum requirements
of the American National Standard for Information Sciences—Permanence
of Paper for Printed Library Materials, ANSI Z39.48-1984.

Library of Congress Cataloging-in-Publication Data

Chase, Cynthia, 1953–
  Decomposing figures.

  Bibliography: p.
  Includes index.
    1. Romanticism—Europe. 2. European literature—
History and criticism. I. Title.
PN751.C5 1986   809'.9145   85-45868
ISBN 0-8018-3136-9 (alk. paper)

For Jonathan

Contents

Acknowledgments

I would like to thank Ellen Burt, Jonathan Culler, Neil Hertz, Richard Klein, and Philip Lewis for crucial help in thinking through the readings that appear in this book. Other friends and teachers gave me generous encouragement: Reeve Parker, Mary Jacobus, Barbara Johnson, Carol Jacobs, Eve Sedgwick, Andrzej Warminski, and J. Hillis Miller.

For invaluable imaginative and practical help in assembling these chapters, I thank my husband, Jonathan Culler. Without him this book would not exist.

My deepest gratitude is to Paul de Man. My debt to de Man for the thinking he made possible much exceeds what this book could acknowledge.

Chapters 1 and 5 first appeared in *Studies in Romanticism,* copyright by the Trustees of Boston University. Chapter 2 is reprinted from *Romanticism and Language,* ed. Arden Reed, copyright 1984 by Cornell University Press. Used by permission of the publisher, Cornell University Press. Chapter 3 is reprinted from *Lyric Poetry: Beyond New Criticism,* ed. Chaviva Hosek and Patricia Parker, copyright 1985 by Cornell University Press. Used by permission of the publisher, Cornell University Press. An earlier version of chapter 6 appeared in the *Oxford Literary Review.* Reprinted by permission of the editor. Chapter 7 is reprinted by permission of the Modern Language Association of America from *PMLA* 93:2 (March 1978), copyright by the Modern Language Association of America. Chapters 8 and 9 first appeared in *Diacritics,* copyright 1979 and 1981 by Johns Hopkins University Press. Another version of chapter 9 appeared in *Difference in Translation,* ed. Joseph Graham, copyright 1985 by Cornell University Press. Used by permission of the publisher, Cornell University Press.

Introduction

Romanticism, more than any other literary historical concept, has been the target and the occasion of a compelling critique of the basic presuppositions of literary history. This book is an attempt to deal with that situation. Its difficulties arise first from the demonstrated invalidity of a familiar conception of history. That demonstration was partly anonymous and diffuse: the practice of close reading, simply, fostered by the New Criticism, hermeneutics, and structuralism alike, made it hard to characterize literary works in the unequivocal, uncontradictory terms that make them illustrate a period or movement. The difficulty was confirmed and compounded by the writings of a small number of theorists carrying out arguments inimical to the assumptions of New Critical close readings—Jacques Derrida, Paul de Man, and Philippe Lacoue-Labarthe and Jean-Luc Nancy (who called the primary concern of Romanticism *l'absolu littéraire*), to name those whose work seemed most inevitable, most impossible to ignore, and most difficult to come to terms with. Their inquiries into the way any work defines, alludes to, and so eludes its genre effectively undercut attempts to claim definitive authority for generic and historical classifications. [1]

Still graver implications arise from the far-reaching critique of teleology that has emerged in the last thirty years in detailed rereadings of certain philosophical texts (Nietzsche and Heidegger, but also Plato and Hegel): [2] a deconstruction of the genetic model that has been at the heart of the concept of history. Here Romanticism plays a decisive role. For Romanticism has been most tellingly identified, beyond considerations of style and theme, precisely with the full emergence and elaboration of the genetic model, whereby we imagine the intelligibility of the cosmos in terms of an ultimate adequation between origins and ends. This would seem to be the Romantic tradition to which we inevitably still belong, a teleological orientation that is the lasting heritage of Romanticism, transmitting ultimately an orientation of Western thought or philosophy "from its beginnings." One can

1

evoke it, as de Man does, in assertions lifted from Wordsworth or from Hegel: the notion that "origin" is "tendency," that "the end is the same as the beginning, because the beginning is an end" (*Zweck* "purpose," "goal"). Though the density and explicitness of the assertion may feel unfamiliar, it spells out what probably remains our habitual way of thinking (postmodernist technologies and sensibility notwithstanding) and what seems the unavoidable assumption of any history-writing. Even histories that stress the discontinuity and incommensurability of a culture or an epoch assume that events and persons described do constitute and participate in the ultimate unity of the movement of history that consists in their totalization, in their interpretation as moments in a process with some shape and meaning.

Romanticism, though, poses a basic threat to this assumption. For the Romantic texts that apparently affirm and enforce it—and mark the historical moment that consists in the apogee of teleological thinking—exceed and undercut the genetic models they appear to follow. This has been the argument worked out compellingly in rereadings of Rousseau, Hegel, Nietzsche, and Wordsworth, by the critics mentioned earlier and by others, but above all by Paul de Man.[3] Those readings locate the contradiction not at the level of statement, in these texts, but in the interplay between a work's statement and its function, including its function or position in the discourse of literary history. What emerges is that analysis of the rhetorical modes as well as the statements of individual Romantic texts generates an inconclusive or unhistorical scheme: a recurrence of works characterized by genetic patterns they simultaneously retrace and decompose. "If this were the case," de Man writes—characteristically posing the difficulty rather than making the assertion—"one may well wonder what kind of historiography could do justice to the phenomenon of Romanticism, since Romanticism (itself a period concept) would then be the movement that challenges the genetic principle which necessarily underlies all historical narrative."[4]

What happens in testing this inference in the analysis of particular works, as this book seeks to do? De Man's work made writing about literature difficult, if irresistible, by inciting a tense awareness of the implicit claims or assumptions entailed in every interpretive move or rhetorical gesture. In his writing, this pressure generates a continual displacement and reinvention of terms and concepts as well as shifts of rhetorical strategy. What if one attempts to bring together and work out a variety of concepts and characteristic moves; what if one takes this work as an impetus to one's own reading, and to the specially complicated enterprise of writing on Romanticism? That is what I have done in these essays.

Through detailed rhetorical analysis of Romantic and post-Romantic texts, this book attempts to clarify the strategies and stakes of the investigation that has emerged as one of the most crucial and complex projects of recent criticism. The individual studies approach works from different angles but identify common problems; they demonstrate the continuity or complicity between canonical Romantic works such as Rousseau's *Rêveries* or Keats's odes and works not generally considered Romantic: Hegel, in crucial passages distinguishing the sign from the symbol and memory from recollection and imagination; George Eliot, whose *Daniel Deronda* displays the metaleptic structure identified with Nietzsche's critique of the concept of cause; and Freud, whose reading of *Oedipus* construes the dilemma of sexuality as the predicament of textuality.

If there is a Romantic tradition, it would consist, these studies suggest, in the recurrence of an attention to problems of reading that undercut the possibility of tradition in the sense of a handing on intact of values, knowledge, functions, and forms. The Romantic tradition would consist in attention to a mode of inquiry that in fact recedes as an explicit philosophical topic during the Romantic period as the topic of aesthetics comes into prominence. It would consist in attention to rhetoric or tropology—to the tropological capabilities of language construed as the very conditions of knowledge and action.

The rhetorical readings carried out in these chapters take their cue from a study of the impact above all in philosophical texts of the confrontation with rhetoric or "literature" as the "other" of philosophy, a study of how an exclusion and at the same time an exploitation of literary strategies and rhetorical modes (for example, narrative and dialogue) have been vital to the self-construction of philosophical discourse.[5] That rhetoric or persuasion or the "force" of language should be primary, rather than its value as presentation or truth, and that it should be at work as much in "philosophical" as in deliberately rhetorical or fictional discourses, disrupts the privileged status and the truth claims of philosophy, dislodging, first of all, the very practical but also fundamental distinction between "philosophy" and "literature." Rather than making this philosophical argument, which has been worked out in studies of Nietzsche, Heidegger, Rousseau, and Plato, by de Man, Derrida, Lacoue-Labarthe, and others, the essays here reflect its impact on conventions of reading; they pursue its consequences for the practice of interpreting literary texts. The style of these readings, intense interrogation or insistent play with the words and figures of poetic and narrative texts, acknowledges the liquidation of a certain boundary or reserve—that of the "serious" use of language, as distinct from its "nonserious" uses, from enunciations in implicit quotation marks, from fictions. For if it is impossible finally to locate a *proper* statement, an utterance proper to its speaker, a meaning coincident with an intention not qualified by the possibility of quotation, of an implied "as if,"—then the fictional status of enunciations in literary texts does not deprive or relieve them of the sharpest possible significance. (Nor does the ultimately rhetorical or fictional status of "philosophical" discourse imply that it henceforth be read as "only" figures, or as literature. One could argue that it is in fact as literature—as stories—that philosophical texts are read in the traditional study of the "history" of philosophy, or intellectual history.)

A familiar conception of literature, then, as well as of history, falls into abeyance in the wake of the confrontation with rhetoric that these readings attempt to maintain. Literary texts, as much as philosophical texts, become exemplary of the conflictual character of language, or of an "impossibility of reading" that "should not be taken too lightly."[6] It arises from the conflict between what a text "says" and what it "does," or between the constative and the performative dimension of language or rhetoric. The rhetorical character of language, the primacy of rhetorical "force" and figure (that is, of *language*) in any art, constrains us to think "art" from the standpoint of language rather than the inverse.[7] The conflict in rhetoric precludes our understanding literature essentially as art, that is, as the harmonious interpenetration of content and form. Rhetoric thus makes a problem out of art or the aesthetic, insofar as the notion of the aesthetic is predicated upon the possibility of fusion or continuity of form and substance, being and doing. Their *dis*continuity—the forcing, in both senses, of their connection—especially troubles interpretation where it appears as an incompatibility between what a text implicitly says about language and figuration and its own figural structures and effects.

Those very works that identify intelligibility as a tropological product, for example, may adopt strategies that prevent this conclusion from being effectively put to work in the reading of them. In compelling the reader to repeat moves that they identify as errors, texts disrupt their formal as well as their discursive intelligibility. Chapters 1 and 5 of this book show how Wordsworth's and Baudelaire's poetic texts scramble the literal and figural and the metaphorical and metonymical axes along which they are composed; chapters 6 and 7 show George Eliot's and Heinrich von Kleist's narratives setting up strategies or devices for their own rhetorical interpretation that come apart or explode as a certain nonfigural or performative element comes into play. The implicit stake here, which becomes explicit in the final essay, is Kant's concept of aesthetic judgment: the possibility of judgment in general or the passage between perception and will. Baudelaire's rewriting of Rousseau reveals in Rousseau's text a framing of Kant's categories that unsettles the form and value of the ethical or aesthetic paragon, "man" or the work of art.

These readings pursue a project different from the classification and description of particular rhetorical figures in a given literary work. Such analysis is in some degree indispensable, but it is circumscribed here by another inquiry. These readings focus on the figures constitutive of the basic literary modes crucial to Romantic writing: lyric, autobiography, and narrative. Lyric, it is argued here, depends upon the figure of voice, the conception of a text speaking, as autobiography depends upon the figure of face, the conception of a name or text that makes itself intelligible. Voice and face, the basic tropes of lyric poetry and of autobiography, are the focus of the first part of the book; causality, the basic trope of narrative, is the focus of the second. These figures are argued here to be constitutive not simply of literary forms but of any act of understanding.

This book shares the premise of much recent interpretation identifying the Romantic tradition with an exacerbated sense of the *problem* of figurative language. Misgivings about language that acts like alienating "garments" rather than "the air we breathe" (to cite Wordsworth's famous figures in his *Essays upon Epitaphs*), and anxiety about themes and strategies invariably borrowed, inevitably preexisting the writer's intention toward meaning—these mark not only the English Romantic poets but also, critical studies have shown, the works of Freud, George Eliot, and Rousseau. But anxiety of influence and hostility toward "rhetoric" need to be reinterpreted as symptoms of a more radical unease about the implications of figure. Or they need to be reinterpreted, rather, as symptoms of a disturbance that cannot be reflected in or assimilated to the experience of a self or a subject (be it the dis-ease of the writer or reader unable to produce a self-consistent discourse), since this disturbance entails the subversion of intentionality itself. Attention to rhetoric or figure comes to mean, then, in these essays, attention to the uncertainly intentional, significative status of the conditions or constituents of meanings—an uncertainty that disturbs the emergence of any recognizable "face" or figure as the origin or the form of a literary work.

What emerges is disfiguration: a theme, or motif, of several texts read here, as well as a rhetorical effect or process.[8] *Disfigurement* (or *defacement*) is not too strong a word for the impact of these texts on a certain anthropomorphism, or for the condition of Wordsworth's Blind Beggar, Freud's Oedipus, Shelley's Rousseau, but these texts engage us not with images of effects of violence but, rather, with intricately contradictory rhetorical operations. The salient term, then, is *disfiguration,* which, in naming both a rhetorical and physical process or effect and leaving uncertain the relationship between them, exemplifies the interpretive predicament it would describe. *Disfiguration* names the impossibility, coincident with the status of language as rhetoric or figure, of fixing a figure's referential status. It is inherently misleading to discuss and define disfiguration in this way, making abstract, ostensibly literal assertions about effects of interference with assertion or representation. It must be encountered instead by way of readings that attend to the vicissitudes of particular tropes—the erosion, for instance, of the figurality of vital rhetorical figures, with the indetermination of meaning that this entails; for the stripping away of figurality is in no sense an emergence or restoration of *literal* language. It is, rather, a disruption of the logic of figure or form—not only a departure from representation, but the decomposition of the figures forming the text.

The effort must be to encounter, rather than to state, the erosion of the distinction between the literal and the figurative on which reading and meaning depend, although that distinction too (encountering or undergoing versus "knowing") gets undercut in the passages of book 5 of *The Prelude*—Wordsworth's book on "Books"—read here in chapter 1. In *The Prelude* the erosion is exemplified in the crucial word *face,* a figure for figure itself, but also the "ghastly face" of the drowned man risen above the surface of Lake Esthwaite. "Books," fundamentally his own past works, enable Wordsworth to see the disfigured face as a figure—to put a face on the effaced figure. This chapter explores how we repeat Wordsworth's error or restoration, in reading the disfigured face as a figure for the literal, an allegory for disfiguration. Both literal and figurative readings of the passage are in effect hobbled, disqualified, by the strictures and entanglements set up by the text's thematization (or wording or figuring) of its rhetorical figures. The first chapter makes conspicuous from the start what emerges repeatedly in this study: far from implying transparency, or a self-presence that would be the privilege of literary texts, which implicitly or explicitly declare and "know" their status as fictions, the text's thematization of its rhetoric—"self-reflection" or self-referentiality—renders it opaque or discontinuous.

The difficulty for reading shows up in a characteristic way in the narratives analyzed in the second part of the book. The function of language as representation or cognition gets complicated by an insistence on the *force* of representation (or the "power" of reading). A passage of *Daniel Deronda* describes Mordecai's inner vision of his "prefigured friend," a scene matching that in which Deronda in fact appears, as a "coercive type"—a "type" or "image" with "foreshadowing power," with the power to "coerce" into existence the event it purports to reflect or represent.[9] Such a "coercive" recognition combines uneasily with the cognitive, constative status of language. The very stress, in Romantic narrative, on the authority or power of recognition undermines the authority of that power, for it brings into play a productive or performative dimension of language at odds with its cognitive and constative representational function. The power to produce an event—even if, as in Eliot's novel or Kleist's narratives about narration or *Oedipus the King,* it is an event consisting precisely in a recognition or persuasion—is essentially at odds with the function of representing preexisting events or entities. The conflict between the performative and the constative dimensions of language takes the characteristic form, in these narratives, of a conflict between the report of prior events and the discursive production of events, posing the question of how events may be the products of discursive structures, or in *Daniel Deronda*'s terms, how narrative structures are "the present causes of past effects."

Here causality itself appears as a figure or a product of narration rather than as a ground. "Accounting for" an event here means both— incompatibly, and impossibly—explaining it and bringing it about. These narratives ask to be read both as the history of the effects of causes and as the story of "the present causes of past effects," the setting up of the structure that causes the event to appear. Thus, though the historical logic must be otherwise, it is, the reader feels, because Deronda has developed an affinity for Judaism that he turns out to be of Jewish parentage. Such a metaleptic plot structure also marks *Oedipus the King,* and it displays the crucial process for the production of textual and psychic significance that Freud identifies as the main-spring of understanding (and repression): *Nachträglichkeit,* "deferred action." The Oedipal drama involves a structure similar not only to Freud's own situation as investigator (analyst, reader) but to trauma as defined in his case histories, such as that of "Emma." Oedipus's accession to genealogical awareness converts, by deferred action, an act of manslaughter into parricide. Accession to sexual awareness converts, by deferred action, an indifferent episode in Emma's past into a seduction. What is also staged is the process of reading, the deferred action—an event, a structure—that brings about the event, or the meaning, of a text.

Such conclusions suggest the inadequacy of these terms *event, meaning, structure,* the extent to which they are emptied out, lose their validity, in being deployed to describe how a represented event is in effect *produced* by a representation, a discursive structure. The structure or representation, then, is the event—of the production of meaning; and the represented event is part of a structure, rather than an event, since it does not occur by itself. The profound disruption of the logic of narrative by narratives staging their rhetorical power, displaying causality as a trope, a metalepsis, entails the disqualification of basic terms like *event* and *structure,* or *form* and *substance,* to evoke the disjunction at work. This aporia drives a rhetorical reading from the question of the relationship between event and structure to what these texts lead one to discuss in terms of accident or random occurrence, and ultimately, as we shall see, the conflict between positing and figuration.

Chapter 4 deals at length with this problematic. What should be stressed here is how the problem raised in the reading of the narrative— the relationship between story and discourse, between event and structure—is a manifestation of the problem posed by language as rhetoric or figure, the relationship between performative and constative.

This relationship ultimately would lie in the conflict between positing and figure. The capacity for language to "posit"—not in the sense of adopting a position or thesis (the gesture of philosophical argument) but in the sense of laying down what had no previous existence—is the distinctive conception of the performative in the writings of de Man. For J. L. Austin, performative utterances do something rather than report something: they accomplish the actions to which they refer. "I promise to pay you tomorrow" does not make a true or false statement but, by performing the act of promising, brings a promise into existence. This is the aspect of performative stressed in de Man's usage. The performative dimension of language ultimately would lie in the capacity of language not only to recognize or represent attributes of things, to "receive them, so to speak, from the entity itself by merely allowing it to be what it is," but also to posit or postulate entities ("posit," or *setzen,* is the word in the passage in *The Will to Power* from which the distinction between cognitive and performative functions of language, *erkennen* and *setzen,* is being drawn).[10] In distinguishing the truth of propositions from the "felicity" of speech acts, Austin identifies a noncognitive element in discourse. The project of classifying localized performative utterances or illocutionary acts,

such as "marrying," each with special conventions to be observed, ultimately spills over into a conception of all language as performative.
"Stating," the uttering of a true or false proposition, the paradigm of
the constative or cognitive, "seems," Austin admits, "to meet all the
criteria we had for distinguishing the illocutionary act" and is, he concludes, "only one among very numerous speech acts of the illocutionary class."[11] The cognitive functioning of language would thus be
inseparable from this performative condition. A permanent tension
and irreconcilability between them emerges in this study in the most
practical and unavoidable problems of reading and interpretation:
conflicts not just between what a text says and what it does, but between what a text says through various aspects of what it "says" and
what it says through various aspects of what it "does"—conflicting
directives for its reading, incompatible enactments of its rhetorical
status.

If the power of language to act is, as much as the power to know,
a fiction, since a text's achievement of speech acts, engagement, persuasion, are interfered with by its cognitive functions (analytical and
self-descriptive) as much as the other way around, the best conception
of the rhetorical force of language would be the uncertain operation
of a certain kind of machine. Not a body (an integral, responsive
form); a machine, for a machine's functioning, or a text's, involves the
complete estrangement of the meaning of the work performed from
its performance. But this machine's workings are not guaranteed to be
mechanical—predictable or automatic. Its force is repeatedly deflected—
its violence not the causing of destruction, but the intervention of incalculable accident, unseizable chance. The work is not a corpus, but a
text: an exploding machine, as Kleist's text suggests. A machine for
exploding, a machine that explodes.

Yet this is the work we live off. The final chapters of parts 1 and 2
concern the peculiar nourishment afforded us by the Romantic tradition. In these chapters it derives from the proximity of certain texts
of Baudelaire and Hegel and of Baudelaire and Rousseau. These texts,
these figures, can certainly not be said to agree, nor, what is more significant, even to understand or to read one another. What they can be
said to do is to translate or repeat, rewrite in another language—a process of intertextual translation occurring apart from any understanding
or interpreting of the other text. The rapport between Hegel and
Baudelaire, between Baudelaire and Rousseau, is the rapport between
two linguistic functions: not writing and reading (the structure of
understanding or "deferred action"), but writing in one language and
writing in another. The reading that makes these languages speak to

each other (as in these chapters) is also part of the model of translation, but as its inevitable mirage or lure. In chapter 5 it takes the form of the argument that a certain section in Hegel's *Philosophy of Mind* says the same thing as Baudelaire's early poem "Le Soleil." In chapter 9 it takes the form of the very perception of what is paradoxically deemed a nonintentional, noninterpretive reinscription or translation of a resonantly ambiguous word of Rousseau's text in Baudelaire's.

These readings go on to elaborate a model of reading that sharply differentiates between the possibility of addressing and understanding one another—or of agreeing, in the course of saying "the same thing"—and the mode of occurrence of "thinking" (Hegel's word), or of texts. What Hegel and Baudelaire would be saying is that memorization and forgetting, rather than understanding or recollection, are the mode in which thinking and composing occur. The mechanical memory thematized in the passages of *The Philosophy of Mind* juxtaposing *Denken* and *Gedächtnis* (memorization power) is exemplified and named again in Baudelaire's essay "Morale du joujou," which reinscribes one double word from Rousseau's *Neuvième Promenade: Morale's* "diligence," for *Rêveries'* "oublie." The latter word is both an effacement and an inscription of the theme of memory and forgetting. What it means is a kind of cone-shaped wafer—edible, and in the time of Rousseau, won in a game, in considerable numbers evidently, after one paid for chances (as Rousseau does in this story) on the turning of a numbered wheel or turntable. Baudelaire—who surely forgets, and surely reinscribes, this word—becomes a figure, in the last chapter here, for the reader in the Romantic tradition. Such a reader can no more read and understand Rousseau than consume Rousseau's *oublies.* What we do, instead, is eat his words. Take them in, and take them back. That is to say, no effort of memory or attention could be adequate to the burden of the rhetorical reading imposed by the Romantic tradition. These chapters try to translate that reflection.

I

Mutable Images

Voice and Figure

The Accidents of Disfiguration

Limits to Literal and Figurative Reading of Wordsworth's "Books"

> The grounds are so disposed as to disguise and to hide: something, always a body in some way. But also to disguise the act of hiding and to hide the disguise: the crypt hides as it holds. Carved out of nature, sometimes making use of probability or facts, these grounds are not natural.
>
> —Derrida, "Fors"

Book 5 of Wordsworth's *Prelude* begins with a lament for the fragility of its titular topic, for an utter vulnerability to damaging accidents:

> Why, gifted with such powers to send abroad
> Her spirit, must it lodge in shrines so frail?
>
> (1805, 5.47–48)[1]

With this prologue, the poem opens into a dream of a final fatal accident, a flood effacing the surface of the earth and all man's works, including the privileged creations of "poetry and geometric truth." The remainder of book 5 displays the fragility of Wordsworth's own most geometric truths, as the poetry shifts from the lament and celebration of "works" to a defense and an enactment of "accidents." Finally, the fatal accident to take place in these pages is an accident to the book's primary imagination of a dream, the dream of an apocalyptic loss and an ultimate rescue effort. The book of "Books" succumbs to a peculiar subversion of intentionality, its effects produced through a process at once overdetermined and accidental, keyed to repetition rather than recovery.

The accident can be located in a certain passage in book 5 that

13

repeats the imagination of calamity in an insistently literal mode. It is Wordsworth's description of the recovery of a corpse from the waters of a local lake, written in a bare, literal language setting it apart from the adjacent passages. What surfaces in the poem with the drowned man's "ghastly face" is effaced figure—lines one can trace neither as literal nor as figurative language, wording that, like the desert traveler in the poet's dream, "Of these was neither, and was both at once." The difficulty in interpreting this episode chances to exemplify a general predicament of the reader of Romantic texts: an erosion of the distinction between literal and figurative modes on which recovery of meaning depends. The text both requires that it be read literally and thwarts attempts to fix its referential status. Trying to retrace Wordsworth's effaced figure discloses the limits of rhetorical categories. A reading of this passage, then, may be offered as an example of what the poet calls accidents in the writing and the reading of literature.

Wordsworth uses the word *accidents* in a defense of the haphazard, spontaneous development of mind, in a polemic against the systematizing educators of the age, "Sages who in their prescience would control/All accidents." The version of 1798–99 mentions "such effects as cannot here/Be regularly classed," which elude Wordsworth's own simple systematizing, "yet tend no less/To the same point, the growth of mental power/And love of Nature's works" (first part, ll. 255-58). When *accidents* appears a few lines later in this version, it carries a concrete, colloquial signification: "numerous accidents in flood or field,/Quarry or moor, or 'mid the winter snows,/Distresses and disasters." The shift in meaning between these two uses of the word marks the peculiar slide of Wordsworth's argument in book 5: a defense of benign chance turns into a defense of chance disasters. Implicitly proffering these episodes as instances of exemplary childhood fostered by accidental influences, Wordsworth in fact recounts two deaths, or two different kinds of fatal accident: that of the Boy of Winander and that of the drowned man whom Wordsworth saw drawn up from Esthwaite Lake. This latter passage—without the elegiac rhythm that makes the Boy's death a destiny—impels us to question how we can account for an accident:

> Seeking I knew not what, I chanced to cross
> One of those open fields, which, shaped like ears,
> Make green peninsulas on Esthwaite's Lake.
> Twilight was coming on, yet through the gloom
> I saw distinctly on the opposite shore

> A heap of garments, left as I supposed
> By one who there was bathing. Long I watched,
> But no one owned them; meanwhile the calm lake
> Grew dark, with all the shadows on its breast,
> And now and then a fish up-leaping snapped
> The breathless stillness. The succeeding day—
> Those unclaimed garments telling a plain tale—
> Went there a company, and in their boat
> Sounded with grappling-irons and long poles:
> At length, the dead man, 'mid that beauteous scene
> Of trees and hills and water, bolt upright
> Rose, with his ghastly face, a spectre shape—
> Of terror even. And yet no vulgar fear,
> Young as I was, a child not nine years old,
> Possessed me, for my inner eye had seen
> Such sights before among the shining streams
> Of fairyland, the forests of romance—
> Thence came a spirit hallowing what I saw
> With decoration and ideal grace,
> A dignity, a smoothness, like the works
> Of Grecian art and purest poesy.

                                            (1805, 5.456–81)

Wordsworth's closing lines ostensibly provide an answer: he could read this like a book. But for us, the contingencies of critical reading and writing will coincide in such a way that the book is irrecuperable. Instead we retrieve a "ghastly face"; we glimpse the surfacing of a disfiguration.

We see written out here the "numerous accidents" of passages: that of the vanished bather, of the boy Wordsworth, who "chanced to cross" beside the lake, and of the language of the passage itself, which succumbs to a spare literalness differentiating it from the surrounding sections of the poem. Words that elsewhere in the book of "Books" resonate with symbolic meaning or imaginative significance here mean physical objects and actions and no more. The effacement of figurative meaning is conspicuous, for these words figure in other passages that are not forgettable:

> Thou also, man, hast wrought,
> For commerce of thy nature with itself,
> Things worthy of unconquerable life;

And yet we feel—we cannot chuse but feel—
That these must perish. Tremblings of the heart
It gives, to think that the immortal being
No more shall need such garments;

(1805, 5.17–23)

Faced with the "heap of garments, left as I supposed/By one who
there was bathing" (1805, 5.461–62), one cannot choose but feel
the divestment of figurative meaning in the literal recurrence of the
noun *garments*.[2] One feels initially, too, a parodic effect in the ironic
repetition of an action: garments are needed no more here not by an
immortal being but by a bather, because he is presently a corpse. The
literal action of drowning also repeats a poetic figure: a report of a
drowned man instead of the vision of "the drowning world" that
opens the book.

Another sort of repetition disconnects this passage and the evocation of the Boy of Winander. That text subtly invokes conceptions of
depth and immersion, in naming the imaginative moment that interrupts the mutual mimicry of the boy and the owls:

And when it chanced
That pauses of deep silence mocked his skill,
Then sometimes in that silence, while he hung
Listening, a gentle shock of mild surprize
Has carried far into his heart the voice
Of mountain torrents; or the visible scene
Would enter unawares into his mind
With all its solemn imagery, its rocks,
Its woods, and that uncertain heaven, received
Into the bosom of the steady lake.

(1805, 5.404–13)

After the blank that supersedes between verse paragraphs, the Boy's
death is named with a gentleness that echoes the gentle reception of
the "uncertain heaven . . . into . . . the steady lake";

Fair are the woods, and beauteous is the spot,
The vale where he was born; the churchyard hangs
Upon a slope above the village school. . . .

(ll. 416–18)

The recurrence of figurative "hanging" suggests a coincidence between
the "pauses of deep silence" and the extended pause of death. The

recurring suspensions of the listening Boy, of the village churchyard, and of "that uncertain heaven" suggest a death by immersion—as if the Boy, suspended in silence, were "received/Into the bosom of the steady lake."[3] The literal repetition of silence and immersion in the episode of the drowned man does violence to these recurrences. One feels a loss of resonance, if not, strangely, of intensity. The coincidence of interruptions, of "chanced" silence and fatality, gets reinscribed as the report: someone had an accident.

The drowned man episode repeats the crucial motions of the Winander Boy's story; interruption, or a thwarting of expectation, and the emergence of death by immersion. The Boy of Winander trusts to an intrinsic responsiveness and continual renewal of exchange with natural voice. The boy Wordsworth expects the reappearance of the bather indicated by the pile of clothes on the shore. Lines among the first of *The Prelude* of 1798-99, which recur in book 1 of 1805 (ll. 291-304), suggest the intimately troubling implications of that particular interruption, the disruption of the continuity of bathing:

> Was it for this that I, a four years' child,
> A naked boy, among thy silent pools
> Made one long bathing of a summer's day,
> Basked in the sun, or plunged into thy streams,
> Alternate, all a summer's day. . . .
>
> (1798-9, first part, ll. 17-21)

The text of the drowned man episode, though, is as devoid of these suggestions as it is devoid of the suggestiveness of the "pause" of the Boy of Winander. While the Boy of Winander, like the "naked boy," is as intimate as "I" with Wordsworth, the drowned man is someone else. The difference between the two texts is that the one invites and the other resists figurative interpretation. Wordsworth sees a great deal at stake in that difference: he identifies it with Imagination itself. In the "Preface of 1815," he delineates the distinction between literal and figurative usage as the difference between ordinary nonpoetic language and the language of the Imagination.

> Imagination . . . has no reference to images that are merely a faithful copy, existing in the mind, of absent external objects; but is a word of higher import, denoting operations of the mind upon those objects, and processes of creation or of composition, governed by certain fixed laws. I proceed to illustrate my meaning by instances. A parrot *hangs* from the wires of his cage by his beak or by his claws; or a monkey from the bough of a tree by his paws

or his tail. Each creature does so literally and actually. In the first
Eclogue of Virgil, the shepherd, thinking of the time when he is
to take leave of his farm, thus addresses his goats:—

> "Non ego vos posthac viridi projectus in antro
> Dumosa *pendere* procul de rupe videbo."
> —"half way down
> *Hangs* one who gathers samphire,"

is the well-known expression of Shakspeare, delineating an ordinary image upon the cliffs of Dover. In these two instances is a
slight exertion of the faculty which I denominate imagination, in
the use of one word: neither the goats nor the samphire-gatherer
do literally hang, as does the parrot or monkey; but, presenting to
the senses something of such an appearance, the mind in its activity,
for its own gratification, contemplates them as hanging.[4]

This passage reasserts a habitual distinction between literal and figurative language, and characterizes the Imagination itself in terms of
fixed functional distinctions between types of word usage. Yet Wordsworth's own examples of word usage here hang between two different
kinds of explanatory power. On the one hand they are meant to be
neutral examples, the content of which is unimportant. On the other
hand, however, they draw a crucial supplementary power of persuasion
from their content, which is not neutral at all. Thus parrots and mon-
keys not only "hang" literally; they are literalists, mimics who produce
sounds or gestures that "render a faithful copy" of what they imitate.
There is a collusion of two kinds of significance here: type of word
usage in the immediate context, and conspicuous connotations of the
content, drawn from other contexts. A collusion of the same kind
adds portent to Wordsworth's description of imaginative activity: "the
mind in its own activity, for its own gratification, contemplates them
as hanging," and in the lines that tell how the Boy "hung / Listening"
in silence, hanging is suggested to be the distinctive situation of Imagination as such. These coincidences lend the argument supplementary
meaning and force; they imply, and insist, that non-imaginative language is parrotlike, while imagination is a choice of precarious suspension. Yet they also subvert the poet's argument. For the persistent
power of sheer reference undermines Wordsworth's claim to situate
the Imagination according to determinate distinctions between figurative and literal word usage. Thus the critical text tells a story that differs from the kind of account it ostensibly attempts.

By this very duplicity, the poet's account raises issues crucial to
our own critical reading. For the coincidences and collusions of
meaning it displays are very like those that frustrate attempts at either

literal or rhetorical reading of Wordsworth's poetic text, the passage
on the drowned man. We are challenged, too, to come to terms with
the implied judgment that that passage is strictly non-imaginative (since
it lacks figurative language). It thus poses the dilemma of how to read
poetry that is literal. How can one read literally, except by merely re-
duplicating the gestures of the writer—like Wordsworth's hanging
monkey?

That dilemma will become more awkward as we begin a reading
of the drowned man episode. We might first take note of an episode
juxtaposed to it in the 1798–99 *Prelude* in which "hanging" imposes
itself literally: the "spot of time" in which Wordsworth confronts
the gibbet on the moor where a murderer had been hung in chains.
The texts of 1798–99 and of 1805 offer two different versions of the
literal, which here, too, Wordsworth "stumbles" on as if by accident:

> We had not travelled long ere some mischance
> Disjoined me from my comrade, and, through fear
> Dismounting, down the rough and stony moor
> I led my horse, and stumbling on, at length
> Came to a bottom where in former times
> A man, the murderer of his wife, was hung
> In irons. Mouldered was the gibbet-mast;
> The bones were gone, the iron and the wood;
> Only a long green ridge of turf remained
> Whose shape was like a grave. I left the spot, . . .
>
> (1798–99, first part, ll. 304–13)

The spot is a scene of effacement, the erosion of the remnants of an
execution, itself the effacement of a murder. Calculated to coincide
and cancel each other, the matched annihilations leave remains instead—
a residue that, strangely, consists not in the instruments or objects of
annihilation ("The bones were gone, the iron and the wood") but in
its site, the spot "Whose shape was like a grave." Nature here, the
"long green ridge of turf," is figured as the remnant of repeated effacements. Repeating his reading of the "spot" for the version of 1805,
Wordsworth rewrites these remains as literal *letters:*

> Hard by, soon after that fell deed was wrought,
> Some unknown hand had carved the murderer's name.
> The monumental writing was engraven
> In times long past, and still from year to year
> By superstition of the neighborhood

> The grass is cleared away; and to this hour
> The letters are all fresh and visible.

(1805, 11.292–98)

The residue is writing. It persists through repeated defacements (of the moor's surface) and effacements (of the letters, as the grass grows back). "Monumental writing" is maintained as the memento of a hanging: the text repeats in a literal mode the message of the Boy "hung/Listening," the theme of how poetic language is produced by a choice of imaginative suspension.

The "long green ridge of turf" and the carved letters are the same residual "spot," the siting or citing of an effacement. Insisting on the citing of the executed murderer's name, Wordworth's second version exploits the peculiar referential status of the proper name. Semiotics distinguishes four kinds of reference, according to four different combinations of "message" and "code." This message can refer to a message, as in reported speech; it can refer to the code, as in definitions; the code (or elements of the code) can refer to a message, as in the case of pronouns; or the code can refer to the code, as in proper names. The proper name is the effect of a binary relation in which the "message" is missing. It designates a class of objects definable only as those objects designated by that proper name. The "proper name" thus entails a peculiarly resistant mode of reference, as the *Prelude* passage suggests in remarking the chronically "fresh and visible" scars that must be repeated recurrently on the spot. Wordsworth comes upon a code without a message, a spot where the medium is the message: letters.

"Letters" and "shape" recur in a different way in the drowned man episode, in a further move by which this passage repeats the story of the Winander Boy. Not just literalization is involved here. Another repetition affects the theme of sound important in the resonant remembrance of the Boy: Wordsworth reports, "I chanced to cross/One of those open fields . . . shaped like *ears*"; and "a company . . . / *Sounded* with grappling-irons and long poles" (my italics).[5] The literal report is not a precise denomination of proper meanings but an exploitation of approximations. The principal quality of ears, their power of hearing, is without relevance, the word's usage here referring only to the accidental fact of their shape. The principal meaning of *sound,* its power of resounding, has no pertinence in this usage of the verb that borrows not its sense but only its letters. Sound "sounded" becomes a mute catachresis, the derived literal verb for soundless probing. In the accidents of repetition, literal language as well as figural is displaced and eroded.

Erosions of significance characterize not only the differences between the drowned man episode and other passages, but also the varia-
tions among different versions of the episode. In 1850 Wordsworth
writes:

Those unclaimed garments telling a plain tale
Drew to the spot an anxious crowd; some looked
In passive expectation from the shore,
While from a boat others hung o'er the deep,
Sounding with grappling irons and long poles.

(1850, 5.443-47)

Mentioning words that carry a powerful charge elsewhere in his poetry—
a spot, a drawing to the spot, and anxiety—Wordsworth's revised version displays another reduction of poetic significance. We can draw a
distinction between this miniaturizing and the askesis of figural meaning that generally characterizes the passage. The revision of 1850 is a
kind of corruption of the text. "There is something peculiar," as Geoffrey Hartman writes, "in the way his text corrupts itself: the freshness
of earlier versions is dimmed by scruples and qualifications, by revisions that usually overlay rather than deepen insight."[6]

The self-corrupting text: Hartman's phrase tells of too much in
this passage, after all, for us to restrict its relevance to revision. Decay
is a fact of the episode. By mere paraphrase, we can state that Wordsworth reports a chance encounter with the emergence of the possibility
of corruption. Just how that factual restatement is factitious requires
interpretation. The corruption of the text, nevertheless, can be a phrase
for two kinds of operation in the paragraph on the drowned man: the
recurrence, disfigured, of figures—the dissolution of images in the accidents of repetition; and the refiguring of a total text, a revaluation of
the textual currency so that it can serve "for commerce of thy nature
with itself." To appreciate the persistence of these two operations (a
decay and an inflation) we must engage in a reading of the passage.

The language of the passage is literal. It is also *about* an encounter
with the literal, with a literal corpse, not, that is, a figure for death
(such as a sunset) or a figural representation of death, like the story of
the Boy of Winander. The language of the passage displays an effacement of figure. It is also *about* the surfacing of an effaced figure, or
"ghastly face." In this episode Wordsworth leaves unreclaimed the
tropes, or "garments," that would mediate the naked facts; and "unclaimed garments" are also the revealing fact in his narrative. We can
interpret the episode as a disruption of the specular structure of

figuration: the effaced figure, or the dead letter, fractures the surface of the space that places sign and meaning. What emerges and breaks the liquid mirror of mimetic or metaphoric reflection is a disfigured face—itself a broken surface. Thus there emerges in the text something that disrupts our conception of literal language in contradistinction to figure. For the literal is revealed as effaced figure, rather than a primary, integral, proper condition of language. Language is from the start the production of decayed or abused figures: not "proper" naming, but catachresis, like Wordsworth's word here—*sounded*—for the act of finding the figure effaced. If Wordsworth's language in this passage is literal, "ordinary" language is not. Language ordinarily covers up the effects of effaced figuration; it erases the effacement of figure. In this text the cover is canceled and the erased effacement reinscribed, in an act of disfiguration.

The "ghastly face" is, however, only one aspect of Wordsworth's statement on the drowned man. Encountering the problem of interpreting an accident, and the very problem of his reader, that of reading literal writing, Wordsworth concludes the passage with an explanation that restores metaphorical status to the episode. As Geoffrey Hartman recapitulates,

> The landscape of fairy story and romance, says Wordsworth, had anticipated such terrors; that ghastly face was, therefore, a poetic rather than soul-debasing spectacle. This interpretation of the episode harmonizes with the argument that imaginative literature continues the child's "natural" maturation by keeping it from being plunged too quickly into the adult world. [7]

The psychological version that Hartman here paraphrases does not figure in the early version of the passage but was composed for *The Prelude* of 1805, to retrieve the episode for Wordsworth's explicit educational theme, "Books." The more fundamental function of the lines is simply to provide a reading of a memory that threatens to remain unreadable. The salient question is not how Wordsworth was able to cope with the corpse as a boy, but how he copes now, as a poet, with that ghastly figure, that literal instance. Referring his explanations to that question, one can infer that what he represents as a series of childhood experiences, an effect of biography, is instead an effect of composition.

Wordsworth identifies as fairy tales and romances, or allegories, the works that enabled him to see the disfigured face as a figure. Allegory is the activity that orders literal language into a sequence of prominent figures, and Wordsworth is engaged in it here, allegorizing in retrospect the literalization he had so literally described. If we must read literally Wordsworth's report of the literal, we should read allegorically his reference to allegory. How can we take at face value Wordsworth's invocation of others' romances? What is the value of such an explanation? Face value, evidently: the interpretation puts a face on the effaced figure of the drowned man. To put it another way, the lines restore "A dignity, a smoothness" to the broken surface of reflection: they resurface eroded figure. Writing "smoothness," Wordsworth enables us to visualize his rhetorical gesture here in the very terms of the literal narrative: poetry smoothes the troubled surface of the lake, smoothes the disfigured features of the ghastly face. Conceived in its rhetorical function, read as allegory, Wordsworth's explanation provides an account of how literal text is interpreted. It is viewed by the "I" as something read before. The relevant "romances" seemingly repeated in the drowned man's surfacing are not, primarily, other books, but this book 5, the book of "Books." What makes the drowned man's "ghastly face" appear as a poetic figure is not the reading of the boy Wordsworth, but the writing—of the Boy of Winander, of the prologue on abandoned garments, and of the dream of drowning books.

These are the texts that provide the figures that he rereads in the effaced figure of the drowned man. What Wordsworth explains in terms of sequential recurrence and reclaims as proof of progress in reading ability is, rather, a nonprogressive, atemporal repetition of *wording* from one passage to another, a repetition at once overdetermined and contingent. Reconstruing effaced figure as the dis-figuration of a previous figure supposes a process of recognition, a perception of the affinity between two different modes of presence, figurative and literal (and past and present), of the same signification. Refiguration, after the effacement and disfiguration of figure, takes the form of a claim of prefiguration. As Wordsworth's explanation proceeds with this recuperative process, the emergence of the drowned man becomes the uncanny appearance, in the real world, of a figure, a "romance," a fiction—but an intact and familiar figure, "hallowed," as Wordsworth says, with the prestige of art. Along with this recovery of figure, the disrupted specular space is also reconstructed, with its familiar distinctions between inside and outside, depth and surface. The figure can now be seen to emerge from the depths of the poet's "inner eye" (which had "seen such sights before") to the surface of external visibility. The episode is also replaced in a coherent temporal scheme: first I read, then eye saw. This reconnects it to *The Prelude*'s intended theme, "the growth of a poet's mind." The poet is enabled to recognize himself even in the broken mirror of the accident.

Even as he makes such a claim, however, Wordsworth is writing something different. He writes that the dead figure's "dignity, or smoothness" is "like works of Grecian art." In this context one can infer that the simile refers particularly to marble statues, to antique nudes. In making such a comparison, the poet invokes a classic strategy for relating loss to value, or effacement to intensity; within a certain long-lasting literary and historical tradition, the sculpture of classical antiquity is treasured precisely in the condition of defacement or fragmentation in which many such works were found. The poet implies that the effaced figure of the risen corpse could produce a similar effect. On the one hand, then, the comparison reintroduces a suggestion of the defacement of the figure at the very moment that it seemingly celebrates it. The very reassertion of the integrity of the figure simultaneously redesignates its effacement. On the other hand, this very reintroduction of the possibility of defacement also functions to lend the effaced figure a supremely high value, which such sculptural figures traditionally take on through their very status as effaced fragments, as if their effacement empowered the viewer's "inner eye" to recognize its own work of recreation.

The perfect duplicity of the gesture performed by the analogy is perhaps Wordsworth's distinction as the poet of *The Prelude*. But the text should have warned us sufficiently against claiming to recognize distinctive features. The recurrence of effacement is a textual effect. It is a matter of the corruption of the text, which is endemic—interminable, even, so this episode suggests, by death. Another such effect is the double reading provided by allegory. Thus Wordsworth's allegory of interpretation in these concluding lines both enacts a retrieval of figurative significance and displays that retrieval as merely an act. As our subsequent self-reading will show, Wordsworth's explanation also predicts the interpretive retrievals of the critical reader.

Wordsworth's explanatory conclusion to the passage first appears in *The Prelude* of 1805, as the episode is shifted from its grouping with the spots of time, in the first part of the 1798–99 *Prelude*, to its position next to the story of the Winander Boy in the book on "Books." As the new context intensifies the effect of repetition, and makes the text's effacement of figure newly conspicuous, the task of refiguration is made more urgent, and the new line on "romance" and reading fulfills that function. In the earlier version, repetition appears differently. It is almost explicitly identified in Wordsworth's concluding remark, which declines to explicate the episode, reading merely:

> I might advert
> To numerous accidents in flood or field,
> Quarry or moor, or 'mid the winter snows,
> Distresses and disasters, tragic facts
> Of rural history, that impressed my mind
> With images to which in following years
> Far other feelings were attached—with forms
> That yet exist with independent life,
> And, like their archetypes, know no decay.
>
> (1798–99, first part, ll. 279–87)

Wordsworth turns from the drowned man to the possibility of turning to other accidents, like this one, that stamp the mind with images linked later and contingently to other forms and feelings.[8] He writes of no feelings initially and intrinsically responsive to the episode, but only of "far *other* feelings" that became "attached": "facts," "images," "feelings," and "forms" are linked in an associative chain fastened merely by metonymy. The passage asserts a repetition of difference. The last line alone implies an affirmation of value, a value in the mode of persistence of the enumerated terms. Shifting diction noticeably, Wordsworth cites as "archetypes" the "numerous accidents" that were the initial instances: he reclaims as models, as metaphor, the initial links of the metonymic chain. Here too then, as in the conclusion to the version of 1805, the refiguration of splintered figure takes place through an assertion of prefiguration. Here too, the repetition of impressions or inscriptions gets represented as a genealogy of readings.

Wordsworth's declaration that they "know no decay" would seem to affirm a kind of immortality for the mind's images, and to celebrate the potency that enables his associations to resist "the decay of images in the mind" described by Locke. But the philosophical term shares the virulence of poetic discourse; the insistent literalism of *decay* refers back to the decay of the risen corpse. The statement becomes an assertion that forms or images cannot figure (cannot "know") the literal decay that was a fact. Or, rather, the statement simply displays so conspicuously the "decay" denied by its syntax that it compels repeated rereading. By disfiguring the syntax of the sentence, shifting its subject, we can read it as the poet's assertion that he knows (recognizes), in these images, no decay—a literal report of the gesture of denial that the line performs. What is the matter here is a certain repetition: (k)no(w)—no—decay.[9] There is *only* decay: the decay of the "ghastly face," of figuration, of the individual incident dissolved among "numerous accidents," and of the initial "facts of rural history" (Wordsworth's phrase in ll. 282–83 of the 1798–99 text) fracturing into "far other" forms. The phrase evokes the mode of persistency that in book 6 of the 1805 *Prelude* will define the Ravine of Gondo: "woods decaying, never to be decayed." "Archetypes," too, will find their place in that context, as "Characters of the great apocalypse."

The phrase "forms that know no decay" means "forms that undergo no decay." We could read this as Wordsworth's attempt to suppress the decay that will not go under, or to "know *no*" in order not to go under himself. What he writes, though, brings to the very surface the distinctive effect of metaphor. For Wordsworth's particular example of "know" for "undergo" calls attention to metaphor's power to confer prestige by giving an aura of intentionality to the action or object in which the metaphor focuses. Metaphor converts undergoing to knowing; it ascribes consciousness. The relation between to "know" and to "undergo" surfaced over in Wordsworth's conclusion poses questions relevant to the initial accident: To "know" that encounter, was it sufficient for him to undergo it? What could it mean to know such an accident?[10] The text of 1798–99 makes these rhetorical questions, repeating the issue in the form of a rhetorical figure. The version of 1805 deals with the issue in another way. The notion of insistent metonymies "which yet exist with independent life," detached from the subject, is not simply reorganized by a final invocation of metaphoric "archetypes"; as statement it disappears altogether, for Wordsworth instead concludes the paragraph with an explanatory reference to reading. The notion of "forms that know no decay" recurs in a new version—in which another use of "knowledge" stresses its proper sense:

> May books and Nature be their early joy,
> And knowledge, rightly honored with that name—
> Knowledge not purchased with the loss of power!
>
> (1805, 5.447–49)

The poet convokes directly knowledge not purchased with decay, or knowledge that does not recognize decay. What is willed in these lines is the reversal of a power structure, a conversion of knowing as undergoing to "knowledge with power." The lines still circumscribe the project of knowing the book of accidents that "Nature" shows itself to be in book 5 of *The Prelude*. The text insists on the rhetorical question. How can we face, or how can we manage not to face, an effaced figure?

This chapter has insistently exploited the collusion of literal reference and illustrative significance that we found noteworthy in Wordsworth's "Preface of 1815." Critical writing can try for an effect of
happy coincidence by using terms that coincide with the wording of
the poetic text. We ought to examine the nature of this coincidence
and the situation of the critical text it generates.

What happens in lines 454–72 of book 5 of *The Prelude* is the surfacing of effaced figure. That statement—a critical reader's interpretive
summary—names three different things at once. It describes the mode
and quality of the language of the passage, the poet's style; it interprets
the significance of the episode read allegorically; and it paraphrases
the poem's literal report of the event. This situation cannot be ascribed
to an ideal transparency of the poetic text (as the density, if not
opacity, of the present paraphrase perhaps sufficiently suggests). It
should not be construed, either, as an instance of the perfect solidarity
of signs and meanings, between surface features of style and the sense
and significance of the referents. The coincidence of mode and meaning is due not to a smooth continuity between style and theme, but to
a displacement between a fictional event in the past, to which Wordsworth refers certain qualities, and another kind of fictional event that
does have those qualities, the writing and reading of the poetic text
itself. This is no language of symbol in which one phrase might mean
simultaneously all it means, and the meaning be present to the word
itself. The structure is, rather, that of homonym, in which disparate
meanings happen to be expressed by the same word. By accident,
here, the signs for the meaning and the signs for the sign can coincide.
Meanings and signs are linked not by intrinsic resemblance but by the
accident of identity.

The coincidence of signs is not a windfall but a dilemma for the
interpreter of Wordsworth's text. The discontinuous sameness of the
passage divides the interpretive act from itself. The pointed accuracy
and multiple relevancy of the poet's words leave one unable to say
what one means, by making one mean several different things at once.
The passage at once requires to be read literally and makes literal reading impossible. It is impossible first of all just because of the conspicuous traces of the effaced figures that provide the key terms of the
text. Reading of "a heap of garments," we necessarily recall the symbolic "garments" of the book's opening; understanding the phrase's
peculiar literalness actually necessitates that we appreciate the repetition and the difference between the two. Yet we thereby appreciate
"garments" as a *figure* for the literal and not as an effaced figure, literal itself. In a similar way, in his concluding comment on the episode,

Wordsworth appreciated the sight of the risen corpse as a literal appearance in the world of a poetic figure from books. We misread the literal as a figure for the literal; Wordsworth misread the literal as a literal manifestation of figure. Thus we duplicate in inverse the very error we claimed to perceive in the poet's reading of the episode. Wordsworth's misreading is a powerful example, a literally compelling rhetorical model. We may see his mistake, but we are bound to repeat it. Monkey see, monkey do.

This encounter with Wordsworth displays how our general dilemma as interpretive readers of poetry is compounded by our unfailing predicament as critical writers about it. The writer cannot state the literal meaning of a passage without simultaneously stating a figurative interpretation, for the rhetorical status of critical discourse automatically lends figurative significance to its terms. Writing figuratively, then, one fails to read literally, and so misses the point of the passage even while focusing on it directly. To read literally would be to halt one's inference at the literal referents of a passage literally written. What *is* the referent, though? Just the literal; the literal is what the passage is about. Wordsworth's text withholds from us a referent distinct from the literalism of the passage itself. The text not only makes a monkey of us, but leaves us hanging. Reading literally, one manages only to read to the letter; and the letter reinscribes the figure it repeats.[11]

Yet the other aspect of this critical predicament is that the writer can do nothing *but* interpret literally. Not only does interpretive transfiguration thwart nonfigurative paraphrase, but literal paraphrase reabsorbs and erases interpretation. For the literal language of the poetic narrative still insists within the figural language of the interpretive text. Writing out our interpretation of the surfacing of effaced figure, we are copying out what is literally written in the poem. Just as the poetic figure of abandoned mortal garments gets literalized, in further writing, as actual clothes; just as the figure of the Winander Boy hanging silent above the lake recurs in some sense, literalized, as an actual corpse; so the interpretive concepts of abandoned tropes and dead figures also get literalized, in the same way, in the process of writing about them with reference to the passage on the drowned man. The slip from figural to literal—the accident—befalls the critical, as well as the poetic, figure. It is as true to say that Wordsworth's text reads its interpretation literally as to say that the interpretation literally reads Wordsworth's text.

While Wordsworth's literal report eludes accurate description, the explanatory section of the passage resists interpretive mastery in another way. For in taking the explanation as a rhetorical gesture, and reading it allegorically, the meaning we thereby infer from it is an account of the error—and the inevitability—of allegorical reading. The passage enables us to construe the disparity between the textual effect of a repetition of wording between different parts of *The Prelude* itself, and the poetic realignment of the episode in a sequence of anticipation and fulfillment, the "romance" of recognition that Wordsworth outlines even as he makes reference to "the forests of romance." We learn from this passage that figurative reading of a literal instance involves the construction of allegories, the inference of a sequence of statements or figures forming a narrative—more precisely, a narrative that one has read before. But figurative reading, and the construction of a narrative sequence, is just what we have been doing—most patently in the very reading of this explanatory passage, articulating its relationship to the preceding narrative as an allegory of reading and misreading. We mimic the misreading we discover, even in the process of discovering it.

At this point the reflexive structure of our own text reaches a certain critical density: we must acknowledge that while we can claim to recognize that our interpretive error merely *mimics* Wordsworth, the recognition really at stake—what lures us to make that claim—is our recognition of our own critical narrative in the mirror of Wordsworth's poem. It is that wish that impels us to demonstrate how the poet himself strives to make the accident into an occasion for self-recognition, seeing himself seeing his own reading in the "ghastly face" before him. If we involuntarily recognize a romance in the drowned man episode, it is not simply Wordsworth's Romantic elegy on Winander, but the romance of our own doomed acts of interpretation. We too would cut a critical figure like the figure of the Winander Boy, and our self-criticism covertly luxuriates in the pathos of that factitious correspondence: if our jocund mimicry of Wordsworth's call is checked, if inexpressible discontinuities baffle our best skill, we console ourselves with the recollection of these memorable Wordsworthian precedents, with a sense of "cutting across the reflex of a star." The seduction of coincidence persists in spite of the fact that the passage we are explicating tells a grimly literal story about accidents. If critical readers are bound to identify with some figure of Wordsworth's, then it ought to be not the youths baffled by silence or unstartled by a corpse, but the trivially exotic pets of the critical "Preface of 1815," who "render a faithful copy of external objects." Thus, we are reduced to saying: better a live parrot or monkey than a dead Boy.

Following through, then, the ambiguous project of noting how our reading of the accident mimics Wordsworth's and how his rhetorical

gesture elicits and predicts our own, we may remark another coincidence: the theme of books as such. Our interpretation, like Wordsworth's, implicitly places this episode in a context of educational
development. If Wordsworth recognizes in the risen corpse figures
familiar to him from allegorical romances, we recognize, in the broken
surface of his text, a figuration familiar to us from allegories of Romanticism—from the interpretive books that are our own most saving
fairy tales. The disruption of the specular surface, the rising of the
dead letter, and the fatality of misreading, all this we have read before, and that fact alone allows us to *see* it, hallowing what we read
"With decoration and ideal grace," as "purest poesy."

For us as for Wordsworth, the act of reading a particular effaced
figure comes to be assimilated to an ongoing educational process,
"the growth of a . . . mind." Yet the book of "Books" begins with a
sharp opposition between books and educators, "accidents" and
"sages," reading process and educational system. The assumption of
antagonism between education and fiction has a long history, and
Wordsworth's revision contributes heavily to a prevalent contemporary
conception of their relationship: his animus against "Sages who in
their prescience would control / All accidents" is echoed in a current
critique of educator-readers who oversimplify the complex contingencies of literary texts. Radicalized, the opposition of educational
process to reading process emerges as an opposition between reading
and books, and a valuing of texts for their very resistance to reading,
their persistence as accidents that elude our accounting. In this perspective, encountering the impossibility of reading is itself authentic
knowledge of literature. Critical interpretation comes to be distinguished, then, by the implicit claim that to "undergo" is to "know":
undergoing the exigencies of reading the text, the interpreter comes to
know the disfiguring accidents of its writing. Such a project can resume
a place within a systematic educational process. A poet can have a
critic; a critic can have a student.

Yet such a conception of interpretation is a seductive delusion
comparable to the illusion that the identity of the poet's and the
critic's wordings could be a happy coincidence rather than a collusion or collision with fatal effects. Moreover, it is a seduction that
always partly fails to work. What the student knows after undergoing
it is that "undergoing" and "knowing" are incommensurable, cleaved
by an unnatural act of reading and failing to form an experience,
which would be that of literature, or of education. What happens to
take place instead is that one or the other goes under: one writer or
reader must take his place under the other—an imposition that impels

readers of Romantic texts, like Wordsworth, to convoke the inversion of power structures and conversion to the experience of "knowledge . . . with . . . power." The outcome of reading in the book on "Books" is an experience that Wordsworth's story leaves unmentioned. One feels impelled to advert to it here.

> Hitherto,
> In progress through this verse my mind hath looked
> Upon the speaking face of earth and heaven
> As her prime teacher. . . .
>
> (1805, 5.10-13)

So Wordsworth writes at the beginning of book 5; now, as he goes on to say, he will acknowledge the precious tutelage of books. The resonant metaphor of a "speaking face" ascribes a human power to nature. In the defense of accidents that becomes the format of his celebration of books, Wordworth comes to write,

> At length, the dead man, 'mid that beauteous scene
> Of trees and hills and water, bolt upright
> Rose, with his ghastly face. . . .
>
> (1805, 5.470-72)

Here, too, nature gets a human face, but quite literally; and not a speaking face but a mute one—an effaced figure unable to articulate any lesson. Annotated texts of *The Prelude* provide us with information about this effaced figure that comes out second as candidate for the writer's "prime teacher"; the drowned man was, in fact, a local schoolmaster.[12] Wordsworth's polemical argument—do away with the schoolmasters!—gets transformed in the course of book 5 into an incident that literally does away with one. The exemplary educational episode consists in seeing a teacher as a dead man. Literary education proves its efficacy in the ability to circumvent mere "vulgar fear" of the "ghastly face" of the schoolmaster risen again. And the effect of writing, as we have written, is the duplicity of a gesture that simultaneously hallows the lost teacher and reinscribes his statuesque disfigurement.

The Ring of Gyges and
the Coat of Darkness

Reading Rousseau with Wordsworth

In *Les Rêveries du promeneur solitaire,* at the end of the *Sixième Promenade,* Rousseau closes a complaint about his inability to appear to his contemporaries as he really is with a fantasy of possessing the power of invisibility:

> If I had been invisible and powerful like God, I should have been good and beneficent like him.

> If I had possessed the ring of Gyges, it would have made me independent of men and made them dependent on me. I have often wondered, in my castles in the air, how I should have used this ring, for in such a case power must indeed be closely followed by the temptation to abuse it. Able to satisfy my desires, capable of doing anything without being deceived by anyone, what might I have desired at all consistently? One thing only: to see every heart contented.

> Always impartially just and unfalteringly good, I should have guarded myself equally against blind mistrust and implacable hate, because seeing men as they are and easily reading at the bottom of their hearts, I should have found few who were likeable enough to deserve my full affection and few who were odious enough to deserve my hate, and also because their very wickedness would have inclined me to pity them out of the sure knowledge of the harm they do themselves in seeking to harm others.[1]

Rousseau conceives this fantasy out of the sense of his intolerable dilemma, that "men insist on seeing me as entirely other than I am":

> As for me, let them see me if they can, so much the better; but this is beyond them, instead of me they will never see anyone

but the Jean-Jacques they have created and fashioned for themselves so that they can hate me to their heart's content.

(p. 1059)

Inclined to "follow blindly my penchant for doing good," Rousseau
has become convinced that "the greatest concern of those who control
my fate having been to keep me entirely surrounded by false and de-
ceptive appearance, any motive for virtuous behaviour is never more
than a lure to draw me into the trap where they want to entwine me"
(p. 1051). The effects of his actions are concealed from him and cut
off from his good intention. This dilemma inspires a fantasy in which
the inability to see or be seen gets reimagined as the ability to see and
act unseen. Instead of "blindly" following his penchant for doing
good, Rousseau would now be capable of "seeing men as they are and
easily reading at the bottom of their hearts." Blindness, which accompanied the inability to *be* seen, is converted to lucidity. Rousseau's
fantasy converts a predicament into a privilege. The invisibility of the
link between the motive force and the effects of his actions, first be-
wailed as the powerlessness to be known for what he is (good), gets
reimagined as a form of power.[2]

The power of invisibility, produced by a wishful reversal, appears
in a passage of Wordsworth's *Prelude* that seems to differ in nearly
every way from Rousseau's *Sixième Promenade,* a passage to which
we are guided by the most superficial resemblance: Wordsworth refers
to a "coat of darkness" operating like the ring of Gyges, making the
wearer invisible. He is describing a performance of *Jack the Giant-
Killer* at Sadler's Wells:

> Nor was it mean delight
> To watch crude Nature work in untaught minds,
> To note the laws and progress of belief—
> Though obstinate on this way, yet on that
> How willingly we travel, and how far!—
> To have, for instance, brought upon the scene
> The champion, Jack the Giant-killer: lo,
> He dons his coat of darkness, on the stage
> Walks, and atchieves [*sic*] his wonders, from the eye
> Of living mortal safe as is the moon
> 'Hid in her vacant interlunar cave.'
> Delusion bold (and faith must needs be coy)
> How is it wrought?—his garb is black, the word
> INVISIBLE flames forth upon his chest.[3]

Wordsworth's tone is satirical, Rousseau's confessional; Rousseau evokes his own lasting dilemma, while Wordsworth apparently describes a momentary distraction; Rousseau's text is claustrophobically self-enclosed, while Wordsworth's giddily appropriates a line from Milton. This line of Milton, however, reveals that the same reversal that stands out in Rousseau's *Promenade* also stands behind this passage of Wordsworth's. For the quoted line comes from Samson's lament for his blindness at the opening of *Samson Agonistes,* "The sun to me is dark," in which he compares the sun's darkness to the darkness of the waned moon, "Hid in her vacant interlunar cave." Wordsworth's appropriation systematically reverses the context of the line he quotes from Samson. Instead of presenting a captive unable to appear to himself or his contemporaries as what he is (a hero of the Lord), the new context in *The Prelude* summons up an adventurer able to appear invisible and therefore able to be a hero. Instead of a giant *killer* (Samson's original and final identity), the new context refers to a "giant-killer." And like Rousseau's fantasy of possessing the ring of Gyges, Wordsworth's description of Jack's "coat of darkness" converts a prior account of blindness and powerlessness to a depiction of omnipotent invisibility. What can be at issue in the peculiar conjunction of wish fulfillment and invisibility presented by these passages from the *Promenades* and *The Prelude?* If Wordsworth's quotation of Milton alerts us to read his lines as more than a good-tempered smirk at a convention of popular theater, is there any clue that we should read Rousseau's lines as other than intemperate self-justification and wishfulness?

Rousseau's *rêverie* has an argument, in fact, about the relationship between the motives and the effects of actions. He does not simply assert their discontinuity; he laments it. It is easy, and in some measure unavoidable, to practice a psychological reading of the *Promenades,* focused on the confessional nature of Rousseau's discourse. It is also possible to focus on his manifest argument about intentions and conventions. The *Sixième Promenade* appears to offer us an account of natural and naturally good motives caught in the trammels of culturally determined and malevolent interpretations and effects. One could suppose one recognized here, as in other more patently philosophical, nonautobiographical writings (such as the First and Second Discourses), a story about nature obscured and degraded by the elaborations of culture. These two ways of reading (psychological and "philosophical") would not have to contradict one another, and they might meet in an account of Rousseau's "ethics of intention." Neither approach, however, enables us to read much in Rousseau's lingering imagination of the power of invisibility. What is at stake in Rousseau's conceiving a situation in which the link between the motive force and the effect of an action is invisible?

A long philosophical tradition, which achieved its classic formulation in Kant's *Critique of Judgment*, identifies the absence of interest or motive as the condition of the existence of an aesthetic object. We might read Rousseau's imagined "invisibility" in this way: as the condition of his writing.

Written marks, to the extent that they are writing, are in some sense invisible—to be read, not seen. We can construe another hint to understand the fantasy of invisibility in this way if we compare Rousseau's description of his motivation in the *Sixième Promenade* and in the *Quatrième*. In the *Sixième Promenade* Rousseau identifies the "penchant for doing good," the wish to make others happy, as his fundamental, primary motivation. In the *Quatrième Promenade* Rousseau identifies the same "primary and irresistible impulse of [my] temperament" in different terms: as the drive to produce an utterance he explicitly identifies as "fiction." In this context Rousseau's concern is to distinguish fiction from lies: "to lie without profit or prejudice to oneself or others," or to invent "an idle fact, indifferent in all respects," would mean to escape the opprobrium of lying. It may seem perverse to identify Rousseau's fantasy of omnipotent altruism in the *Sixième Promenade* with this scathing description of not-lying in the *Quatrième*, in order to call them both "fiction." Yet the two *Promenades* do move among the same concerns: at issue in them both are truth and falsehood, statement and interpretation, and guilt and innocence; epistemological and ethical issues are combined. More tellingly, both situations (invisibility and not-lying) are ascribed the same intentional status with regard to motive. Rousseau describes how he is driven to talk, to produce nontruths, by a "mechanical effect" quite distinct from the motive to influence or deceive, simply under the pressure of the social situation of conversation, which comes to compound a "primary and irresistible impulse." Thus the originative motivation, itself motiveless, which Rousseau in the *Sixième Promenade* calls his "penchant for doing good," is identified in the *Quatrième* as the impulse to produce fictions.

We will have occasion later to notice an odd similarity in the turn of the argument of the two *Promenades*. At present we are committed to a working hypothesis: that Rousseau's imagination of invisibility is a conception of the condition of his own writing as fiction.

The wishfulness of Rousseau's fantasy does not preclude its interpretive function. We can hazard an account of the significance of the transformation worked by the ring of Gyges before determining the status of that transformation. Let us speculate, then, that in reimagining his predicament as a writer as possession of the ring of Gyges, Rousseau's *rêverie* suggests that the incomprehensibility of the mode of intention animating his writing (his inability to be seen as he is) can be imagined as a radical abstraction of intention (such as characterizes fiction) lending that writing a unique productive and interpretive power. If our reading of the *Sixième Promenade* can proceed along these lines—if the intentional mode of Rousseau's writing is indeed at issue—it will be all the more important, finally, to interpret the nature of the wishfulness involved in his evocation of the ring of Gyges.

The *Sixième Promenade* is about Rousseau's relation to others in the world, which is essentially determined by his status as a writer. Let us suppose, then, that Rousseau is writing about his relation to his readers. This approach may prove more productive than those that first seemed most plausible (attending to the psychological and "philosophical" statements of the text), for it enables us to identify the stakes of Rousseau's fantasy of invisibility. That fantasy has to do with the power to read. Rousseau imagines himself "reading at the bottom of their hearts" ("lisant au fond des coeurs").

The ability to read is quite literally part of Wordsworth's topic in his lines on the performance at Sadler's Wells. The story of Jack the Giant-Killer can be performed because the audience can read, and willingly accepts an actor's marking with the word *invisible* as a real state of invisibility.

While ethical judgments are conspicuous in Rousseau's *Promenade,* in the *Prelude* passage the implications of the acts of reading and writing as an ethical issue must be inferred from shifts of tone and from the gesture represented by citation. Wordsworth's citation changes the associations of Milton's phrase from failure to success and displaces it from a context of tragic seriousness to one of satire. He stresses the actor's facility in representing the magical power of invisibility with the simplest stage device, a cloak with a labeling word, and he flaunts his own facility in recycling the language of Milton—not only the phrase from *Samson Agonistes* but also the "darkness visible" of *Paradise Lost.* The stage at Sadler's Wells is the scene, then, of a travesty. (That travesty situates the pantomime among the other "London" spectacles, which are all presented as distorted or degraded forms of imaginative energy.) The very effectiveness of the stage prop "coat of darkness"—and the very ease of Wordsworth's deployment of Milton's line—are rather disturbing.

This turns out to be the case for the ring of Gyges, too. Although

Rousseau initially pictures the effects of his magical power as wholly good, he ends by qualifying and reversing that judgment:

> There is only one point on which the ability to go everywhere un-observed might have made me seek temptations that I should have found it hard to resist, and once I had strayed into these aberrant ways, where might they not have led me? It would be showing great ignorance of human nature and myself to flatter myself that such easy opportunities [*facilités*] would not have seduced me or that reason would have halted me on this down-ward path. I could be sure of myself in every other respect, but this would be my ruin. The man whose power sets him above hu-manity must himself be above all human weaknesses, or this excess of power will only serve to sink him lower than others, and lower than he would himself have been had he remained their equal.

> All things considered, I think I will do better to throw away my magic ring before it makes me do something foolish.

(p. 1058)

The coyness of this passage is unpleasant. Rousseau is evidently following up a claim about the highest, freest privilege of serving the general happiness with an unstated allusion to the advantages of invisi-bility for reaping private sexual benefits, requiring him to renounce his aspiration to omnipotence. The well-known story of Gyges—whose first use of his ring was to perform adultery with the queen—allows Rousseau to make us take his meaning without actually spelling it out. The Gyges legend also gives Rousseau's retraction a predictability that makes his initial presumption of altruism seem coy as well, and the entire fantasy a double self-indulgence.

The passage has to be taken as a coy allusion to sexual license, but it cannot be left at that. The break in tone with the previous paragraph does not release us from the text's implicit concern with the power of fiction. Rousseau's determined avoidance of particularizing the antici-pated wrongdoing can be taken not only as false *pudeur*, but also as an injunction to read the passage in the abstract terms he provides: "*facilités*" and the inducement to "seek temptations." Invisibility, then, turns out to entail the danger of degradation, and both Words-worth and Rousseau imagine a certain facility as a threat associated with the power of invisibility. Wordsworth shows this facility distinctive of effects achieved by being read—by using a mere written word to pro-duce belief and construct imaginary events; Rousseau too describes a magical facility of reading ("easily reading at the bottom of their hearts"). What can it possibly mean that both Wordsworth and Rousseau associate the power of reading with an effect of travesty or degradation? This is the enigma that will aminate our reading of Wordsworth's lines on Jack the Giant-Killer and Rousseau's *Sixième Promenade.*

The predicament evoked by Rousseau in the *Sixième Promenade* is a state of radical discrepancy between intentions and meanings. Rousseau's desire to exercise generosity, for example, cannot be fulfilled, for the very act of satisfying another's desire retroactively establishes an implicit contract according to which one's action becomes simply the fulfillment of an obligation: "But from these first acts of charity performed with an overflowing heart arose chains of successive obligations which I had not foreseen and which it was now impossible to shake off. My first favours were in the eyes of those who received them no more than an earnest of those that were still to come" (pp. 1051–52). Rousseau complains that every intention promptly becomes entangled in a web of conventional meanings alien to it, since an intended meaning must take the form of an action that stands as a sign, deriving its signification not from an intention but from the other signs that form its context.

Avoidance of such a subversion of his intention is the motive Rousseau claims to discover for the first action of the *Promenade,* his detour past the spot where previously he had often given alms to a lame boy. This anecdote is the warrant for the statement with which the text begins: "We have hardly a mechanical movement whose cause we cannot find in our heart, if we really knew how to look for it." This statement seems to set up a contrast and a hierarchy: there is "our heart," the realm of desires and intentions, and "mechanical movements," which take their meaning from such intentions. As the context is elaborated, however, motive and mechanism turn out to have "another and a finer connection than that of contrast."[4] The anecdote and explanation that follow reveal that the intention motivating Rousseau's "mechanical movement" is nothing other than the impulse to avoid having an intention—to avoid an intention that will be a repeated action in an established context, hence a sign not effectively invested with intention.

> This pleasure become by degrees a habit was somehow transformed into a sort of duty which I soon began to find irksome, particularly on account of the preamble I was obliged to listen to, in which he never failed to address me as Monsieur Rousseau so as to show that he knew me well, thus making it quite clear to me on the contrary that he knew no more of me than those who had taught him. From that time on I felt less inclined to go that way, and in

the end I mechanically adopted the habit of making a detour when I approached this shortcut.

(pp. 1050–51)

The motive for the mechanical movement is simply the negation of motivation—the suppression or elision of the motive to do good.

Not only does the suppression of a generous motive produce a mechanical movement; acting in consistency with that motive produces the same kind of motion: Rousseau refers to his tendency "to follow blindly my penchant for doing good." This penchant, according to Rousseau, is the original motive that defines "my character and my nature." What is the content of this original motivation? It is described as a desire for "public felicity," for general happiness—described as fundamental generosity. It is a desire to gratify others' desires, a desire for a correlation between desire and gratification and between motive and realization. It is the motive to discover desires and to make them into motives for action. What Rousseau identifies as his originative motive, then, is the motivation to postulate motives.

Such a motivation to find motives is the cause or condition of the very predicament of which Rousseau complains, the subversion of the correlation between intention and meaning. This is the paradox that promptly appears in Rousseau's account of his dilemma: it is the energy for motivating signs, the drive to ascribe motives to actions, that saturates the complex of significations which Rousseau describes as irreparably subverting his intentions. The motive to establish motives is the very condition of their ruin. The beginning of the *Sixième Promenade* thus requires a different reading than its opening sentence seems to invite. The opening, which initially appears to announce an argument in favor of motivation, claiming and hoping to find particular intentions behind the apparently automatic movements of the self, turns out rather to introduce an account of the motivation to *suppress* motivation. The opening anecdote depicts a mechanical reflex that reacts against the mechanical character of motivation itself, motivation as a mere mechanism for the production of motives. What has to be avoided, then, is precisely motivation. Rousseau arrives at this inference: "a motive for virtuous behavior is never more than a *lure* to draw me into the trap where they want to entwine me." Hence the only possible motive, for Rousseau, must be the avoidance of motivation.

This will be the motive for Rousseau's fantasy of possessing the ring of Gyges, of being "invisible," "all-powerful," and "disinterested for myself." This state is conceived to escape the double bind of motivation. It is an escape from a predicament not of bad faith but of error: what matters is not that Rousseau's *own* motivation powers the complex of significations that subvert his intentions, but rather that the meaning of his actions, when apprehended according to a conception of localized motives, must invariably be misinterpreted.[5] The *Sixième Promenade* relates that Rousseau's action—his writing—will be systematically misinterpreted so long as its meaning is construed as the correlative of particular intentions or motives. Rousseau's writing is "motivated" in a manner invisible in such a perspective: it is motivated only with regard to motivation itself, which it may either posit or negate.

Rousseau's fantasy of possessing the ring of Gyges would then name the truth of the following predicament: inasmuch as his writing is not generated by the particular intention of a particular agent, but rather by a stance in regard to motivation in general, it is indeed—within a system conceiving meaning as intentional or motivated—action generated by an invisible agency. Rousseau's fantasy of invisibility would interpret the intentional structure of his writing, correcting the error inherent in the interpretive process that seeks to visualize the agent and motive for the production of meaning. Possession of the ring of Gyges signifies that condition of language in which no motive can be ascribed as the meaning of an utterance: it is an allegory for the state of fiction. Rousseau's imagination of being invisible is an insight into the fictional status of his own writing.

His evocation of the effects of the ring of Gyges must then be read as an account of the effects of fiction. It is an allegory recounting the consequences of the radical abstraction of intention involved in the production of a fictional text, or, which may amount to the same thing, in the reading of a text as primarily self-referential, the "vision" of a text as "invisible." Rousseau describes an access of power and lucidity: with invisibility comes the power of vision, and more particularly the power of reading ("seeing men as they are and easily reading at the bottom of their hearts"). Rousseau thus draws a connection between a text's fictional, self-referential status and its power to "read" other texts. Some such connection is suggested by one's own experience reading fiction and criticism: it is often less productive to interpret the fictional text by means of the critical text than to do the reverse.[6] Why should this be so? Rousseau's allegory of altruism suggests that a fiction, free of the intention to impose the communication of its own particular meanings, can refer rather to its conditions of signification. These are the conditions, too, of the signifying strategies of other texts designed to conceal rather than to display their rhetorical structure, which the fictional text brings to light. Rousseau's own writing can be shown to have this extraordinary interpretive power.[7]

In what sense might fiction be, like invisibility, singularly equipped to produce "public felicity"? Fiction has the ability to "see all hearts contented" through its power to exemplify virtually any meaning that may be wanted by another text or reader.

It would seem that Rousseau need have no misgivings in imagining himself invisible—in identifying his writing as fictional. The text whose status is fictional or self-referential would seem to hold a powerful position. Yet the next paragraph goes on to describe that position as intolerably precarious. Being invisible comes to entail, here, something that closely resembles the power to *lire au fond des coeurs:* the power to "seek temptations." The danger was already inherent in the effects of invisibility as described in the first part of the ring of Gyges fantasy, which itself reinterprets the dilemma we have already analyzed in one version, in the opening paragraphs of the *Promenade,* where we discovered the intrication of motivelessness and motive. Freedom from motive, it appeared, could be the only motivation for Rousseau; freedom from motive will itself operate as a motive, and as a motive to posit, not just to negate, motivation. In Rousseau's fantasy, the power to fulfill others' desires becomes a drive to produce them—to "seek temptations." At the beginning of the allegory, freedom from motive went along with omnipotence, with the power to fulfill the desires, to realize the motives, of others; now the power to realize motives becomes an impetus to look for them. What does this mean in relation to Rousseau's writing? Freedom from motive gave Rousseau's self-referential writing the power to "read" other texts. But that very power of reading is grounded in a practice of motivation (an ascription of motive to the meaning of texts) that must inevitably entail, so Rousseau concludes, the remotivation of his own text as well, with the lapse into error and the loss of power that that involves—the liabilities of the first form of "invisibility" that were Rousseau's complaint in the rest of the *Promenade.* [8]

The lucidity of the self-referential text is complete except with regard to the figural status of lucidity itself. Lucidity as an attribute of magical invisibility is a figure for the endemic "invisibility" of the text whose intentional status is indeterminate, in an indeterminate relationship to motivation. The ability to fulfill desires will have the effect not only of suppressing them but also of producing them; so the power of language (distinct from any intention) to designate meanings will produce intentions toward meaning.

Just as the idea of the invisible is part of a conception of the world as visible, so the idea of fiction, or of an unmotivated text, is solidary with a conception of writing defined by its relationship to motive—of writing motivated, always, in some way, if only by the negation of motives. What Rousseau's text shows us is not only that these conditions (motivated or unmotivated) are part of the same system but that one produces—demands—the other. The insight into the radically fictional nature of language and the error of motivating texts with intentions thus occur close together.

Rousseau's misgivings about fiction have to do with the fact that fiction above all provokes literal reading and a passage into action, as if the very vacuum of motive inevitably drew toward it a very powerful motive indeed. Rousseau describes how the interpretation of a discourse as fictional takes place at the same time as its manipulation in the service of a compelling motive. This strange occurrence characterizes the type of response produced by an action set on stage and read as fictional. The intense yet disengaged response of the spectator is associated, in Rousseau's "Lettre à d'Alembert sur les spectacles," with murderous slander:

> Tacitus reports that Valerius-Asiaticus, accused calumniously at the order of Messalina, who wanted to make him perish, defended himself before the emperor in a way that moved that prince extremely and drew tears from Messalina herself. She went into a neighboring room to recover herself, after she had, all the while weeping, in a whisper given notice to Vitellius not to allow the accused man to escape. At a play I never see one of those weepers in the boxes [pleureuses de loges] so proud of their tears without thinking of those of Messalina for that poor Valerius-Asiaticus.[9]

In the Sixième Promenade Rousseau describes his own stance as that of a spectator at a theatrical performance. Here he adduces as evidence of his intact moral impulses the same imaginative sympathy detached from participation that he attributes to the "pleureuses de loges":

> Even my indifference to them only concerns their relations with me; for in their relations with one another they can still interest me and move me like the characters in a play I might see performed. My moral being would have to be annihilated for me to lose interest in justice. The sight of injustice and wickedness still makes my blood boil with anger; virtuous actions where I see no vainglory or ostentation always make me tremble with joy, and even now they fill my eyes with precious tears. But I must see and judge them for myself, for after what has happened to me I should have to be mad to adopt the judgment of men on any matter or to take anyone's word for anything.
>
> (p. 1057)

The ability to see everything himself, the position of omniscient spectator, is the privilege of the possessor of the ring of Gyges that Rousseau goes on to imagine. It is accompanied by invisible and absolute power, like the power of Messalina to determine, by a word to the emperor, the death of Valerius-Asiaticus.

In the *Quatrième Promenade* Rousseau refers to an occasion on which he brought about not the death but the dismissal and disgrace of a fellow servant, even while feeling intense sympathy for her predicament. The incident is recounted in book 2 of the *Confessions*. Accused of stealing a ribbon, Rousseau declares that it has been given to him by Marion, a pretty servant girl employed in the same house: "Never was spitefulness farther from me than in that cruel moment, and when I accused that unlucky girl, it is bizarre but it is true that my friendship for her was the cause of it. She was present to my mind, I excused myself on the first object that offered. ['Elle était présente à ma pensée, je m'excusai sur le premier objet qui s'offrit']" (p. 86). Like the double gesture of Messalina, Rousseau's action combines two incompatible positions: a speech act promptly effective in protecting the speaker and destroying its object; and a spectator's appreciation of a scene of unmerited suffering. Rousseau not only sees the scene as a spectacle, he speaks his lines as a figurative statement. This is what Rousseau is concerned to explain in the *Confessions:* "I accused her of having done what I wanted to do and of having given me the ribbon because my intention was to give it to her."

In the interest of making his excuse, Rousseau closely identifies the motive for an utterance with the meaning one wishes to communicate by it. Rousseau implies that his judges misunderstood his meaning in misunderstanding his motive, in failing to infer that his liking for Marion was the sense of his mentioning her name in connection with the ribbon. Rousseau claims that the statement "Marion gave me the ribbon," was a figure for "I would have liked to give the ribbon to Marion." And behind the inverted substitute statement produced by Rousseau stands not simply a particular motive—the intention of giving Marion the ribbon—but the wish that such inversions or substitutions should come into play, as they would if Marion reciprocated Rousseau's affection. Behind the figurative statement stands a desire that there be desire in circulation (between himself and Marion)—a desire that there be motives (for taking a ribbon). Rousseau's explanatory account implies that Marion was not the only victim in this episode, that his words, too, fell victim to a hasty literal interpretation by his employers (who failed to infer his wish to give Marion the ribbon). More fundamentally, however, they also failed to understand the order of motivation at work: one consisting not in particular motives, but in an orientation toward motivation itself. Rousseau makes nearly the same claims here about his act of speaking as he does about his writing in the *Sixième Promenade*. Even while accusing himself of slander, he declares his language to have been subjected to misreading.

But in the very midst of his account in the *Confessions,* Rousseau offers another version of how the slander occurred: "I excused myself on the first object that offered." Rousseau declares that his pronunciation of Marion's name was a matter of accident; it was the first sound that came out of his mouth when he was under pressure to open it. Instead of explaining what he said in terms of his motivation toward motivation, this half-sentence adduces no motivation at all for the enunciation "Marion." It was an altogether arbitrary expression: not even figure, a substitute name motivated by the wish to find a resemblance, but fiction in the most radical sense—without referent and without motive. According to this description of Rousseau's utterance, it was not simply misunderstood by his listeners; it was a misunderstanding to seek to understand it at all, for nothing at all stands behind it.

This reading of the passage in the *Confessions* follows the same sequence as the *Sixième Promenade:* a description of the predicament produced by a practice of interpretation based on the inference of motives, followed by an evocation of the state of fiction. The question arises whether Rousseau's two accounts of his utterance of the name "Marion" are related to each other in the same way as his diagnosis of his dilemma in the first part of the *Sixième Promenade* and his imagination of possessing the ring of Gyges in the second part. We saw that the predicament of being perpetually misinterpreted in an interpretive system matching meanings with motives impelled Rousseau to imagine a condition free of motivation. In imagining that condition—the fictional status of his language—Rousseau was at once realizing a certain motive (that of escaping motivation, which was bound to ensure his guilt), *and* actually replacing an erroneous conception of his language with a truer one. It is possible—almost—to read Rousseau's "second" account of his slander (as sheer accident) in much the same way. Thus, on the one hand Rousseau's description of his utterance as arbitrary and unmotivated can be interpreted as correctly designating the status of his language (as fictional); and on the other hand, this description functions as an excuse, and thus apparently realizes a motive (that of excusing Rousseau in the reader's eyes for his role in the dismissal of Marion). When one distinguishes between the act of accidentally saying "Marion" and the act of saying that one accidentally did so, it appears that whereas the first is unmotivated, the second is motivated— to escape motivation, in order to deny guilt. The second act and not the first would then be of the same order as Rousseau's fantasy of invisibility in the *Sixième Promenade*.

Rousseau's fiction "Marion" is an instance of the danger of fiction. The danger is not only that a fiction may invite its audience to read into it a particular motive (as Rousseau's employers do), but also that it may write a particular proper name. The most arbitrary fiction can coincide with the most efficient slander, and the account of the production of a fiction (the identification of an utterance as fiction) can function as the most effective denial of guilt.[10] Such an account is therefore powerfully motivated. In this way fiction does enter into the system of interpretation according to motive; the accident, which can be fatal, does enter retroactively into an economy in which the victim's identity is not arbitrary. The capacity to count one's acts as fictions is the power to deny any guilt—but without the power to control those acts or to elude the guilt that attaches to that account itself. Therefore Rousseau finally calls "inexcusable" his practice of producing fictions. This judgment comes in the next to last paragraph of the *Quatrième Promenade* (which begins by reinvoking the episode of the slander of Marion). It comes as a surprise after the preceding paragraphs, which distinguish persuasively between lies and fictions. The same pattern of last-minute retraction occurs near the end of the *Sixième Promenade* where Rousseau renounces his fantasy of possessing the ring of Gyges. We seem to know the reason for this renunciation of fiction: its power arbitrarily to engender guilt that cannot finally be excused. The claim that one's language is fiction has to be retracted because of the way it becomes implicated after all in the order of motivation.

Something in Rousseau's account of the Marion episode resists this reading, however, and resists being read in the same terms as Rousseau's imagination of the ring of Gyges (and this resistance might lead us to suspect that our reading of the latter passage has not gone far enough). If we look again at Rousseau's second account of his slander—the half-sentence positioned between the start and the finish of his confession of his motives, "I excused myself on the first object that offered"—we must conclude that guilt is not the greatest danger to the integrity of the speaker here. It is simply that he has no control over the act of utterance, which is described as if it were an involuntary physical motion. This intimation must alter our estimate of the relationship between uttering a fiction, in this sense, and claiming to have uttered one. To account one's utterance fictional, in this sense, is to evoke a dispersal of the speaking subject too drastic for there further to exist a speaker who would be acquitted, by the alibi of fiction, from the charge of willful slander. The claim that an utterance was fiction may still occur as an excuse, but as an excuse that is merely the material of a fiction, for there is no subject (no agent with a mode of motivation) to be excused.

We were wrong, then, to think that the identification of an utterance as fictional could be adequately accounted for in terms of a motive to deny motivation in order to defend the integrity of the speaker. The loss of control evoked by such a claim can in no way be motivated. Rather, the claim itself repeats the unmotivated gesture of the fiction "Marion." Rousseau's half-sentence "je m'excusai sur le premier objet qui s'offrit" is a repetition of the accident of saying "Marion." It cannot be accounted for, either, as a true estimate of the status of Rousseau's utterance coming to replace an erroneous estimate (as we read Rousseau's fantasy of invisibility). It must be read neither as a motivated, interested negation of motive nor as a motiveless, disinterested, in some sense inevitable disclosure of the truth about Rousseau's language. This is as much as to say that it must not be *read*. The clause on "Marion" interrupts Rousseau's account of the episode rather than follows it. This interruption differs entirely from the articulation of the *Sixième Promenade,* which we must no longer attempt to read in terms of the structure of the passage in the *Confessions.*

We have been led to repeat the gesture of last-minute retraction performed by Rousseau at the conclusion of his celebrations of fiction in the *Quatrième Promenade* and in the passage on the ring of Gyges. Does coming upon his fiction "Marion" have any effect on our reading of his allegory of invisibility? We read that passage in the light of the concept of motivation, taking a cue from the terms proposed by Rousseau in the course of the *Promenade* ("any motive . . . is never more than a *lure*"). We found Rousseau's fantasy of invisibility to be motivated as an escape from the order of motivation, an order that permanently threatened the subject with errors of interpretation. We read the imagination of invisibility as an imagination of the condition of fiction or an order of meaning dissociated from motives. We then interpreted Rousseau's renunciation of this imagined invisibility in terms, once more, of the danger of motivations, for the very negation of motive instituting fiction turned out to take its place in an economy of motivation all the more powerful for being denied. Throughout our reading, the order of motivation appeared as the danger, of error or of guilt, that Rousseau's *Promenade* attempted to circumvent.

But Rousseau's ultimate wariness of his position as invisible spectator led us to passages describing that position in the "Lettre à d'Alembert" and in the *Confessions;* and, in the latter text, fiction appeared in a form that could not be connected, by any means, with the order of motivation but, rather, occurred as an accident—as the incursion of sheer contingency into the activity of speech, a fatal accident to the idea of a subject in control of his utterance. We must note at once that no such accident takes place in the passage invoking the ring of Gyges in the *Sixième Promenade.* Here Rousseau writes an allegory on fiction as invisibility, an allegory that can be read, and read to designate the order of motivation as a permanent threat to the writing subject, and especially to the writing of fiction. Our perspective on this passage about the danger of motivation must shift once we have encountered, in Rousseau's fiction "Marion," the danger of accident—of a fiction that falls outside the order of motivation altogether. What falls outside such an order is also excluded from the passage of the *Sixième Promenade.* In that passage we discover the motivated negation of motive, which belongs to the order of possible motivations, even as the invisibility conferred by the ring of Gyges is a possibility included within the system of visibility in general. What we do not discover in the passage is the accident that does not take place there. But the exclusion of accident leaves a trace: in the peculiar pattern of retraction that ends the fantasy with a repetition of the finish of the *Quatrième Promenade,* and in an image not of guilt but of degradation: "this excess of power will only serve to sink him lower than others." We have as yet no term to identify the excluded accident and to differentiate it from the invisibility we have consistently interpreted as the condition of fiction. Invisibility is a sign, however, pointing us to another text where the "invisible" actually appears as a sign—Wordsworth's. His lines on the "coat of darkness" may spell out for us what was occulted by Rousseau's ring.

Wordsworth's lines on invisibility raise two issues absent from Rousseau's: the question of how it may be represented and the question of the pertinence of another text, the passage Wordsworth quotes from *Samson Agonistes.* Wordsworth describes with ironical amusement how easily invisibility is represented on stage, and his irony here also touches Milton:

How is it wrought?—his garb is black, the word
INVISIBLE flames forth upon his chest.

(1805, 7.309–10)

Invisibility can be represented with the greatest of ease abbreviated in
language, in a written word. Milton is the master of such an effect: he
makes "darkness visible" precisely by means of that formula, which
becomes a label as reusable as "Jack's." Juxtaposing a Sadler's Wells
pantomime and the poetry of Milton typifies Wordsworth's imagination of London, where all human inventions appear equalized by their
common denominator, the capacity to be displayed as signs:

The comers and the goers face to face—
Face after face—the string of dazzling wares,
Shop after shop, with symbols, blazoned names,
And all the tradesman's honours overhead:
Here, fronts of houses, like a title-page
With letters huge inscribed from top to toe;
Stationed above the door like guardian saints,
There, allegoric shapes, female or male,
Or physiognomies of real men,
Land-warriors, kings, or admirals of the sea,
Boyle, Shakespeare, Newton, or the attractive head
Of some quack-doctor, famous in his day.

(1805, 7.172–83)

Just as Shakespeare's shape can be set beside a quack doctor's, Milton's text can be set beside a quack Jack's. Wordsworth is writing in
the tradition of *The House of Fame,* not only Pope's satirical *reprise*
but Chaucer's ironical allegory, which places "Omer" and the other
immortal poets in Fame's palace along with the horde of rumor-
mongers and ambitious fakes. Wordsworth's irony embraces the fact
that any work of poetry, including Milton's, depends for its effects on
rhetorical devices requiring the complicity of the reader. That reading
effect is magically efficient in presenting the idea of invisibility, not
so much despite as because of the very paradox that when invisibility
is made visible (by becoming readable) its invisibility becomes invisible.
Language is the neatest trick. Wordsworth's quote reveals that a quite
specific trick is at issue here: producing invisibility from blindness by
means of an act of reading. Wordsworth too creates invisibility from
blindness, using Samson's lines on blindness to describe the actor's
fictive invisibility. As easily as invisibility becomes visible, blindness

turns to invisibility by another act of reading, Wordsworth's reading of the phrase from *Samson Agonistes.*

While Rousseau condemns the error of visualizing a particular agent and particular intention behind a text, Wordsworth satirizes the inverse misreading. Jack the Giant-Killer's invisibility makes his deeds seem to his victims to be caused by an impersonal agency such as destiny, and this invisibility is all too easily accepted and appreciated by the audience reading the actor's label. Wordsworth's account of the scenario shows it to be a trick of writing. His text reveals the blindness involved in *not* identifying a particular agency behind what can be read as "invisible"—read as the unmotivated action of language itself, the nonintentional and nonreferential language of fiction. (Wordsworth's poetry characteristically provokes and seems to celebrate such a reading, which occurs, for instance, in critics' and in Wordsworth's own interpretation of his encounter with the blind beggar in book 7.) Although Rousseau's passage on the ring of Gyges initially proposes the truth in the invisibility of the agency of Rousseau's language, Wordsworth's lines on the "coat of darkness" stress how wishful that conception of language is—one all too easy to write and to read, as Wordsworth indicates in showing the ease with which Jack's invisibility can be *visualized,* thanks to writing. As it happens, Wordsworth's judgment of the collusion between performers and audience—"Delusion bold! and faith must needs be coy"—could serve as an epigraph to Rousseau's fantasy of possessing the ring of Gyges, marking its slide from a bold faith to a coy concession of delusion. Wordsworth's judgment implies (as the final turn of Rousseau's text also suggests) that the notion of unmotivated, nonreferential language falls within the conception of motivation, belongs to the system of visibility, to the specular system conceiving language as the reflection of a subject.

Like the kind of misreading described by Rousseau, such as the error of his employers in taking literally his accusation of Marion, the misreading described by Wordsworth also has violent, if not serious, consequences. One can compare the Sadler's Wells *Giant-Killer* with Odysseus, who escaped unscathed after putting out the eye of the giant cyclops Polyphemus, thanks largely to a similar technique: he introduced himself to Polyphemus by the name of "No Man." When Polyphemus bellowed for help to his fellow cyclopes and they asked him who had injured him he replied, "No Man"; they replied that if no man injured him, then it must be an act of the gods: he must be either sick or mad. Because none of the other cyclopes came to take revenge on him, Odysseus was able to pass out of Polyphemus's cave invisibly (eluding Polyphemus's touch as well by hanging beneath the belly of one of his rams going out to pasture). It was Polyphemus's listeners who effectively transformed the name No Man to the meaning "no man." In the same way, it is Jack the Giant-Killer's audience who transforms the label "Invisible" into effectual invisibility, enabling the killing—on stage, to be sure—of several more giants blind to their adversary. If reading *in* a particular motive can be a dangerous error of interpretation, so can the reverse: ascribing an action to a disinterested agency, accounting it inevitable, or necessary.

In the case of Odysseus's feat as in the case of Jack's, the establishment of signification (with its prompt consequences) depends on a reading that must pass by way of an audience, a third party, a third reader distinct from the reader who is directly concerned (the giant) as well as from the producer of the sign. There is a further dimension, then, to the danger of reading (the enigmatic suggestion that initially induced our reading of these texts). It would seem to lie not only in the destructive action to which it may offer immunity, but in the elision of the speaking (or writing) or the reading (or listening) subject, bypassed for a third instance that functions more or less mechanically.

Wordsworth's evocation of the reading process as producing invisibility concerns not only the effects of language in general but Miltonic effects in particular, as his quotation suggests. The feat of converting blindness to invisibility is originally and peculiarly Milton's. Milton's literal blindness figures as a sign for his blindness to natural continuities, a blindness that operates, in turn, as visionary power. Like Jack the Giant-Killer, Milton becomes the invisible agency of extraordinary feats. "Miltonic blindness to the identity of the self as creator and the self being objectively represented in the process of wavering growth"[11] makes possible the poetry of *Paradise Lost*.

Miltonic blindness and visionary invisibility are so closely identified, and so different from the resources required by the autobiographical poet of *The Prelude,* that it would be wrong to suppose that Wordsworth's passage is designed (like Rousseau's) to fulfill the wish to produce invisibility from blindness. Rather, such blindness itself may appear as the content of a renounced wish:

> These beauteous forms,
> Through a long absence, have not been to me
> As is a landscape to a blind man's eye: . . .[12]

Here Wordsworth's affirmation of his own distinctive gift as a poet takes the form of a denial of Miltonic blindness. The denial that seeks to be an affirmation has the resonance of regret or renunciation. The tone is very different in the lines from the prospectus to *The Excursion,* where Wordsworth deliberately compares his project with Milton's.

> Not Chaos, not
> The darkest pit of lowest Erebus,
> Nor aught of blinder vacancy, scooped out
> By help of dreams—can breed such fear and awe
> As fall upon us when we look
> Into our Minds, into the Mind of Man—
> My haunt, and the main region of my song.[13]

To write the "more lowly matter" of *Tintern Abbey* and *The Prelude,* an account of "the Mind and Man contemplating," Wordsworth abandons comparison with Milton's project—to engage in a different kind of passage past "blind vacancy."

The structure of such a passage may perhaps be inscribed in the phrase Wordsworth selects to cite in his lines on the Sadler's Wells pantomime:

> He dons his coat of darkness, on the stage
> Walks, and atchieves [*sic*] his wonders, from the eye
> Of living mortal safe as is the moon
> 'Hid in her vacant interlunar cave.'

> (1805, 7.304–7)

The phrase from Milton is an oxymoron designating two contradictory spatial situations: the moon is "hid in her vacant interlunar cave," yet the cave is nonetheless "vacant." The moon and her cave are a radiant source and the site of its withdrawal, an inner agency and an outer site. The phrase simultaneously negates and affirms the persistence of an inner agency that is absent; absent, it either is, somewhere, or is not. The phrase asserts both these alternatives. In addition, the site of this absence is not in fact spatial but temporal: her "interlunar cave" is that phase of the moon in which the moon is intermitted, left out.

Is there a "hidden" agency or is there no agency—rather, a "vacant" site? Wordsworth's citation makes the question undecidable. The question and the assertion of both its contradictory answers constitute a gesture that we have traced in the text of Rousseau's fantasy on the ring of Gyges. That gesture is also enacted by the two texts taken together, as we are reading them here: whereas Wordsworth's lines on the "coat of darkness" first of all display the operation of a "hidden" agency, Rousseau's account of his ring first of all maintains the vacancy of its site. We can read Wordsworth's citation as an emblem of the issue raised between his text and Rousseau's.

We can also read it as an emblem for the "blinder vacancy," unlike Miltonic blindness, that takes place in *The Prelude*. One place it occurs is in "London," in a passage not far from the scene at Sadler's Wells. Wordsworth here is "smitten" by a spectacle—the spectacle not of imaginary invisibility but of literal blindness.

> 'twas my chance
> Abruptly to be smitten with the view
> Of a blind beggar, who, with upright face,
> Stood propped against a wall, upon his chest
> Wearing a written paper, to explain
> The story of the man, and who he was.
> My mind did at this spectacle turn round
> As with the might of waters, and it seemed
> To me that in this label was a type
> Or emblem of the utmost that we know
> Both of ourselves and of the universe,
> And on the shape of this unmoving man,
> His fixed face and sightless eyes, I looked,
> As if admonished from another world.

(1805, 7.610–23)

As at Sadler's Wells, it is a man wearing a label that Wordsworth finds so powerfully diverting ("My mind . . . turn[ed] round"). Once again the impact of the scene depends on an act of reading. The blind beggar, like Jack the Giant-Killer, cannot read his own label. In the other passage it was the imaginary magical power of an actor that depended on an audience's participation, which seemed to function according to a guaranteed mechanism. Here it is the man's very identity that depends on the mediation of a third person, a spectator, a passerby who may happen to turn his gaze from the blank face and read the written figures. Or rather, there can be no identity in this composite of "fixed face and sightless eyes" and "written paper." The blind beggar displays the separation between functions as intimately interdependent as writing and reading and shows that the text exists precisely by virtue of this division.[14] In the blind beggar, Wordsworth confronts an image of the autobiographical poet unable to read his own text.

It appears that Wordsworth's "coat of darkness" is a wishful inversion of blindness after all. Yet the role in both passages of a written label reveals that the crucial inversion at stake is, rather, the conversion of the arbitrariness of mere chance, in the generation of meaning, into the arbitrariness of a mechanism, the mechanics of rhetorical and theatrical tricks. The spectators who guarantee special power to the Giant-Killer of Sadler's Wells are there to supplant the absent or vacant spectator who would confer intelligibility on the beggar with his written paper. In the case of the blind beggar, the connection between text and meaning is intermittent and contingent. But Wordsworth's response to the "spectacle" promptly reaffirms their connection: his mind "turn[s] round," to pass from the vacancy of the accidental encounter between himself and the beggar and the darkness of the fatal juxtaposition of "sightless eyes" and "written paper" to the plenitude of an ulterior sense: "a type / Or emblem of the utmost that we know. . . . I looked, / As if admonished from another world." It is as if the label in its role as "type" had made the literal blind beggar invisible, like the actor playing Jack the Giant-Killer, and enabled him to appear, like Jack, as the operation of a supernatural agency. (It should be noted here that our own acceptance of the composite image of the beggar as an emblem for autobiography performs, inevitably, a similar recuperative gesture. Yet the conjunction of "emblem" and "autobiography"—of the autobiographical and the pictorial or visual—proves, in Wordsworth's text, to resist restorative responses.) That final line, however, can also be read another way. The "other world" from which the poet is (paradoxically) "admonished" might be a world in which reading occurs or fails to occur by accident rather than for cause. This is the world, or the time, in which the condition of the possibility of meaning is "hid in her vacant interlunar cave." Reading occurs by accident: the cave is vacant; but that accident occurs in a reading (such as the reading that it occurs by accident): a condition for meaning *is* there, "hid."

The lines that recount Samson's final action in *Samson Agonistes* share the same narrative perspective as Wordsworth's description of the scene at Sadler's Wells in book 7 of *The Prelude*. The scene at the temple of Dagon is recounted afterward by an eyewitness, the Hebrew messenger. Samson is absent; from blind subject he becomes, in effect, the invisible agent of the closing scene. That is, the same conversion that takes place between Milton's lines and Wordsworth's also takes place within Milton's poem itself. The question arises of what Wordsworth is converting and what he is repeating. The Hebrew messenger tells of a hero's deed requiring self-destruction.

The building was a spacious theatre,
Half round on two main Pillars vaulted high,
. . . .
At length for intermission sake they led him
Between the pillars; . . .
                              . . . which when Samson
Felt in his arms; with head a while inclined,
And eyes fast fixed he stood, as one who prayed,
Or some great matter in his mind revolved.
At last with head erect thus cried aloud,
Hitherto, lords, what your commands imposed
I have performed, as reason was, obeying,
Not without wonder or delight beheld.
Now of my own accord such other trial
I mean to show you of my strength, yet greater;
As with amaze shall strike all who behold.
This uttered, straining all his nerves he bowed,
As with the force of winds and waters pent,
When mountains tremble, those two massy pillars
With horrible convulsion to and fro
He tugged, he shook, till down they came and drew
The whole roof after them, with burst of thunder
Upon the heads of all who sat beneath,
Lords, ladies, captains, counsellors, or priests,
Their choice nobility and flower, not only
Of this but each Philistian city round
Met from all parts to solemnize this feast.[15]

This is the performance of a giant killer, and one that exploits his
rhetorical manipulation of his audience. Jack the Giant-Killer's feat
requires that his audience read him literally and referentially (taking
the label to mean "this person is invisible"). Samson invites his audience to understand his words in their ordinary figurative sense, to assume that he will "strike them" with amazement, rather than strike them
in such a way as to amaze them. At last Samson effectively both destroys
and becomes the "tongue-doughty giant" who had been his antithesis
(personified by the giant Philistine Harapha). Samson's alienation from
his own language finally takes the form of mastery of a rhetorical device in the service of effective action. Yet this reuniting of language
and power produces no *Aufhebung* but spectacular downfall and
destruction.

The change from lack of control of one's own language to mastery of a rhetorical device is the transformation at issue in Wordsworth's metamorphosis of Samson and the label-wearing beggar into the label-wearing actor at Sadler's Wells. This transformation is an instance, rather more intricately condensed than usual, of that "discourse . . . sustained *beyond* and in spite of *deprivation*"[16] that characterizes Wordsworth's autobiographical writing in *The Prelude,* which orders, for example, the passage of the Winander Boy from "pauses of deep silence" to "the bosom of the steady lake" and the village churchyard, and the passage of the drowned man's "ghastly face" to "purest poesy." One could work out the recurrence of this scheme in book 7: the discourse of autobiography, as a process of self-reading, is interrupted by the shock of "London," by an accident like the blind beggar's deprivation of sight with which to read his own story; discourse is sustained by the theatrical trick that passes by way of an audience reading and identifying the text with its wearer. The trick also inverts the relation between the two subjects, so that the blinded writer is replaced by a blinded reader, in a reading process that transfers authority to the writing subject.

"Half-rural Sadler's Wells" thus serves, in Wordsworth's "London," to assimilate the compulsion of accident, as it appears for example in the "mill" and the monsters of the "true epitome / Of what the mighty City is herself" (the Fair), to a visible scene revealing a specular structure. Wordsworth's very ability to distinguish himself from the simple spectators at the performance ("Nor was it mean delight / To watch crude Nature work in untaught minds") gives him the security of finding himself beyond the confines of the theatrical performance, like the pleasure of self-consciousness he recalls from the "country-playhouse" of his childhood, when "having caught / In summer through the fractured wall a glimpse / Of daylight, at the thought of where I was / I gladdened" (1805, 7.482–85). This pleasure depends on a stable distinction between the inside of the theater and the space outside it, between sunlight and the artificial lighting that by itself becomes sinister, like the glare of the theater in the scene in which the beautiful baby boy appears to Wordsworth "Of lusty vigour, more than infantine . . . a cottage-child," miraculously immune to his position "environed with a ring / Of chance spectators" (1805, 7.379–87). Wordsworth shares some of Rousseau's mistrust of the theater. Spectacle is associated for him with the tyranny of the eye, "a transport of the outward sense, / Not of the mind."[17] Hence it is unlikely that a theatrical spectacle should serve primarily in Wordsworth's writing to restore a disrupted specular structure, as in the reading we have just suggested—unless, indeed, that specular structure itself were to turn out to share the disturbing qualities of spectacle, rather than serving to stabilize a self-conscious subject.

A theater is the scene, a spectacle the pretext, of Samson's heroic deed. The very theatricality of Samson's final act could threaten to diminish its tragic effect. Irony encroaches on the drama not only because the hero's action is one of mass destruction that also destroys himself. The more corrosive irony lies in the rhetorical character of Samson's feat. Not that his feat is easily trivialized; a theatrical performance, and an act of language, become the pretext for actual annihilation. Language and power coincide here in an act of destruction. But what is also threatened with destruction, in Milton's text, is the meaningfulness of their momentary convergence. For good reason Samson's play on the word *strike* is not conspicuous in Milton's lines: his feat must not seem to depend on an arbitrary mechanism. Such a reading would deprive the disparity between "eyesight" and "strength" of pathos and make Samson's tragedy an essentially linguistic predicament, a matter of the way language functions or fails to function. That functioning is the very topic of Wordsworth's passage on Jack the Giant-Killer, which deliberately empties of pathos the phrase from *Samson*. Wordsworth's lines repeat and make explicit the depiction of the theatrical and rhetorical devices at work in Samson's plot. Yet the workings of such devices threaten the pathos and meaning not only of Milton's tragedy, but of the discrepancy between "knowledge" and "power" and the impossibility of self-reading that are themes of Wordsworth's autobiographical writing.

A greater threat to self-reading or autobiographical writing emerges in Wordsworth's text by way of what it precisely declines to repeat: the exact wording of the blind Samson's enigmatic opening monologue. Wordsworth's citation of *Samson Agonistes* in fact entails a crucial discrepancy. We shall find that Wordsworth's revision reveals the stakes of his reading of Milton, and even more, of the act of reading in general.

The citation designs to turn us away from its source as much as to turn us back to it. Milton writes,

> The sun to me is dark
> And silent as the moon,
>
> . . . .
>
> Hid in her vacant interlunar cave.

(ll. 86–9)

Wordsworth, in the text of 1805, writes,

> safe as is the moon
> 'Hid in her vacant interlunar cave.'

Wordsworth's rewording converts *silent* to *safe;* his revision of Samson's lines follows the affirmative negation composed by Milton in a passage evoking his own blindness:

> Half yet remains unsung, but narrower bound
> Within the visible diurnal sphere;
> Standing on earth, not rapt above the pole,
> More safe I sing with mortal voice, unchanged
> To hoarse or *mute,* though fallen on evil days,
> On evil days though fallen, and evil tongues;
> In darkness, and with dangers compassed round. . . .[18]

Wordsworth might well have wished to appropriate these lines for his own project, and his revisionary citation of Samson's lines might appear consistent with such an attitude. Something else, though, is at stake.

In Milton's text, *silent* interrupts the already contradictory spatial image (further complicated by a temporal description) with a term from a different order, that of sound. It is as though Samson's lament for being blind suddenly shifted to a lament for being deaf. Samson does lose the sense of the meaning of others' utterance: "I hear the sound of words, their sense the air / Dissolves unjointed ere it reach my ear" (ll. 176–77). The true strangeness of these lines, however, lies in the fact that the interruptive part of Samson's complaint might truthfully be echoed by anyone: "The sun to me is silent." Just this Wordsworth will not repeat. For what Samson makes a measure of the most terrible deprivation is the condition of anyone who hears and sees. To lament that the sun is silent is to identify the condition of *sense,* the possession of physical senses and the ability to conceive sense or meaning, as a state of deprivation. Samson's disorienting complaint for the very orientation of language is a lament for the unintelligibility of the most fundamental figure, whereby *light* is imagined as intelligibility conceived as *voice.* To refer to the silence of the sun as a catastrophe is to point to how vital is the identification of light with meaning conceived as voicing, and how fatal the strictly figurative, rhetorical status of that identification.

That identification is imposed by "decree." Samson's lament

associates the deprivation of sense with the Word that imposes meaning even as it gives light. Here Milton's lines link the issue of "sense" (of figuration and meaning) with the issue of motivation—to suggest that the imposition of sense is *un*motivated, or, rather, that for the "prime decree" the question of motivation is unmotivated and arbitrary. Since it is without intentional status, its figurative status is also indeterminable, and its truth status undecidable. As the imposition of "sense" through an arbitrary speech act, the "prime decree" is a bereavement. In this passage, the moment in which the system of motivation is exceeded and the moment in which the system of figuration is exceeded come into play together.

If sense is identified as a state of deprivation, the restoration of sense becomes a meaningless project. Lamentation that "the sun . . . is silent" threatens both Milton's tragedy and Wordsworth's autobiography. In particular, it subverts the project of restoring and maintaining the identity of the subject beyond death, which is the theme of *Samson Agonistes'* final lines and of Wordsworth's *Essays upon Epitaphs.* The first essay states that an epitaph is composed in a "belief in immortality" yet designed "to be accomplished . . . in close connection with the bodily remains of the deceased." The mediation between the two ideas depends, in Wordsworth's essay, on an analogy between the "journey" of life (toward death and immortality) and journeys following the sun—"voyage toward the regions where the sun sets," which will ultimately approach the east, and "voyage towards . . . the birthplace . . . of the morning," which will ultimately approach the west.[19] Such "lively and affecting analogies of life as a journey" are meant to give "to the language of the senseless stone a voice" (p. 54). A meaningful epitaph, a text that achieves restoration of meaning, is supposed to have a voice. (Manoa, too, imagines inscribing "sweet lyric song" on Samson's grave.) Voice is the value threatened by the inalterable silence defined in Samson's complaint about the sun. In describing a lack constituted by sense itself, by the very condition of meaning, that complaint describes language, the condition of intelligibility, as a deprivation. The subject's relation to his own language is lacking; the privation at issue here is muteness, the subject's deprivation of his own voice. This is the silence that Wordsworth censors when he quotes Samson in *The Prelude.*

In concluding the last of the *Essays upon Epitaphs,* Wordsworth quotes himself, and here he designates the inalterable silence mentioned by Samson. The lines Wordsworth cites are a passage from book 7 of *The Excursion* ("The Churchyard among the Mountains") concerning the life, death, and grave of the Dalesman, a deaf-mute:

> When stormy winds
> Were working the broad bosom of the lake
> Into a thousand, thousand sparkling waves,
> Rocking the trees, or driving cloud on cloud
> Along the sharp edge of yon lofty crags,
> The agitated scene before his eye
> Was silent as a picture: evermore
> Were all things silent, whereso'er he moved.

(p. 94)

One's own muteness is as such inconceivable (just as one cannot conceive oneself incapable of meaning anything). Yet the way the Dalesman's lack is described here suggests, like the interruptive part of Samson's lament, a condition not peculiar to him but inevitable. "Silent as a picture," "the sun is silent"—these lines require us to think the very forms of intelligibility—the visible, the figural—as forms of privation.

Wordsworth's lines on the deaf-mute go on to describe his compensations. Though we have already inferred from the format of Samson's complaint that compensation or restoration must lose their meaning if sense is a deprivation, it is important to be explicit about the forms such compensation takes. Wordsworth's lines on the Dalesman are explicit on the matter, and what we find ourselves reading is a description of reading:

> books
> Were ready comrades whom he could not tire,—
> Of whose society the blameless Man
> Was never satiate. Their familiar voice,
> Even to old age, with unabated charm
> Beguiled his leisure hours; refreshed his thoughts;...[20]

(p. 95)

Muteness is compensated for, Wordsworth tells us, by means of books. That is, books do not have a voice themselves; they provide a substitute "voice," once they have been personified (as "ready comrades," in the phrase of The Excursion). This is a voice only according to a rhetorical device—one on which the intelligibility of language depends, for it is impossible (or lunacy) to conceive of language without reference to the idea of voice. Books, however, are precisely a voiceless language, as the very nature of their "voice" indicates, and as Wordsworth's focus on their role as "ready comrades" for a deaf-mute emphasizes. Wordsworth's phrase here stresses simultaneously the personifying figure that lends books a voice and the fact of their muteness.

Books themselves, the means of compensation or restoration, install the very deprivation for which they were meant to compensate. When Wordsworth quotes Milton's poem *On Shakespeare* in the first of the *Essays upon Epitaphs*, he leaves out the following lines:

> For whilst to the shame of slow-endeavouring art,
> Thy easy numbers flow, and that each heart
> Hath from the leaves of thy unvalued book
> Those Delphic lines with deep impression took,
> Then thou our fancy of it self bereaving
> Dost make us marble with too much conceiving; . . .[21]

The "book" makes its reader mute. To *hear* a monument, to hear its "easy numbers flow," is to take on ourselves the mute fixity of a text. By revealing the figurative and fictive nature of its voice, the book exposes the voicelessness of language, which is an unthinkable conception, "bereaving" the reader of his relationship to language.

One's relation to one's own voice is not a specular one. The projection of voice in a text, however, installs a specular structure. Just as "light" must imply intelligibility conceived as voice, as meaning, so "voice" must imply meaning conceived as light, as the presentation of an intelligible figure; otherwise the very sense of voice or light is lost. But this means that voice must be projected in a text or a figure. In Milton's account, "voice" is substituted for voice: the articulate reader becomes the mute marble of an epitaph. As the nonspecular relation to voice becomes a specular structure, it becomes a trope.

Specularity does turn out, then, to have the disturbing effect Wordsworth associates with spectacle, "the transport of the outward sense." The very textual structure that was supposed to compensate for or restore the relation to voice definitively subverts it. The epitaph's visual and figural language, and its figural and literal orientation toward the sun, was supposed to guarantee it a genuine voice. In effect it installs the voice of a silent reading: "The sun looks down upon the stone, and the rains of heaven beat against it." In this sentence, which seems to celebrate the natural condition of the epitaph, "the sun . . . is silent" and the inscription "silent as a picture." The epitaph itself is revealed in this light to install, by the very achievement of the "voice" of legibility, a voicelessness that is a more radical privation than death.

In the context of the citations in the *Essays upon Epitaphs*, it becomes possible to determine the significance of Wordsworth's citation of *Samson Agonistes* in the passage on Jack the Giant-Killer. It becomes evident, in the first place, why Wordsworth changes *silent* to *safe:* not because Milton's powerful voice threatens his own with silence, but because this "silent" moment in Milton's text designates Wordsworth's peril from his own writing. This is also the case in the omission of the lines on the "unvalued book" from Milton's poem *On Shakespeare.* To identify the "book" as Milton's poetry, making it Milton's presence that threatens Wordsworth with self-"bereaving" through "too much conceiving" so that he censors these lines, is to adopt as a final explanation what is rather an explanatory figure in the poetry itself. Milton's figure is not a reassuring one: "we" readers are portrayed as being turned to stone by reading another's book; yet simply by differentiating the names of writer and readers, it preserves a notion of the individual subject that remains informed with the idea of individual voice. In this sense it is more reassuring, and more explanatory, than the idea of a muteness induced by one's own language.

Wordsworth turns to quote Milton when his own voice is threatened. Wordsworth is then like the Dalesman turning to his "ready comrades," the "books he could not tire," for a compensatory "voice." Yet that very supplement confirms the deprivation, as the instance in the lines on Sadler's Wells makes clear: the cited passage designates the very privation at issue, so that Milton's writing must be censored in turn.

What, specifically, in Wordsworth's own writing, in the passage on Jack the Giant-Killer, threatens his voice and impels him to borrow Milton's? It is the spectacle of the voiceless efficacy of writing that has such an impact, the actor's role played out "silent as a picture" through the written label on his coat. It is not simply the effectiveness of theatrical or rhetorical trickery that is involved. The lines on the deaf-mute spell out what was "silent as a picture": "stormy winds . . . working the broad bosom of the lake," "the agitated scene before his eye"—nature. The lines on the quality of his enjoyment at Sadler's Wells spell out that the same order of reality is at issue: "Nor was it mean delight/To watch crude Nature work in untaught minds." "Crude nature" is crude literacy, the ability to read a written sign. Language is nature, and language as such, not simply the rhetorical device, is silent, a deprivation of one's own voice. This deprivation is the very scenario at Sadler's Wells. For the power that is "invisible" ought to be the power of voice. It must take the form, however, of writing. Not invisibility, not blindness, but visibility itself is the predicament, the system of visibility that is the system of literal and figural language. Intelligible language, intelligible nature, is mute—an idea that makes no sense, that mutes the mind that articulates it, and that Wordsworth therefore silences.

To silence it, though, Wordsworth repeats the very gesture that was disturbing: he displays a label, a phrase detached from its context in the speech of Samson, and flaunted, like the actor's label, to produce an image of invisibility. The poet's irreverence toward Milton resembles the actor's irreverence about invisibility. The trivializing of potentially serious themes gets contrastingly stern treatment in *Essays upon Epitaphs,* where Wordsworth recurrently denounces the subversion of taste "by the artifices which have overrun our writings in metre since the days of Dryden and Pope." Wordsworth's satirical writing in "London" has a Popeian resonance in the very lines where he is criticizing this culture of wit and satire, and his gesture in citing *Samson Agonistes* in his lines on Sadler's Wells could be described as he describes the unpardonable fault of writing bad epitaphs:

> Energy, stillness, grandeur, tenderness, those feelings which are the pure emanations of nature, those thoughts which have the infinitude of truth, and those expressions which are not what the garb is to the body but what the body is to the soul, themselves a constituent part and power or function in the thought—all these are abandoned for their opposites,—as if our Countrymen, through successive generations, had lost the sense of solemnity and pensiveness (not to speak of deeper emotions) and resorted to the Tombs of their Forefathers and Contemporaries only to be tickled and surprized.
>
> (p. 84)

The practice of citation in this present exercise at times may have seemed to invite the same reproach. The fault finally at stake, though, is the act of reading. Quoting is a would-be reading aloud, an effort to give voice to language. Such an effort is doomed to make sense—sense that is a state of deprivation, as Wordsworth characterizes the sense that resides in language.

Such sense is senseless. Wordsworth writes this out in a passage that must be quoted here, in a conspicuously final position, as if to serve as the telos of a certain trajectory—imitating a gesture that occurs more than once in current writing on Wordsworth and on language.[22]

> Words are too awful an instrument for good and evil to be trifled with: they hold above all other external powers a dominion over thoughts. If words be not (recurring to a metaphor before used) an incarnation of the thought but only a clothing for it, then surely will they prove an ill gift; such a one as those poisoned vestments, read of in the stories of superstitious times, which had power to

consume and to alienate from his right mind the victim who put them on. Language, if it do not uphold, and feed, and leave in quiet, like the power of gravitation or the air we breathe, is a counter-spirit, unremittingly and noiselessly at work to derange, to subvert, to lay waste, to vitiate, and to dissolve.[23]

At Sadler's Wells, language is "noiselessly at work," as the Giant-Killer achieves his wonders "silent," precisely, "as the moon." This threat to the "body" of *The Prelude* Wordsworth displaces by citing and censoring Milton—only, indeed, to designate by omission the very effect that threatens him: clothing the gap with a quote only gives it more permanent outline. The poisoned vestments Wordsworth mentions refer to the tunic of Nessus, that compensatory garment supposed to ensure the wearer's love for the giver, but which in fact guarantees its wearer's lunacy.[24] The Giant-Killer's coat of darkness is a comparable garment, a compensatory device that installs a still worse deprivation. Samson too, with his "redundant locks," risks the mad death of the other giant-killer, Hercules.[25] Autobiography becomes as mad a gesture as the blind beggar's appears to be when, by wearing his story in written form rather than uttering it, he compounds blindness with muteness. Wordsworth's *Essays* and *The Prelude* are such "poisoned vestments": autobiographical writing does not "leave" a life "in quiet," but through the very process of giving it a "voice" in language, which is voiceless, makes it mute.

Rousseau's possession of the ring of Gyges is another such project. (It was supposed to ensure the mutual love of the giver and his recipients, his dazzled readers.) As in Wordsworth's case it is the silent voice of language that exposes its voicelessness, in Rousseau's case it is the system of motivation itself that reveals its lack of motivation. The condition of invisibility imagined by Rousseau is one of unmotivated motivation, unmotivated inference of motives, a gratuitous act of reading "au fond des coeurs" that is mad in the sense that it reinstalls the conception of the motivation of meaning that as "invisible" fictional writing it had begun by renouncing. The very omniscience and omnipotence that should free one of unrealized motives, unsatisfied desires, and temptations becomes a compulsion to "chercher des tentations." The unintentional intending evoked here by Rousseau can also be read in the last word of *Samson Agonistes:*

Oft he seems to hide his face,
But unexpectedly returns
. . . .
    whence Gaza mourns

> And all that band them to resist
> His *uncontrollable intent;*

(ll. 1749–54; my italics)

Here in the voice of piety, under cover of the idea of necessity, once again we come upon the language of "prime decree" and unreadable motive.

The term we were seeking, for a fiction distinct from fiction as "invisibility," could be *muteness*—fiction as language deprived of voice. The accident that occurs, in Rousseau's lines on "Marion," is an incoherence that interrupts his relation to his own voice. This moment actualizes the *impossibility of excluding the possibility of accident:* the impossibility of excluding from language—which is "perceived" in being read, and which is motivated by reading—the effects of sheerly random pattern. Rousseau's "inexcusable" ceding to "le babil de la conversation," like Samson's, is but the inverse of muteness. The degradation that Rousseau realizes to be the ineluctable effect of using the ring of Gyges is muteness or madness—being a vegetable, as Shelley will put it:

> I turned and knew
>
> . . . .
>
> That what I thought was an old root which grew
> To strange distortion out of the hill side
> Was indeed one of that deluded crew,
> And that the grass which methought hung so wide
> And white, was but his thin discolored hair,
> And that the holes it vainly sought to hide
> Were or had been eyes. [26]

Shelley has Rousseau tell us how this degradation came about: because he "joined the dance" of "Life." He joined in motivation; he joined in the process of reading. This joining in occurred through the very lucidity of an "invisible," unreadable fictional text, capable of reading other texts and finally voicelessly reading its own. Shelley is also evoking another madness, the inevitable misreading of Rousseau's texts that came "in the guise"[27] of the French Revolution. The "Rousseau" at issue here for Shelley is also a certain Wordsworth. For, as the end of *Essays upon Epitaphs* suggests, the effort to give voice to language can give rise only to a voiceless "language unremittingly and noiselessly at work . . . to vitiate, and to dissolve" the condition of the possibility of meaning.

Viewless Wings

Keats's *Ode to a Nightingale*

The difficulty of interpreting Keats's poetry is closely bound up with its loveliness, its power to gratify our wish for beauty. This is a power to provoke nearly unanimous value judgments together with widely disparate accounts of their occasion. Modern criticism of Keats presents a curious picture: a clear consensus on the harmonious tenor of the development leading from *Sleep and Poetry* to the ode *To Autumn,* together with strong disagreement on the meaning of its individual moments. I will begin by sketching one such disagreement— about how to characterize Keats's situation in the exquisite fifth stanza of the *Ode to a Nightingale*—to help us ask: what investments can we discern here, important enough to be common to such opposite critical readings? For if critics give incompatible accounts of key passages, and yet end with the same judgments, their conclusions must be motivated by some other kind of constraint than the acts of reading from which they ostensibly arise. The nature of such constraints on critical reading can emerge for us, I suggest, if we attend to the tropes and the rhetorical gestures that Keats's ode cites or repeats—if we carry out a certain kind of intertextual reading.

How does one characterize the gesture of the ode's peculiarly Keatsian fifth stanza—naming flowers in the darkness, guessing each sweet, "White hawthorn, and the pastoral eglantine"? It depends on how one reads the fourth: it depends on that notorious crux where— as typically in Keats—the most lovely *and* the most variously interpreted lines of the poem coincide: [1]

Already with thee! tender is the night,
   And haply the Queen-Moon is on her throne,
     Cluster'd around by all her starry Fays;

But here there is no light,
Save what from heaven is with the breezes blown
Through verdurous glooms and winding mossy ways.

The fifth stanza continues, "I cannot see what flowers are at my feet.
. . ." The question of how to take this passage is loaded by the lines at
the opening of stanza 4 with the issue of Keats's commitment to poetic
flight:

Away! away! for I will fly to thee,
Not charioted by Bacchus and his pards,
But on the viewless wings of Poesy,
Though the dull brain perplexes and retards:

The decision how to read what follows amounts to a judgment upon
the speaker's commitment to "the viewless wings of Poesy." It is here
that one finds an incipient consensus, not upon the function of the
viewless wings in these lines, but upon the desirability of Keats's ultimately giving them up. Interpretations of the fourth and fifth stanzas
converge in a final value judgment—that Keats ought to abandon
poetic flight—after diverging widely on just *how* these stanzas mean
that. Keats's lines effectively resist attempts to determine the matter
more precisely by appealing to them alone, for at this decisive juncture
the ode's syntax turns radically ambiguous. To judge the effects of
recourse to the viewless wings of poesy we have to decide how to
voice the exclamation point after the fourth stanza "thee." A mute
mark stands at the place which is *either* an exclamation at arrival *or*
a statement of distance. The punctuation mark doesn't tell us how to
hear it: whether as an expression of passionate satisfaction, or as a
mere pause for differentiation, like a heavier comma or displaced
italics. To have an *ear* for this can only be to have a stake in a story
about the nightingale and Keats.

Earl Wasserman's cold ear—rigorously attentive to the program by
which the ode distances the poet from his addressee—can hear that
"thee!" as no more than a stressed difference: with *thee* the night is
tender; with me, meanwhile, it's not. For Wasserman the fifth stanza,
with the poet's evocation of "The coming musk-rose, full of dewy
wine, / The murmurous haunt of flies on summer eves," matters chiefly
as a deferred and imagined season that cannot match the summer sung
"in full-throated ease" by the nightingale.[2]

More typically this "guessing" of "what flowers are at my feet" is
taken as a reward, and as a characteristically Keatsian achievement
something like the luxurious surmise of the ode *To Autumn.* Leslie

Brisman takes this stanza as a reward for "the demystified *rejection* of transcendent flight" he finds in the fourth stanza. Casting off the "viewless wings" of the visionary imagination together with "the dull brain [that] perplexes and retards" brings Keats at once to the resonant resources "at my feet"—to a "poetry of earth," "to the significant earth whence all sign-constructions take their origin."[3]

We find the same conclusion at the end of an entirely different reading by Jack Stillinger, for whom the speaker's situation in stanza five is not a reward but a bereavement: he sees in it "the speaker's vivid realization of what he has lost by crossing the boundary into an imaginary ideal"—"the transient natural world he has *left behind* and now longs for."[4] Rejection of wings, return to the earth, or adoption of wings, loss of the earth; diametrically opposed as they are, both readings feed into essentially the same account of Keats's accomplishment. He is praised for renouncing finally the Romantic vision of poetry as transcendent flight, and so inaugurating the demystifying gesture of modernism. Critical unanimity about Keats reflects an agreement on how to place Romanticism in the literary tradition. It is seen as a predominantly symbolic and recurrently visionary and escapist mode, to be valued insofar as critical moments of its greatest men, Keats and Wordsworth, anticipate the undeceived modernist vision that marks our own historical moment.

Keats is the poet most assertively invoked where the Romantics are judged from the standpoint of their consistency with a certain note sounded in Stevens and Williams: a "poetry of earth," committed to the intensities and truths of perception. I would suggest that Keats gets invoked in this context because his poetry has to be appropriated, since in fact it *questions* the status of perception, makes the nature of sensory evidence a difficulty. But at the same time Keats's poetry richly gratifies that wish for beauty that impels us to ascribe epistemological authority to the aesthetic, to presume the continuity of perception with knowledge. It is this that makes Keats's texts peculiarly hard to read.

The predominant critical account would reassure itself about a quite intractable issue. We find Brisman and Bloom, as well as Stillinger (along with other less strikingly disparate critics), praising what Stillinger describes as Keats's "final opting for the natural world, where all the concrete images of poetry come from and where melodies impinge on 'the sensual ear' or not at all."[5] The resemblance to Brisman's praise of stanza 5 is striking: Keats returns to "the significant earth whence all sign-constructions take their origin." These very affirmations indicate what constrains such different critical readings to conclude with the same affirmation. It is vital that signs be seen to "take their origin" or find their expression in the phenomenal world, just as it is vital that "melodies"—or language—"impinge on 'the sensual ear.'" The intelligibility of language and the meaningfulness of sensory experience require it. But does Keats's text make this guarantee? The problem is indeed that "melodies impinge on 'the sensual ear' or not at all." At stake is the possibility of *hearing* writing—of hearing a voice in, and putting a face or a name to, linguistic signs. At stake is the assumption on which reading depends, the continuity between perception and cognition—and Keats's poetry treats it as an *issue* rather than an assumption. The Nightingale Ode ends with a question about the status of the intense perception it has evoked: "Was it a vision or a waking dream?"

The question of whether perception is not hallucination surfaces often in Keats's poetry, but it arises with special force through the prominence of that paradigmatic lyric mode, the ode. The ode's distinctive trait is a special kind of prosopopoeia, or personification, the gesture of address. Odes generally entail apostrophe, sometimes to the reader, sometimes to a nonhuman or an inanimate object. Now, this trope that usually works to "make the objects of the universe potentially responsive forces"—that characteristic lyric function—tends to be not interrogated, but dismissed as meaningless cliché. Critics as various as George Shuster (in *The English Ode from Milton to Keats*) and Michael Riffaterre (in *La Production du texte*) have tended to dismiss apostrophe as being insignificant because it is simply conventional; they tend, as Jonathan Culler and Paul de Man point out, to try to "transform apostrophe into description."[6] But in the characteristic discourse of the lyric, description of objects' sensory qualities—perception—only follows upon the primary apostrophic gesture. "The address frames the description it makes possible" (writes de Man); "the figuration" in the text "occurs by way of address."[7] Apostrophe expresses the lyric presupposition that the object may be addressed as a subject, and it makes that vital presupposition "independently of any claims made about the actual properties of the object addressed."[8] The figural logic of the lyric as it appears in its paradigmatic form, the ode, would make us grasp the sense of Vico's assertion that poetry— and specifically the trope that "gives sense and passion to insensate things"—is the origin of language.[9] Why, then, are critics uncomfortable about making the figure of address conspicuous? For good reason: what we suppress when we ignore apostrophe is the dependence of all discourse, including what we call *perception,* on the figure of address. For what the address does is to claim the existence of an addressee capable of *hearing* it: capable of giving ear, of giving voice, to a text; passing from a sign to a sound and a sense; passing between cognition and perception. The trope of address, a prosopopoeia, institutes the intelligibility of language by engendering the figure of a reader; that is, by letting us conceive of the reading of a text as an intelligible perceptual process like hearing.

Keats's Nightingale Ode plays on the presupposition that the addressee can *hear* by addressing a being that has a *voice*. The address to a creature that sings enforces the assumption that to be able to sing is to be able to listen, that to have a voice is to be able to hear. This kind of reciprocity does *not* exist between a text and a reader, as the *Phaedrus* pointed out: we hear its assertions, but it doesn't hear our questions. The nightingale, by implication, can, and at the same time the ode represents its own action as an act of listening. Keats's poem is full of phrases and figures from Milton and Shakespeare (seventeen by one count), and one way they function is as echoes: they enforce the ode's basic trope, persuading us that Keats is "listening" by persuading us that we hear what he hears. What motivates this rhetorical strategy? Continuity between singing and listening is desirable in both senses: if to be able to listen is to be able to sing, then Keats's own position in literary history—listening to older voices—is a favorable one. But an intertextual reading will show us that the power to pass from hearing to singing is one the ode ascribes not to the poet himself but to Milton, the "immortal bird" to whose phrases Keats's ode "listens," "darkling," more than any other.

The poet's sense of distance from the nightingale can then be read as Keats's sense of the discrepancy between his own and his precursor's power of song. Morris Dickstein, among others, is persuasive in linking Keats's adieu to the nightingale with an adieu to "another music he had left behind," as he puts it, and quotes Keats, "I have but lately stood on my guard against Milton. Life to him would be death to me." "Like his tutelage to Milton," Dickstein writes, "Keats's enchantment with the song of the nightingale had in the end turned into a struggle for survival."[10] But the struggle in the ode is of a different sort. We need an intertextual reading less eager to evoke persons and more attentive to recurrent rhetorical patterns. Such reading suggests that the mixed praise and blame in the ode reflects not a struggle with a deafening precursor, but radical ambivalence about the poem's chosen trope. Critics noting Keats's ambivalence about the nightingale frequently approve the poem's final stanza for marking a stage in his renouncement of the visionary imagination and renewed concern for real life: "Adieu! the fancy cannot cheat so well / As she is fam'd to

do, deceiving elf." But it is not the nightingale as the symbol of the
visionary mode that is the "deceiving elf" for Keats. The deceiver is
not the addressee of the ode but its "fancy," the address itself. And
the deception is rather, we might say, a *déception:* it dismays and deceives us by not deceiving us thoroughly enough. The appeal to voice
leaves precariously evident the rhetoricity, the fictitiousness, of the
vital supposition it imposes. The gesture of address in the Nightingale
Ode functions like the "tongueless nightingale" Keats summons up in
The Eve of St. Agnes. With that trope Keats collapses the narrative of
Philomel's *recovery* of voice into an emblem expressing how the *figure*
of voice is, precisely, voiceless. The intelligibility of language depends
on a figure itself mute, unable to make itself intelligible.

The ode's ambivalences mark Keats's confrontation with the fundamental trope that Milton and Wordsworth, as well as Keats, deployed
with notable misgiving. We find the same stance toward listening in a
turn in Wordsworth's Immortality Ode: "I hear, I hear, with joy I
hear!/—But . . ." But, indeed: Keats's ode envisages death in these terms:
"*Still* wouldst thou sing, and I *have ears in vain*"—asserting the futility
of the very stance he assumes, and measuring that futility as one out-
lasting the very difference between life and death. Keats's most grimly
apostrophic poem, *This Living Hand,* deeply resembles Milton's epitaph *On Shakespeare.* Milton's fancy here is that Shakespeare's own
writings form the one sufficient monument to his name, a monument
that has the fluency of speech. This epitaph, like Keats's ode, credits
its addressee with a voice. Wordsworth quotes half the poem in his
Essays upon Epitaphs; he omits a passage that, like Keats's *This Living
Hand,* conceives a poetry that can induce the wish to die, in these telling lines:

> For whilst to the shame of slow-endeavouring art
> Thy easy numbers flow, and that each heart
> Hath from the leaves of thy unvalued book,
> Those Delphic lines with deep impression took,
> Then thou our fancy of itself bereaving
> Dost make us marble with too much conceiving;
> And so sephulchred in such pomp does lie,
> That kings for such a tomb would wish to die.[11]

The passage represents the dangerous implication of these texts' chief
figure, prosopopoeia, or the figure of address, the "thou" we accord a
body of writing: that "thou," "our fancy of itself bereaving/Dost
make us marble"—monumentalizes us in turn. To *hear* a monument,

to hear its "easy numbers flow," is to take on ourselves the mute fixity of a monument or a text.[12]

In *The Fall of Hyperion* Keats writes, "Poesy alone can tell her dreams,/With the fine spell of words alone can save/Imagination from the sable charm/And dumb enchantment" (ll. 8–11). But *The Fall* goes on to show that poesy's spell, the gesture of address, is also spellbinding: when the narrator of *The Fall* invokes the poets, "pledging all the dead whose names are in our lips," the draught brings on a swoon, and a dream-vision entailing further perils of ultimate stillness. ("Die on that marble where thou art," Moneta tells him, and his chief act is to take up Saturn's immobile posture "in the unchanging gloom.") The first stanza of the Nightingale Ode stresses that the voice he lends the nightingale works on him like the "domineering potion" of *The Fall*.

Its effect would seem to culminate in stanza six, with the passage, "Darkling I listen. . . . Now more than ever seems it rich to die." What do we make of the fact that this wish to die follows directly upon the ode's single deliberate allusion to Milton? I would suggest that we must look to the exact context to tell us more than that. Keats alludes to a passage in which Milton himself is apostrophizing, the invocation of book 3 of *Paradise Lost,* where Milton frames a regret for his blindness with an address to heavenly light. "Darkling I listen"—"Nightly I visit": the echo runs from Milton's evocation of *his* pledge:

> Thee Sion and the flowery brooks beneath
> That wash thy hallowed feet, and warbling flow,
> Nightly I visit: nor sometimes forget
> Those other two equalled with me in fate,
> So were I equalled with them in renown,
> Blind Thamyris and blind Maeonides,
> And Tiresias and Phineus prophets old.
> Then feed on thoughts, that voluntary move
> Harmonious numbers; as the wakeful bird
> Sings darkling, and in shadiest covert hid
> Tunes her nocturnal note.

                                                                    (3.30–40)

What matters here is not simply that Milton identifies himself with the bird, who *sings* darkling, while Keats distinguishes himself from the bird, and listens darkling. John Hollander puts it: "The word is transformed in the echo, not merely by being applied to the response

rather than to the act of eloquence, but by including in its sound
somehow an acknowledgment of its source, as if to say . . . 'Darkling,
I listen to Milton's *darkling.*'"[13] Keats's allusion tells us that he is
hearkening to the Milton whose claim to sing issues directly from an
address to the heavenly muse.

Prosopopoeia and apostrophe are in fact the central devices of the
poems echoed in the ode's earlier stanzas as well, *L'Allegro* and *Il
Penseroso* and *Lycidas.* But the Milton invoked with "Darkling I
listen" has also mobilized the powerful trope of blindness. Blindness
means the invisibility of language become pure voice or inner light; it
stabilizes prosopopoeia in a ratio where the perceptual and the cognitive, and the visible and the audible, hold fixed places. In the total
absence of literal light the troubled connection between perception
and cognition is dissolved, in the single certainty that voice represents
illumination. The nightingale singing in darkness, named "immortal
bird" in the next stanza, is the "self-begotten bird" of *Samson Agonistes* (ll. 1687–1707): Samson's blindness gets linked in this passage
to his being "With inward eyes illuminated . . . into sudden flame,"
like the phoenix, the "secular bird of ages" whose "*fame* survives" although "her *body* die," a clear-cut compensation in which identity is
totally preserved, in a "self-same song" (Keats's phrase) "that no
second knows nor third" (Milton's). It is in response to this rhetorical
figure, rather than to Milton or to the precursor as such, that Keats
recalls his impulse to call *death* "soft names in many a muséd rhyme,"
and "to cease upon the midnight with no pain."

But it is the lines following these in which the misgivings about
prosopopoeia reach their greatest intensity, as the conception of death
shifts radically: "Still wouldst thou sing, and I have ears in vain;/To
thy high requiem become a sod." What is remarkable about these
lines, as I suggested earlier, is that the crucial futility, which is the very
condition of the poem, to "have ears in vain," is identified as a condition common to both death *and* life. Devastating in the same way is
an expression in the opening lament of *Samson Agonistes:* "The sun
to me is dark/*And silent* as the moon." Samson laments as desperate
blindness an ordinary condition of perception, the silence of the sun.
The sun is silent, literally, not just to Samson; to cite this as a catastrophe is to point to how vital is the identification of light with intelligibility conceived as voice. Thinking of the *light* of the senses as
speaking meaningfully is our way of conceiving phenomenal, perceptual experience to be continuous and consistent with knowledge. This
is what we do in ascribing epistemological authority to aesthetic experience; we credit as natural and as given the figure of speaking light,

the identification of light, voice, and intelligibility. Samson's describing the silence of the sun as a catastrophe indicates how fatal is the strictly figurative, rhetorical status of that identification. His sentence makes explicit the assumption that to "have ears" or to *see* the sun is as good as to be dead if one does not also *see* and *speak the sense of* what one hears, if one does not also *hear* in one's own voice the significations of "light." Keats's phrase, like Milton's, describes the perception of the phenomenal world as a hopeless deprivation and signals the precariousness of the trope required to make it meaningful. As Samson puts it, he is "bereaved thy prime decree," "Let there be light, and light was over all" (ll. 84-85). Perception is a deprivation because it hangs on a decree, the primary positing of a "thee" whose word brings light.

Thus, when the notorious crux in stanza four hangs our estimation of "the viewless wings of poesy" on a radically undetermined "thee!" it checks interpretive judgment in an exemplary, revealing way. Still more is revealed by the Miltonic pre-text for the same figure. "Viewless wings" echoes (as we say) the same figure in the last stanza of Milton's unfinished poem *The Passion:* it reads,

> Or should I thence hurried on viewless wing,
> Take up a weeping on the mountains wild,
> The gentle neighborhood of grove and spring
> Would soon unbosom all their echoes mild,
> And I (for grief is easily beguiled)
>   Might think the infection of my sorrows loud,
> Had got a race of mourners on some pregnant cloud.
>
>   (ll. 50-56)

The poem breaks off there. Margaret Ferguson defines its pertinence to the Nightingale Ode: "excessive pregnancy lapsing into silence." The lapse after flight on viewless wings, only to arrive "already with thee," but find that "here there is no light"—that lapse has a precedent in the effects of the same figure in Milton's poem.

Moreover, these lines disclose the system of assumptions involved in how we describe them, in our calling such a repetition an "echo." Echo is a nymph, initially, with a story much like Philomel's, the tongueless girl who wove her tale into a tapestry before she turned nightingale. These are stories of the victory of voice over meaningless repetition or over mute textile and mutilated figure. Milton's conceit has "the gentle neighborhood of grove and spring/ . . . *unbosom* all their echoes mild": echoes are not simply sounds bounced off surfaces but responses issuing from a "bosom," from an inward state. Echoing is at once natural and human; to speak of a person *echoing* another's feeling is to *naturalize* a discursive and not inevitable response, while to speak of a landscape echoing a speaker is to personify a natural element. To speak of a *text* "echoing" another naturalizes and humanizes at the same time what is essentially a semiotic structure. Reading—our conception of reading on the model of a perceptual process, like hearing or seeing—depends on this prosopopoeia; signs must be actualized by an act of perception in a responsive subject. The "listening" reader functions like "the gentle neighborhood of grove and spring," and is just as figurative an entity. Milton's intricate conceit here images echoes as "a *race* of mourners" begotten by the coupling of a human lament and a natural object. Both metaphors presume the same stable primacies: the same generational hierarchy places a sire at the origin of his "race" and a voice at the origin of its echo. Milton's combination of the two metaphors reveals the investments that underlie discussion of "echoes" as well as allusions to poetic "fathers."

To produce echoes is to engender readers, and vice versa. But just here Milton is cut off. The poem breaks off in imagining its unlimited seminal power. Where the text makes the fullest claims for its fundamental trope is also where its statement and its action split entirely. It seems no accident, then, that Keats's poem attains its greatest unintelligibility at the point at which it repeats this figure.

Keats's flight on viewless wings can be situated in another intertextual dimension as well. Eamon Grennan traces the shift in the conception of death in stanza 6 to Claudio's shift in attitude in act 3, scene 1 of *Measure for Measure,* where Claudio first proposes to "embrace the darkness like a bride," and then imagines death with dread: [14]

> Ay, but to die, and go we know not where,
> To lie in cold obstruction and to rot;
> This sensible warm motion to become
> A kneaded clod . . .
> . . . .
> To be imprisoned in the viewless winds,
> And blown with restless violence round about
> The pendent world. . . .
>
>   (3.1.116–19, 122–24)

What authorizes deducing an "echo" here is not the similar sound of *wings* and *winds* but the similar rhetorical patterns. Leslie Brisman takes up the phrase "viewless winds" to convoke another kind of intertext, a text unread by Keats, a revision for the 1850 *Prelude* that introduces the word *viewless* into the passage in book 5 celebrating "the great Nature that exists in works / Of mighty Poets":

Visionary power
Attends the motions of the viewless winds,
Embodied in the mystery of words:
There, darkness makes abode, and all the host
Of shadowy things work endless changes. . . .

(5.595–99)

"Viewless winds" is a curious pleonasm. "Viewless *wings*" calls poetry an invisible means of transport: not by any literal vehicle but by the transport of words from literal to figural significations, from visible to viewless referents. Poetry or figurative language is an invisible mechanism for rendering things invisible and hence meaningful. (Placing this trope in an ode to a nightingale compounds its circularity or tautology: the poet says in effect that he will fly on viewless wings to viewless wings.) "Viewless *winds*" calls figurative language *breath,* the medium of voice. What both these figures do is spirit away the visible and the material status of language, its existence as writing or signs. For acknowledgment of that material dimension, one would have to turn to other texts of Keats's or Wordsworth's—Wordsworth's *Essays upon Epitaphs* and poems that title themselves inscriptions, Keats's *This Living Hand,* the opening of *The Fall of Hyperion,* perhaps, and even the *Ode on a Grecian Urn.* The *Ode to a Nightingale,* rather, confronts the consequences of the figure of *voice* that is our habitual and essential conception of language.

Brisman cites the passage from *The Prelude* in order to contrast Keats's direction with Wordsworth's. "Wordsworth is pointing us 'there'—in signs, in the space separating signs from significance—while Keats returns us 'here'—to the significant earth whence all sign-constructions take their origin."[15] He quotes Heidegger to credit Keats with what *The Origin of the Work of Art* calls "setting forth the earth" and "setting up a world"—and declines to recall that for another Heidegger Being-in-the-world is a condition of *Dasein,* no such thing as a *hiersein;* but one need not stray farther than *Lycidas,* really, to dispute Brisman's sanguine reading of stanza 5. What he does achieve, though, in adducing the *Prelude* passage, is to charge the question of Keats's stance toward flight on viewless wings with the loaded issue of Keats's stance toward the visionary imagination. Brilliantly, too, he connects visionary power with death, by showing that the images in which Wordsworth describes imagination resemble those with which Shakespeare describes being dead.

Yet these alignments still make up a surprisingly predictable story. They enable Brisman to tell, about stanzas 4 and 5 of the Nightingale Ode, the story critics have mostly wanted to tell about Keats's development. Keats's renouncement of visionary transport can now be identified as an evasion of death as well, and his recourse to the earth and its natural objects can be construed as a saving return to the *origins* of imaginative life associated too with *originality,* with independence of the precursor. For this story to stick, the reading has to stop with stanza five, to ignore the turn toward death in the sixth stanza. Yet Brisman cites a text that can make us see the ironic logic of this entire sequence. In the second stanza of Wordsworth's *A Slumber Did My Spirit Seal,* he points out, we find again the image of being confined in a placeless place, rolled round the earth rather than embedded in it, that marked Claudio's conception of death:

A slumber did my spirit seal;
  I had no human fears:
She seemed a thing that could not feel
  The touch of earthly years.

No motion has she now, no force;
  She neither hears nor sees;
Rolled round in earth's diurnal course,
  With rocks, and stones, and trees.[16]

In the first stanza, a human being is imagined as like a natural "thing," exempt from change, from "the touch of earthly years." In the next stanza it turns out that she is indeed exempt from touch and shares the state of natural objects—and that this is to be, not safe from death, but dead.[17] Identification with natural objects, in an evasion of temporality and death, instead brings on or constitutes that very death— which is not a state of rest but a state of constant motion, precisely like the endless change and placeless place of words or the imagination.

Though we may not hear anything like Wordsworth's toneless irony in Keats's exquisitely inflected middle stanzas, it is productive to read stanzas 4–6 in the same way. Thus the movement from precarious flight on the viewless wings of poetic language, to sensing the incense of the palpable objects growing "at my feet"—that shift in fact situates the speaker in an "embalmed darkness" that reappears a stanza later as the state of death, as the equivalent of being a senseless "sod."

And the sod is still accompanied by the nightingale's "high requiem"—
pursued by "viewless wings"—even as to be a "kneaded clod" in Claudio's vision gives no respite from being blown by "viewless winds,"
and even as the dead "she" of Wordsworth's poem is "rolled round in
earth's diurnal course" rather than at rest from the drive of direction
toward meaning. In short, these stanzas share with Shakespeare's and
Wordsworth's texts a figurative sequence linking imagination, earth,
and the appeal to natural objects. The appeal to the natural object—
whether by imagining a human being as a perceivable thing or by
imagining nonhuman things as expressive beings—is shown to be not
an escape from but only another mode of precisely the commitment
to figurative language that it sought to avoid, a commitment to the
vital and deadly trope of prosopopoeia.

To read Keats's stanzas according to Wordsworth's in this way,
though, is to risk overlooking the utterly distinctive qualities and
Wordsworthian preoccupations of the Nightingale Ode. Keats is par-
ticularly concerned with the status of perception. Compare the end
of the *Ode to a Nightingale* with the end of *The Solitary Reaper:*
"The music in my heart I bore / Long after it was heard no more."
For Wordsworth perception is subsumed in the act of recollection.
For Keats it is made critical, and tentative, by its dependency on an
Erinnerung felt not as recollection but as guesswork and anticipation:

> I cannot see what flowers are at my feet,
>   Nor what soft incense hangs upon the boughs,
> But, in embalmed darkness, *guess* each sweet
>   Wherewith the seasonable month endows
> The grass, the thicket, and the fruit-tree wild;
>   White hawthorn, and the pastoral eglantine;
> Fast-fading violets cover'd up in leaves;
>   And mid-May's eldest child,
> The coming musk-rose, full of dewy wine,
>   The murmurous haunt of flies on summer eves.

To name these unseen flowers is to guess them, call them, greet them.
This straitened tentative perceiving is an act of reading, reminiscent of
the closing address to Melancholy in *Il Penseroso,* the request for
some "mossy cell,"

> Where I may sit and rightly spell
> Of every star that heaven doth shew,
> And every herb that sips the dew;

Till old experience do attain
To something like prophetic strain.

(ll. 170–74)

Keats attains "to something like prophetic strain" in naming "the
coming musk-rose, full of dewy wine," and his doing so depends, like
the Penseroso poet's, on "old experience" of the sweets "*endowed*"
by every season—"endowment" resting the natural process on a con-
tractual one, the rhetorical contract whereby the months restore to
us what we greet as "seasonable." The poet's wishful naming of
"sweets" is a willful greeting that recalls the flowers he has "spelled,"
not just the flowers he has seen. His calling recalls the anthology in
Lycidas, framed by its apostrophe:

Ye valleys low where the mild whispers use,
Of shades and wanton winds, and gushing brooks,
On whose fresh lap the swart star sparely looks,
Throw hither all your quaint enamelled eyes,
That on the green turf suck the honied showers,
. . . .
Bring the rathe primrose that forsaken dies,
. . . .
The musk-rose, and the well-attired woodbine. . . .

(ll. 136–46)

Keats's stanza only suspends, it does not forget, the question posed
from Milton's poem: "false surmise" or true. (The "dewy wine" of
the musk-rose is not named "the true, the blushful Hippocrene," like
the "beaker full of the warm south"; stanza 5 holds off from too
assertive hints that for a thing to blush, to have a face to lose, is for it
to be "true.")[18]

The pastoral of *Paradise Lost* affirms "Hesperian fables true;/ If
true, here only." The guessing of sweets in the Nightingale Ode, like
the calling of flowers in *Lycidas,* is a "*false* surmise" in the sense
that it diverges from the poem's main act of attention: attention to
the unnatural death of Lycidas "under the whelming tide," to the
"dread voice[s]" that "touch" the poet's "trembling ears," and to the
whelming voice of the nightingale. The "uncouth swain" of *Lycidas*
has declared explicitly that his song is a gesture that disrupts seasonal
time, that shatters its leaves before their "season due," compelled by
the occasion of a poet's death. Hence Lycidas's elegist can renounce as
false the surmise that the earth's flowers might gather to provide the

poet a seasonable grave. But the elegist and celebrant of the Nightingale Ode can make no such assured distinction between false and true surmises of perception, nor between the guesswork that lends names and face and the surmise that lends its *voice* to viewless things. Keats's text displays the effects of knowing that naming or describing an object implies the primary figure of address: the gesture of conferring intelligibility upon a collection of signs by endowing them with an *outline* having the power to *address* us—a face and a voice.

Wordsworth acclaims the visionary power of words insofar as they *embody* thought—and names this function in words naming the medium of voice as the power of death, Shakespeare's "viewless winds." And so "the very word" leaves Keats "forlorn": "Forlorn! the very word is like a bell/To toll me back from *thee* to my sole self!" John Hollander points out that even as Keats echoes his own poem, he also echoes Milton's one more time.[19] He is forlorn in the very impossibility of being alone in his forlornness. For the self-reflection in the weighing of that word dates from Adam's self-delusion, loving Eve:

> How can I live without thee, how forgo
> Thy sweet converse and love so dearly joined,
> To live again in these wild woods forlorn?
>
> (9.908–10)

In applying *forlorn* first to a place ("faery lands") and then to himself, Keats reenacts the effect of Milton's syntax, where the *forlorn* applied by Adam to himself makes the wild woods of paradise forlorn too, fallen with him even as he speaks. This is the ode's question also: how can *I* live without *thee*? This passage also suggests how little it signifies when we impose our own unwarranted personification—when we succumb to the tempting simplification of calling the "I" of the poem "Keats." Here "Keats" is tolled back to the "sole self," but not just to *his* "sole self," for his way of doing it shows us that he cannot say "I" without also saying Adam's "I," the first *I* and all *I*'s. *I* and *thee,* like *here, now, there,* are deictics, terms that designate absolutely general categories even as they point to particulars. This linguistic feature makes naming the self a gesture as problematic as affirming the certainty of perception—as futile as asserting the particularity of what "I hear *this passing night,*" or of any here and now. (So in the chapter of the *Phenomenology* entitled "Sense-Certainty" Hegel invites us to write on a piece of paper, "Now is the night.")[20] In the final stanza of the ode, the emptiness of Keats's "sole self" is matched with the emptiness of sensory evidence: "Was it a vision or a waking dream? . . . Do I wake or sleep?"

Let me conclude by distinguishing very explicitly between two ways of interpreting the prominent presence in the ode of both invocation and the description of perception. The fundamental trope of the figure of echo is prosopopoeia: the persuasion that a text has a voice. This is the same figure that invests responsiveness in a natural object, which can thereby elicit our perception. One way to take the prominence of this trope in Keats's ode is to point to his double concern for the perceived object and the precursor poet, and to conclude that he is nostalgic for the freedom from linguistic contingencies which those two imaginary entities enjoy. Keats's ambivalence toward the visionary mode is not then a realism and wisdom inaugural of modern poetry, as in the critical consensus first described here, but a nostalgia for pre-Romantic or non-Romantic conditions. This reading at least has the virtue of contradicting the celebration of Keats as the celebrant of "our perishing earth" and of perceptual reality. But it performs another unnecessary characterization, ascribing to Keats himself a psychological configuration that we simply project as the plausible correlative of certain conflicting rhetorical structures in these texts. This account also charges interpretation with an ethical judgment, contrasting Keats with the "greater" Romantics insofar as his poetry "evades" its temporal or linguistic predicament.

We do better to read the conjunction of perception and echo in Keats in another way, pointing to his highly conspicuous rendering of the figure of address. The *Ode to a Nightingale* does not celebrate perception but displays its dependence on prosopopoeia and plays out the implications of that trope. To infer, as Keats's ode leads us to do, the primacy of the figure of address, is to infer that understanding depends on the possibility of imagining a sign as a voice or an image, and a sound or an image as a sign. And it implies that this is a rhetorical moment rather than a natural given, and rather than, in the first place, a moment in the *experience* of an individual subject (such as Lacan's "mirror stage").

Many other poems of Keats's bring together the same indeterminacies as those of the ode's last stanza. We might, for instance, reread the apostrophic sonnet *O Thou Whose Face* as spoken by the nightingale. Could we ignore what seems to sound like the familiar proposal of a negative capability, or a poetry of sensations rather than of thoughts, we should hear this poem offering something quite other than reassurance:

> O fret not after knowledge—I have none,
>   And yet the evening listens.
>
> . . . .
>
> And he's awake who thinks himself asleep.

The equation in the last line oscillates indefinitely. No music, only poetry, so leaves us hanging. Intertextual interpretation, too, must attend to effects like these. It should serve not just to heighten our characterizations of certain voices (blind bard, belated poet), but to uncover the necessities of those other recurrent figures, those sequences of tropes that recur in more than one text. Perhaps one should also reread Keats's letters, looking not at the familiar thematics of "Negative Capability," or "the Vale of Soul-making," but rather at the fleeting comments on the conditions of writing—the condition of writing poems in *letters,* for instance: "I know you would like what I wrote thereon—so *here* it is—as they say of a Sheep in a Nursery Book."[21]

Giving a Face to a Name

De Man's Figures

How do the names for rhetorical figures function in the writings of Paul de Man? What order of effects do they point to; what pressures are they made to bear? Such questions have been answered in some detail for the figures most often at issue in contemporary criticism and theory: metaphor and metonymy, symbol and allegory. But they have yet to be posed for a less familiar set of names that takes on prominence in essays published after *Allegories of Reading:* prosopopoeia, apostrophe, and anthropomorphism. The identification of a prosopopoeia or of an apostrophe marks a key moment, a turning point, in essays dealing with subjects as varied as autobiography, the lyric, stylistics, and the sublime. The arrival at such a moment itself becomes the subject of the concluding sentences of de Man's essay on Wordsworth's *Essays upon Epitaphs,* "Autobiography as De-facement":

> As soon as we understand the rhetorical function of prosopopoeia as positing voice or face by means of language, we also understand that what we are deprived of is not life but the shape and the sense of a world accessible only in the privative way of understanding. Death is a displaced name for a linguistic predicament, and the restoration of mortality by autobiography (the prosopopoeia of the voice and the name) deprives and disfigures to the precise extent that it restores.[1]

This conception of understanding—as a "privative way" of access to the world that more surely than death deprives us of its sense—is the burden of de Man's late essays. The significance here ascribed to prosopopoeia could hardly be greater, since its understanding is identified with that of "understanding" itself. What we shall attempt to identify in the reading that follows is the nature of the "linguistic predicament" condensed in the trope that de Man (alone) translates as *"prosopon-poiein . . . to give a face."*[2]

The Oxford English Dictionary cites as a synonym for *prosopopoeia* "personification"; it defines the word as "a rhetorical figure by which an imaginary or absent person is represented as speaking or acting"; and it gives the derivation from the Greek as *"prosopon*—face, person, and *poiein*—make." De Man's translation or definition of prosopopoeia is already a reading, and is in fact a giving of face. Translating *prosopon* as "face" or "mask," and not as "person," is to imply that a face is the condition—not the equivalent—of the existence of a person. The face that de Man gives the word *prosopopoeia* comes from Wordsworth.

> Hitherto
> In progress through this verse my mind hath looked
> Upon the speaking face of earth and heaven
> As her prime teacher. . . .
>
> *(Prelude, 5.10-13)*

"Face" is, first of all, a *"speaking* face," the locus of speech, the necessary condition for the existence of articulated language. These lines are not simply an anthropomorphism, a conceit by which human consciousness is projected or transferred into the natural world. They assume the recognition of an entity or agency that bridges the distinction between mind and world by allowing them to exist in the proximity, in the dialogue of this distinction.

> *(RR, 89)*

These comments specify that the figure in Wordsworth's lines is a prosopopoeia, not an anthropomorphism and not exactly a personification, and they suggest the crucial significance of that distinction, elaborated in the later essay "Anthropomorphism and Trope in the Lyric." If a critique of humanism is to be traced in de Man's writing, it should be located in moves like this one, the sharp distinction between alternative descriptions of certain lines of poetry. The "conceit" of anthropomorphism, as this passage goes on to characterize it, lies in the fact that this particular rhetorical conceit excludes or denies the role of *tropes* or *figures* in the process of representation, in favor of the recognition of *essences*. Anthropomorphism "is not just a trope but an identification on the level of substance," "the *taking* of something for something else that can then be assumed to be *given*" (*RR*, 241). Taking the natural as human, it takes the human as given. This is to take the human as natural, to create a naturalness of man from

which man and nature in effect disappear as the distinction between
them is effaced. The entirely different effect of Wordsworth's lines
is to describe the human as dependent upon the giving of a figure,
that of "face." De Man's usage of *prosopopoeia* is distinctive and unfamiliar, but the usage of *face,* in this essay on Wordsworth is stranger,
more defamiliarizing, still: "Man can address and face other men,
within life or beyond the grave, because he has a face, but he has a
face only because he partakes of a mode of discourse that is neither
entirely natural nor entirely human" (*RR,* 51). De Man not merely
reads *prosopopoeia* as the giving of face; he reads *face* as that which
is given by prosopopoeia. Face is not the natural given of the human
person. It is given in a mode of discourse, given by an act of language. What is given by this act is figure. Figure is no less than our
very face.

   "Face" is a figure. In de Man's writing, face, like prosopopoeia, is
a figure from *The Prelude:* its meaning derives from the reading of the
Blest Babe passage that de Man characterizes as "Wordsworth's essay
on the origins of language as poetic language" (*RR,* 51).

> Blessed the infant babe—
> For with my best conjectures I would trace
> The progress of our being—blest the babe
> . . . who sleeps
> Upon his mother's breast, who, when his soul
> Claims manifest kindred with an earthly soul,
> Doth gather passion from his mother's eye.[3]
>
>   (1805 *Prelude,* 2.237–43)

The decisive term here is *claims.* De Man comments, "What is later
called a 'mute dialogue with my Mother's heart' begins here in the
exchange of a gaze, a meeting of 'eyes.' But this encounter is not a
recognition, a shared awareness of common humanity. It occurs as an
active verbal deed, a *claim* of 'manifest kindred' which is not given in
the nature of things" (*RR,* 52). Prior to any perception—prior to the
perception of nature, prior to seeing the mother's face—is the "*claim*
of 'manifest kindred,'" "the starting, catachrestic *decree* of signification." De Man's conception of language as figure includes the conception of language as act. The *claim* of relationship sets up a process
of comparison and substitution, the system of tropes and figures,
whereby language functions as representation or cognition. In Wordsworth's words,

> hence his mind,
> Even in the first trial of its powers,
> Is prompt and watchful, eager to combine
> In one appearance all the elements
> And parts of the same object, else detached
> And loth to coalesce.
>
> (2.245–50)

The claim of demonstrable relationship sets up a capacity to see entities as interchangeable parts of a whole. It inaugurates a process of
totalization that "in the span of a few lines," de Man observes, "can
grow to encompass everything, '*All* objects through *all* intercourse
of sense' (2.260)" (*RR*, 91). The capacity to compose, from her
"eye," the mother's face, opens the way to compose the entire intelligible world.[4] In *Allegories of Reading* this process of totalization is
identified with metaphor or "metaphorical synecdoche," as the positing of resemblance between terms that erases their differences and
integrates them into wholes, into concepts or entities, including such
concepts as the self or time. A rhetorical reading deconstructs these
concepts by revealing their dependency on the figure of metaphor.
The unlimited capacity of representation or figuration in fact is (as
for the Blest Babe) a total dependency; this is the significance of the
figure of "face": "Face, then in this passage, . . . designates the dependence of any perception or 'eye' on the totalizing power of language. It heralds this dependency as 'the first/Poetic spirit of our
life.' The possibility of any contact between mind and nature depends
on this spirit manifested by and in language." (*RR,* 52). This passage
momentarily seems to describe the dependence of perception on figurative language as an enabling possibility rather than a predicament.
Yet the reading is deeply disquieting because of de Man's use of precisely the familiar word *face* to designate the figure. The face given by
an act of language is the only face in de Man's reading; this usage bars
retreat to a word for an independently existing phenomenon, the face
we think we always have.

Prosopopoeia, or the giving of face, is *de*-facement, then, insofar as
if face is given by an act of language it is "only" a figure. Such might
seem to be the sum of the argument of "Autobiography as De-facement." But the dependency of perception upon language is not necessarily disturbing. Why dependency on *figurative* language should be
disturbing is more effectively intimated in de Man's usage of *face* in
"Wordsworth and the Victorians" than it is explained in the essay

that describes the disturbance most explicitly, "Autobiography as Defacement." Bound up with the question of the implications of the interpretation of *prosopopoeia,* or *face,* is the question of its grounds. The interpretation does not simply converge, as it sometimes appears to do, with the statement of directly quoted or paraphrased passages of Wordsworth, though it is part of the meaning of these essays to show how compelling and precise such language can be. As the first essay draws upon the Blest Babe passage, the second draws upon the famous passage on language as counterspirit:

> Words are too awful an instrument for good and evil to be trifled with: they hold above all other external powers a dominion over thoughts. If words be not (recurring to a metaphor before used) an incarnation of the thought but only a clothing for it, then surely will they prove an ill gift; such a one as those poisoned vestments, read of in the stories of superstitious times, which had power to consume and to alienate from his right mind the victim who put them on. Language, if it do not uphold, and feed, and leave in quiet, like the power of gravitation or the air we breathe, is a counter-spirit, unremittingly and noiselessly at work to derange, to subvert, to lay waste, to vitiate, and to dissolve.[5]

For de Man the significance and authority of this statement arises from its very inconsistency with the strategy of the text in which it appears. Such is also the significance of the assertion in book 3 of *The Prelude* that the face-making power of the eye "Could find no surface where its power might sleep" (3.164). This describes a *"function"* of face—"as the relentless undoer of its own claims"—hardly to be reconciled with "the *meaning* of face, with its promise of sense and of filial preservation" (*RR,* 92). Wordsworth's warning against the destructive agency of the "clothing" of thought marks another such aporia. "Clothing" is the visible outside of the body, as body or "incarnation" is the visible outside of the soul; both figures describe the function of language as figuration, as the capacity for making thought visible or accessible to the imagination. This is what the passage warns against, and what is the strategy and subject of these *Essays upon Epitaphs* no less than of *The Prelude.* A condemnation so far-reaching and self-indicting takes on, in de Man's reading, the authority to generate a question:

> The language so violently denounced is in fact the language of metaphor, of prosopopoeia and of tropes, the solar language of cognition that makes the unknown accessible to the mind and the senses. The language of tropes . . . is indeed like the body, which is

like its garments, the veil of the soul as the garment is the sheltering veil of the body. How can this harmless veil then suddenly become as deadly and violent as the poisoned coat of Jason or of Nessus?

(RR, 80)

Or in the terms of the essay's title: how does the giving of a face to a name—the achievement of an autobiography or an epitaph—become a disfiguration or "de-facement"?

The conclusion of "Autobiography as De-facement" gives us an answer that perpetuates the question rather than laying it to rest. It is offered in the form of an allegory. From Wordsworth's allusion to "poisoned vestments" de Man retells the story of the coat of Nessus, given to Hercules' wife so that she might regain her husband's affection, but which brought about his madness and death. "It was supposed to restore the love which she lost, but the restoration turned out to be a worse deprivation, a loss of life and of sense." And the epitaph on the deaf-mute Dalesman that Wordsworth places at the close of his *Essays* must be understood to tell "a similar story, though not to the end" (RR, 80).

For the Dalesman's story closes, indeed, with a loss of life and a *restoration* of sense. After his death,

>   yon tall Pine-tree, whose composing sound
> Was wasted on the good Man's living ear,
> Hath now its own peculiar sanctity;
> And at the touch of every wandering breeze
> Murmurs not idly o'er his peaceful grave.[6]

With the murmuring pine tree we recover "the speaking face of earth and heaven." But this figure—the condition of the possibility of speech, in the reading of the Blest Babe passage—has now to be understood as also the condition of its impossibility. Figure as such (like the "outside equivalent" or figure for the Dalesman's deafness: a mute nature, a "valley . . ./ Soundless with all its streams") is "silent as a picture" (ll. 509-10, 520); writes de Man,

> To the extent that language is figure (or metaphor, or prosopopoiea) it is indeed not the thing itself but the representation, the picture of the thing and, as such, it is silent, mute as pictures are mute. . . . Wordsworth says of evil language, which is in fact all language including his own language of restoration, that it works "unremittingly and *noiselessly*" (154). To the extent that, in writing, we are dependent on this language we all are, like the Dalesman . . . , deaf and mute—not silent, which implies the possible manifestation of

sound at our own will, but silent as a picture, that is to say eternally deprived of voice and condemned to muteness.

(RR, 80)

In the assertiveness of its statement and the opacity of its key terms, this passage gives us to understand the necessity of discovering another mode of understanding for its assertions. Why, in fact, should the function of language as figure, as the visibility of thought, contrast with the function of articulation or speech? Why should the silence of writing imply that language as such is mute? What, since speaking and meaning certainly take place, can this "muteness" signify? For answers to these questions we must turn to arguments carried out elsewhere in de Man's work, where the notion that language fails because "it is not the thing itself" is elaborated through an analysis of cognition as predication, as the establishment of a link between subject and predication, as the establishment of a link between subject and predicate. It is de Man's readings of Hegel on sense-certainty and on the sign that explicate the understanding announced or warned of in the closing lines of "Autobiography as De-facement": "As soon as we understand the rhetorical function of prosopopoeia as positing voice or face by means of language, we understand that . . . we are deprived of . . . the sense and shape of a world" (RR, 46). The specific significance of "positing," of "figure," and of "writing" emerges in an argument from the text of Hegel that will help to explicate the reading of prosopopoeia in Wordsworth: that face is a figure; that voice is a fiction, arising from the figure of face.

The figurality of face is implied by the etymology of prosopopoeia; the fictionality of voice, by its definition. De Man points to a collusion of prosopopoeia with apostrophe and to its "disruptive" overlapping with catachresis. Catachresis coins a name for an unnamed entity by an "abuse" of figure, the use of a figure, a name transferred from another entity, as a name. Naming takes place by the production of figures whose figurative status is simultaneously effaced. Catachresis thus describes a dependency and conflict between name and figure that is present in the concept of "giving a face." The definition of prosopopoeia links it with apostrophe: like the gesture of address, which assumes the possibility of reply, it confers upon "an absent, deceased, or voiceless entity" the power of speech (RR, 75). As the only face, in de Man's reading, is the face conferred by catachresis, the only voice is the voice conferred by apostrophe. Our perception of voice is entirely bound up with a concept of comprehension conceived on the model of an exchange between an author and a reader; that concept cannot effectively be stabilized by appeal to the natural phenomenon of voice; it has to be actualized in a text, in the fiction of a monologue or a dialogue with a reader. De Man's readings of Hegel, Hugo, and Baudelaire (in "Hypogram and Inscription" and "Lyrical Voice in Contemporary Theory") are designed to show how this actualization of voice is undercut, how the process of reception is at odds with the text's production as writing and as figure. Reception theory founders on the irreconcilable discrepancy between the function and meaning of texts disclosed in Wordsworth's figure of face: the incompatibility of *sagen* and *Meinung* detailed in Hegel's analysis of the deictic function. De Man dwells on prosopopoeia, rather than apostrophe, because these texts do not simply disclose that a voice is "only" a figure, that understanding is an illusion. They disclose the predicament inherent in the fact that understanding takes place figuratively, that voice *is* a *figure*—which is, in other terms, "the logical difficulty inherent in the deictic or demonstrative function of language."[7]

Voice, or the notion of a speaking consciousness, is a figure for the deictic function of language that itself involves a conflict between the function of language as postulation or act and its function as figure or representation. The distinction emerges in a reading of Nietzsche's critique of the identity principle (the foundation of logic) as posited, postulated, predicated, by an act of language, rather than discovered or known and simply represented in language. Once the representational function of language is seen to take place by means of figure—by the assumed and imposed resemblances, the "aberrant totalizations" of metaphor—language has to be conceived not only as representation, cognition, or constatation, but also as act. Predication entails not simply knowing, *erkennen,* but positing, *setzen.*

> To know [*erkennen*] is a transitive function that assumes the prior existence of an entity to be known. . . . It does not itself predicate . . . attributes but receives them, so to speak, from the entity itself by merely allowing it to be what it is. . . . It depends on a built-in continuity within the system that unites the entity to its attributes, the grammar that links the adjective to the noun by predication. The specifically verbal intervention stems from the predication, but since the predicate is nonpositional with regard to the properties, it cannot be called a speech *act.*
>
> . . . On the other hand, language can also predicate entities: in this Nietzsche text, this is called "*setzen*" (to posit).[8]

It will turn out that predication (in Wordsworth's words) "Of these was neither and was both at once," for de Man goes on to read Nietzsche as showing that "the possibility for language to perform [to act] is just as fictional as the possibility for language to assert [to know]" (*AR*, 129). Predication involves the necessary but impossible combination of these two functions: the *positing* of a *relationship*. To posit a relationship, de Man implies, is a contradiction in terms, since to posit or to postulate implies an arbitrary act not determined by any existing relationships, which sets up what had no previous existence, no relationship with other existing things.

De Man's essays on Hegel ("Sign and Symbol in Hegel's *Aesthetics*," "Hegel on the Sublime," and "Hypogram and Inscription") examine the difficulties of the notion of a predication that posits. The question is how the link between a subject and a predicate can be established, if it is not received from the entity itself or built into a grammar whose structure mirrors relationships existing apart from it. De Man's analysis shares its point of departure with Hegel's critique of the inadequate linking of subject and predicate in the language of sense-certainty and of *Vorstellung*, or "picture-thinking," the ordinary thought Hegel distinguishes from conceptual or speculative thinking in the preface and first chapter of the *Phenomenology*. Hegel appears to go on to describe the process whereby subject and predicate are effectively bound together through determinate negations performed by conceptual thought. Yet this process is described not as what does but as what "ought" (*soll*) to happen,[9] and, as Andrzej Warminski's "Reading for Example: 'Sense-Certainty' in Hegel's *Phenomenology of Spirit*" forcefully argues, the conditions of predication are spelled out in terms that describe its subversion even as they affirm its achievement.[10] For Warminski as for de Man, Hegel's text signifies the impossibility of an achieved predication. De Man's strategy is to read the analysis of the deictic function in chapter 1 of the *Phenomenology* and in paragraph 20 of the *Science of Logic* with definitions of the status of the sign in the *Encyclopedia* and the *Aesthetics*. De Man will associate the problem of how a subject is linked with a predicate with the incompatibility of sign and symbol: the arbitrary link between sign and meaning in the sign is at odds with the determined link between them in the symbol. "Sign and Symbol in Hegel's *Aesthetics*" describes "the necessity, which is also an impossibility, to connect the subject with its predicates or the sign with its symbolic manifestations."[11] The arbitrary nature of the sign will be associated, further, with the positional power of language; the determined relation between form and meaning in the symbol will be associated with the function of representation.

The "necessity" and "impossibility" of connecting subject and predicate can be traced in Hegel's critique of the rhetoric of sense-certainty, an analysis of the deictic function in statements about the "here" or "now."[12] De Man recalls Hegel's account of the discrepancy between the generality of what a deictic term such as *this* in fact says and the singularity of what it is meant to mean. "It is as a universal . . . that we give utterance to sensuous fact. What we say is: 'This,' i.e., the universal this. . . . Of course we do not present before our mind in saying so the universal this, . . . but we *utter* what is universal; . . . we do not actually and absolutely say what in this sense-certainty we really *mean*."[13] The deceptiveness of the figure of a speaking consciousness comes to light in an analysis of the contradictory conditions of the deictic function that it names.[14] Voice is a figure that covers over a muteness, an irreparable split in the function of speech, the incompatibility between *sagen* and *meinen* in deixis.

The functioning of deictics such as *this* or *here* or *now*—speaking of what is radically general even as they mean to speak of what is absolutely particular—implies "the impossibility of saying the only thing one ever wants to say, namely the certainty of sense perception."[15] Hegel writes, "One who makes such an assertion [that the reality or being of external things in the sense of particular sense objects has absolute validity for consciousness] really does not know what he is saying [*spricht*], does not know that he is stating [*sagt*] the opposite of what he wants to say [*sagen will*]."[16]

Do we not in fact say, and sometimes also mean to say, something other than the certainty of sense perception, even if the idea of certainty remains associated with the possibility of sensory evidence? The split between meaning and saying lies not only, though, in the invalid and dispensable rhetoric of sense-certainty, but in the indispensable demonstrative function of language. Language as deixis or "speech . . . has the divine nature of immediately inverting [*verkehren*] the meaning and making it into something else and thus not letting it get into *words* at all."[17] An earlier passage in chapter 1 of the *Phenomenology* identifies this "divine nature" of language as the production of a universality that is truth: "Language, however, is the more truthful; in it we ourselves refute directly and at once our own 'meaning'; . . . since universality is the real truth of sense-certainty, and language merely expresses *this* truth. . . ."[18] Because language states only what is general, the preface to the *Phenomenology* affirms (discussing the self-effacement of the philosopher, who does not offer his opinions, but rather allows general truths to come to light), "ich kann nicht sagen was ich nur meine": "I cannot say what is only my opinion [*Meinung*]," but also, "I cannot say what I . . . mean."

These passages seem to describe not only a predicament but a

progression. But does the confrontation between language and meaning indeed take place as the inversion of "mere" opining or meaning
into generality and "truth"? Not only such a dialectical conversion is
at issue in the operations of language described in Hegel's text. Andrzej
Warminski traces "another *Verkehren*—one more like *per*version than
*con*version"—in the simultaneous functioning of two discrepant senses
of "example" (*Beispiel*) in the achievement of knowledge of immediate knowledge worked out in chapter one of the *Phenomenology*. [19]
De Man turns to the discussion of the deictic function of the first person pronoun in paragraph 20 of *The Science of Logic*. Nietzsche's
account of the sheer positing of the identity principle undermines the
authority of the first principle of logic. Hegel's reading of "I," de Man
writes, excludes the articulation of the conscious with the logico-
grammatical subject and thereby paralyzes at the very start the project
of logical and of dialectical thought:

> "When I say 'I' I mean myself as *this* I at the exclusion of all
> others; but what I say, I, is precisely anyone; any I, as that which
> excludes all others from itself [ebenso, wenn ich sage: 'Ich,'
> meine ich mich *als diesen* alle anderen Ausschliessenden; aber was
> ich sage, Ich, ist eben jeder]" (74). In this sentence, the other-
> ness of "jeder" does not designate in any way a specular subject,
> the mirror image of the I, but precisely that which cannot have a
> thing in common with myself; it should be translated, in French,
> not as "autrui," not even as "chacun," but as "n'importe qui"
> or even "n'importe quoi." [20]

The "I" which is *said* differs utterly from the "I" which is *meant,* but
is not its determinate negation, the condition for a dialectical conversion. Rather, "the position of the I, which is the condition for thought,
implies its eradication . . . as the undoing, the erasure of any relationship, logical or otherwise, that could be conceived between what the I
is and what it says it is." [21] What is erased is the possibility of relating
subject and predicate. The position of the "I" implies the erasure of
identity as the identity-in-difference of "what it is" and "what it says
it is," its status as an entity with properties or as a subject with
predicates.

    "Position" here names the positional power of language as "posit-
ing," or *setzen,* that is inherent in the arbitrary nature of the sign, as it
is contrasted by Hegel with the symbol. In referring to the position of
the "I," de Man draws upon a comparison between the status of the
sign and the status of the thinking subject argued in the opening pages
of "Sign and Symbol in Hegel's *Aesthetics.*" In a section of the

Encyclopedia distinguishing thinking from perception, imagination, and understanding (par. 458), Hegel stresses the arbitrariness of the relationship between the sensory dimension and the intended meaning of the sign, and goes on to identify the most free "activity of the intellect," thought, with the use of signs rather than symbols. De Man writes,

> To the extent that the sign is entirely independent with regard to the objective, natural properties of the entity towards which it points, and instead posits properties by means of its own powers, it illustrates the capacity of the intellect to "use" the perceived world for its own purposes, to efface (*tilgen*) its properties and to put others in their stead.[22]

> Just as the sign refuses to be in the service of sensory perceptions but uses them instead for its own purposes, thought, unlike perception, appropriates the world and literally 'subjects' it to its own powers. The agent of this appropriation is language.[23]

The agent of this *meinen* (*mein-en,* to make mine; *meinen,* to mean) is *sagen*—its subversion, we saw in the analysis of deixis. Thought "subjects" the world in producing signs that signify: that take on significations, in the way that the subject, arbitrary in its first position, takes on predicates. Signs signify only as they convey a meaning that is general, recognizable, part of a system of preestablished relationships—relationships that are determined, like the relationship between form and meaning in the symbol. "Thus the sign, random and singular at its first position, turns into symbol, just as the I, so *singular* in its independence from anything that is not itself, becomes, in the general thought of logic, the most inclusive, plural, general and impersonal of subjects."[24]

It becomes in fact a subject incapable of functioning as a subject, an "I" that cannot say an "I" that stands in any relation to it. This "eradication" of the subject can be understood in terms of the difference between sign and symbol:

> As we saw, the I, in its freedom from sensory determination, is originally similar to the sign. Since, however, it states itself as what it is not, it represents as determined a relationship to the world that is in fact arbitrary, that is to say, it states itself as a symbol. To the extent that the I points to itself it is a sign, but to the extent that it speaks of anything but itself, it is a symbol. The relationship between sign and symbol however is one of mutual obliteration.[25]

For the sign to operate as a symbol, in signifying, is for the functioning of language as signification to cancel what allowed it to come into being in the first place, the arbitrary power of position of the sign.

This is the predicament named in the statement that *voice* is *figure*. To say what it means, the sign must take on a face, must present a figure, but in being a face, it loses the power to mean, to speak. Language functions as the representation of meaning only in blotting out the positing power that enables it to act as language.

The aporia is sharply stated in de Man's readings of passages in Hegel's "The Symbolism of the Sublime"[26] and Shelley's *The Triumph of Life* that describe the origin of language as "light." The shapes of light in Shelley's poem, figures, in de Man's reading, for the figurative dimension of language, originate in a dawn that the opening of the poem presents not as a gradual natural event but as a single sudden moment, an act:[27]

> Swift as a spirit hastening to his task
> . . . the Sun sprang forth
> . . . and the mask
> Of darkness fell from the awakened Earth.
>
> (ll. 1–4)

This moment has the suddenness and the originary force of the Creation described in Genesis, which Hegel quotes: "And God said, Let there be light, and there was light." Hegel is presenting as the purest expression of the sublime the idea that God is the creator (*Schöpfer*) of the universe: not by a natural generative process (*zeugen*) but by an act of creation (*schaffen*) that is an act of language. "The figure is not naturally given or produced but . . . posited by an arbitrary act of language" (*RR*, 117). What is posited is figure: that which is perceptible or intelligible, but also, mute. This implication of the analysis of deixis enters Hegel's text on the sublime with the theme of radical asymmetry between creator and creation: "Let there be light" is "the word . . . whose command to be also and actually posits what is without mediation and in mute obedience."[28] The muteness of the creation is implied by the notion that the Word speaks:

> The word speaks and the world is the transitive object of its utterance, but this implies that what is thus spoken, and which includes us, is not the subject of its speech act. . . . To say that language speaks, that the grammatical subject of a proposition is language rather than a self, is not fallaciously to anthropomorphize language but rigorously to grammatize the self. The self is deprived

of any locutionary power; to all intents and purposes, it may as well be mute.[29]

But de Man's reading is aimed at a muteness that is not only represented or thematized in the text, but occurs there. In "The Symbolism of the Sublime," de Man argues, intelligibility breaks down when Hegel's first and second quotations are juxtaposed. The second quotation is an apostrophe from the Psalms: "Light is your garment, that you wear. . . ." *Garment* implies a mere covering, a dispensible outside surface. But this light said to be a mere garment was identified, in the first quotation, with the Word itself. (This is the difficult part of the reading: "Let there be light and there was light" has to be read not only as a speech act that posits the phenomenal world, but as a decree in which the Word posits itself as light.) De Man concludes:

> One can understand this, as Hegel does, as a statement about the insignificance of the sensory world as compared to the spirit. Unlike the *logos,* it does not have the power to posit anything; its power, or only discourse, is the knowledge of its weakness. But since this same spirit also, without mediation, *is* the light (p. 481), the combination of the two quotations states that the spirit posits itself as that which is unable to posit, and this declaration is either meaningless or duplicitous. One can pretend to be weak when one is strong, but the power to pretend is decisive proof of one's strength. One can know oneself, as man does, as that which is unable to know, but by moving from knowledge to position, all is changed. Position is all of a piece and moreover, unlike thought, it actually occurs. It becomes impossible to find a common ground between the two quotations.[30]

What has occurred is the erasure of the positing power of language by the position, the positioning, of (a) figure. "Light is your garment" is a figure, an apostrophe, describing—or rather, ascribing—figure. As such it functions like a prosopopoeia, which emerges explicitly in Hegel's next quotation, "Thou hidest thy face. . . ." The quotation of an apostrophe, in particular, renders the affirmation of the positional power of language meaningless or duplicitous, and this is due not only to the content of the apostrophe ("light," "garment," figure) but to its mode, that of a figure ascribing figure. This mode of operation disrupts not only the conception of language as representation but also the conception of language as possessing the absolute power of position.

The result of the reading of Hegel is consistent with the conclusion of the reading of Nietzsche, in which the conception of language as *setzen* (positing) displaces that of *erkennen* (knowing) but provides no

truer model for the functioning of the text. Nietzsche's passages operate not as *setzen* but as the negation of *Voraussetzungen* (presuppositions or assumptions) (*AR,* 125, 129). Hegel's text, de Man finds,
describes a shift from *setzen* to "*das Gesetz*"—"a law of differentiation (*Unterscheidung*), not the grounding of an authority but the un-
settling of an authority which is shown to be illegitimate. . . . the main
monarch to be thus dethroned . . . is language, the matrix of all value
systems in its claim to possess the absolute power of position."[31] The
critique is located not only in the works explicitly concerned with law
and the political (Hegel's *Principles of the Philosophy of Law* and *Lectures on the Philosophy of Religion*) but already in the sections of the
Aesthetics following "The Symbolism of the Sublime," where the
homology of trope with symbol (the conception of art as symbol that
dominates the *Aesthetics*) gives way to the requirement of an explicit
specification of the difference and disjunction between sign and meaning. In the *Aesthetics,* after "the sublime relationship is completely
eliminated (*vorständig fortfällt*),"[32] what follows, called "The Conscious Symbolism of Comparative Art Forms" (including "allegory,"
"metaphor," and "simile") is the functioning of language in the construction of figures or tropes: rather than *setzen, nebeneinandersetzen,*
the deliberate "comparison" or juxtaposition of a literal and a figurative meaning. Instead of a Word that posits—what the text on the sublime (with the quotation from Genesis) represents—there is a figure
that gives face or figure: the text functions, performs, by addressing
such a figure.

How such a giving of figure can take place is precisely the problem
identified as "the necessity, which is also the impossibility, to connect
the subject with its predicates or the sign with its symbolic significations."[33] De Man's interpretation of the predicament of predication
entails a double gesture. On the one hand there is an insistence on the
fact that for language to exist, there must be the possibility of a "position" absolutely independent and arbitrary in relation to the sensory
world: a sign. The concept of the sign entails the concept of a trace or
space produced arbitrarily: by chance (or by an intention always
established only after the fact), not by necessity (not arising by nature
as a necessary part of the physical world). The arbitrary relation between the meaning and the sensory component of the sign implies a
moment in which the sign stands free of its significations. On the
other hand, de Man stresses that this moment can never exist as such.
The sign exists only insofar as it signifies, enters into a determinable
relationship or system of relationships. The sign's standing apart from

its significations is named, in a chapter on Rousseau in *Allegories of Reading*, "fiction." Such a fiction—"the absence of any link between utterance and a referent . . . causal, encoded, or governed by any other conceivable relationship" (*AR*, 292)—is indeed a fiction, but an indispensable one. Only the possibility of the emergence of marks that are random, in no way determined until their form and meaning is determined by an act of reading, makes possible the existence of a text. As de Man writes, "without this moment, never allowed to exist as such, no such thing as a text is conceivable" (*AR*, 293).

While the conclusion of "Hegel on the Sublime" stresses the fictionality of this moment (or of the possession, by the Word or language, of the absolute power of position), the conclusion of "Shelley Disfigured" stresses its indispensability, together with the inevitability and the invalidity, of the imposition of meaning that succeeds and conceals it. "The initial violence of position can be only half erased," de Man writes, "since the erasure is accomplished by a device of language [the figure that confers figure, prosopopoeia] that never ceases to partake of the very violence against which it is directed" (*RR*, 118–19). The gesture that infers relationship and ascribes meaning is as violent, as unwarranted and alogical, as the arbitrary positioning of the sign.

> How can a positional act, which relates to nothing that comes before or after, become inscribed in a sequential narrative? How does a speech act become a trope, a catachresis which then engenders in its turn the narrative sequence of an allegory? It can only be because we impose, in our turn, on the senseless power of positional language the authority of sense and meaning. But this is radically inconsistent: language posits and language means (since it articulates) but language cannot posit meaning; it can only reiterate (or reflect) it in its reconfirmed falsehood. Nor does the knowledge of this impossibility make it less impossible. This impossible position is precisely the figure, the trope, metaphor as a violent—and not as a dark—light, a deadly Apollo.
>
> (*RR*, 117–18)

The passage *narrates* the giving of figure even as it states its impossibility. This paragraph condenses the movement that de Man describes as the way in which Hegel's analysis of the position of the "I" (par. 20 of the *Encyclopedia*) "forgets its own statement": "by describing the predicament it states, which is a logical difficulty devoid of any phenomenal or experiential dimension, as if it were an event in time, a narrative or a history."[34] Here where de Man writes that "we impose, *in our turn,* on the senseless power of positional language the authority of sense and meaning," the analysis of the logical difficulty inherent in the status of the sign is restated as it is in "The Triumph of Life," in "the narrative sequence of an allegory" (*RR*, 117).

De Man's text repeats the rhetorical strategies it reads. Thus what is next at issue is the gesture of questioning performed at the start of the passage just cited: How does a speech act become a trope? How does the senseless positional power of language give way to the imposition of the authority of sense and meaning? These questions rearticulate those asked at the beginning of each episode of the allegory by the speakers within the poem ("I" and "Rousseau"); "'Whence camest thou? and whither goest thou?/How did thy course begin,' I said, 'and why?'" (ll. 296–97). It is precisely "in the form of the questions that served as a point of departure for the reading," de Man now asserts, that the violent imposition of meaning occurs. Questions presume the possibility of answers. In de Man's text they are displaced (as in Shelley's text they are framed) by assertions that revoke the meaningfulness of questioning. To question or to "put in question" is the virtually inevitable mode and goal of contemporary criticism and theory. De Man's strategy not only unsettles the rhetoric of critical discourse but also challenges the basic terms of the project in which Heidegger precedes him, the departure from an anthropological conception of man: the focus on the "entity . . . which includes inquiring as one of the possibilities of its Being," "the inquirer," *Dasein*.[35] De Man's critique of questioning is aimed at the very conditions of the project marked by such a definition, as well as the assumptions implied by the act of questioning. This passage in "Shelley Disfigured" concludes in the voice of the allegorist: "To question is to forget" (*RR*, 118).[36]

To question is to forget the arbitrary power of position at the origin of language or the senseless positional status of the sign. To question is to give a voice or a face, to "claim manifest kindred" with an entity thereby assumed to be capable of response and reply. This "trope of address," prosopopoeia, "is the very figure of the reader and of reading."[37] No reading can occur without it, but every such reading effaces the condition of existence of the text it reads. "Shelley Disfigured" draws a distinction between the inevitable operation of reading and the belief in its value: "What *would* be naive is to believe that this strategy, which is not *our* strategy as subjects, since we are its product rather than its agent, can be a source of value and has to be celebrated or denounced accordingly" (*RR*, 122). De Man's way of naming the process of reading or understanding undertakes to thwart and elude this valorization. The impulse to value the operation of reading or any one of its moments is discouraged by de Man's characteristic

designation of reading or rhetoric in terms that are "mutually obliter-
ating" (like the structures of the sign and the symbol): the giving of
face as de-facement, the conferral of meaning as the erasure of the
power to mean. To affirm that to question is to forget, in a passage
that begins by posing questions that recall a complex interpretation,
is to show that the writer never eludes the erasure of meaning that he
describes.

The forgetting or erasure entailed in the gesture of ascribing meaning is explained in "Sign and Symbol in Hegel's *Aesthetics*" in terms
of the incompatibility of symbol and sign. In "Hypogram and Inscription: Michael Riffaterre's Poetics of Reading" it is explained in terms
of the disparity between the figural and the material modes of being
of the sign, between figure and inscription. Saussure's notion of a
hypogram (the term borrowed by Riffaterre to describe the poetic
text as an expansion and concealment of a "matrix," or semantic
given, whose referential meaning is suspended) is found to include the
meaning "souligner au moyen du fard les traits du visage"—to confer a
face, like *prospopoiein*—and to imply a model of the performance of
language through a figure that confers or ascribes figure. This model,
de Man argues (which is similar to the model that emerged in Hegel's
text with the elimination of "the sublime relationship"), implies the
annihilation of the phenomenality of meaning that it seeks or appears
to ensure. "Hypogram and Inscription" reads in Hegel's chapter on
sense-certainty and Hugo's poem "Ecrit sur la vitre d'une fenêtre fla-
mande" (a poem analysed by Riffaterre) an "allegory of cognition"
that recounts a misreading of the phenomenality of the signifier—such
as the glass pane on which the poem is said to be "*écrit*" or the "piece
of paper" on which Hegel's words "Now is the night" are said to be
written down—as a guarantee of the phenomenality of the signified
and the referent, ultimately, the mind and its concepts, space and
time.

Hypogram is a term that surfaces in the portions of Saussure's
notebooks published in 1971 by Jean Starobinski under the title *Les
mots sous les mots: Les anagrammes de Ferdinand de Saussure.*[38]
Saussure explores the notion that Latin poetry is structured by the
coded repetition of the phonemes or syllables of proper names. The
text would be produced by a process of formal elaboration and not
primarily as a process of representation. This idea is familiar in contemporary conceptions of poetry (such as Riffaterre's) as suspension
of reference. The nonreferential text remains intelligible, readable, so
long as it is possible to distinguish between those of its elements that
are encoded—produced in obedience to rules of composition—and

those that are generated by the laws of probability. But Saussure's inquiries revealed not only the suspension of reference, but something more disruptive: the disappearance, under the pressure of inquiry, of the significative status of the sign. The grounds for a distinction between encoded and random elements proved to be impossible to establish. Saussure could find no external historical evidence of the existence of such rules of composition, nor could he prove, on the basis of the internal evidence of the texts, "whether the structures were random, the outcome of mere probability, or determined by the codification of a semiosis."[39] Saussure's attempt to limit and describe the anagrammatic phenomenon that the poetry displayed was undercut by the capacity he came to recognize of discovering further, potentially endless anagrams or anagrammatical patterns of recurrence in a text.[40] The texts were made up of patterns that might or might not be significative, of elements that might or might not be signs. The term *hypogram,* in its resemblance to the term *prosopopoeia,* suggests (de Man implies) the impossibility Saussure discovered of perceiving the semiotic process, of identifying it as a phenomenon, without *conferring* on some patterns of recurrence (and not on others) the status of meaningful articulations. Saussure's discovery implies the undoing of the distinction between sign and trope:[41] the hierarchical relationship between signifier and signified is seen to be set up by the same order of gesture as that which connects a literal and a figurative meaning.

The arbitrary and aleatory character of the material of signification would be what is ultimately implied by the performative status of language. The power of language to posit, rather than to receive or represent entities, implies the possibility for the linguistic sign to occur as an entirely arbitrary position, even if it will necessarily be construed as a structure or pattern—a figure. In this sense figuration is in conflict with the very condition of existence of language or the linguistic sign. Whence the peculiar asymmetry of the term *disfiguration:* figuration as such is disfiguration, insofar as it mutes language, in effacing the arbitrary power of position of the linguistic sign. But moreover, the capacity for language to posit (with the necessary possibility of random position that that entails)—the performative power which, also, is implied in the status of language as "figure" or rhetoric—this disfigures, too, language as cognitive structure, as meaningful pattern, as face.

In the potentially endless proliferation of anagrammatic patterns that Saussure finally had to acknowledge, the text as principle of *articulation* disappears. The text's formal overdetermination is demonstrable; but its form, or rather the laws of its determination, are not phenomenally or mathematically perceivable. "We would then have witnessed, in effect," writes de Man, "the undoing of the phenomenality of language": [42] the undoing of the perceivability, the intelligibility, of linguistic structures—the undoing of the conditions of cognition.

This undoing was inherent in the "arbitrary nature" (Saussure's terms) of the sign, in the "position" of the sign, the subject, the "I." With this undoing we reach the conception of language that emerges in Hegel's *Aesthetics* after the elimination (with the eradication of "the sublime relationship") of the absolute power of positing. Conceived as a figure that gives figure (as "hypogram" or as the prosopopoeia of "light") "the principle of signification . . . is no longer a sign-*producing* function (which is how Hegel valorized the sign in the *Encyclopedia*) but the quotation or repetition of a previously established semiosis; it is reduced to the preordained motion of its own position."[43] Saussure mentions, among the meanings of *hypogram* that make it suitable to designate what he seeks to describe ("genre d'anagramme à reconnaître dans les littératures anciennes") (including "souligner au moyen du fard les traits du visage") "soit *faire allusion; soit reproduire par écrit* comme un notaire, un secrétaire."[44] Allusion *or* reproduction; quotation *or* repetition; *hypogram* elides, and undoes, the crucial distinction between the effect of an intentional codifying activity and that of an automatic process. So does the model of signification as quotation that de Man finds in the description of language as trope that emerges in the last section of the *Aesthetics*. Quoting (like questioning) entails assuming the independent prior existence of a meaningful (or intelligible) articulation. But calling a text a quotation entails assuming a possible disjunction between text and meaning. (The text's meaning is not the speaker's, but that of the text quoted.) If the quotation cannot be identified with the intention of the speaker, this ultimately puts in doubt whether it is an intentional structure, a meaningful articulation, at all: whether it is not in fact merely the repetition (by chance or by necessity) of a pattern without meaning that is intelligible (or perceptible) only insofar as it is repeated.

The anagram might, in short, be a fiction: a random occurrence of syllables (mis)read as a key word or proper name. De Man's account of the text as "inscription" that only a figure (ascribing figure) transforms into description rejoins his account of Rousseau's text as "fiction" that only a (mis)reading transforms into a confession or an accusation. The claim by Rousseau in the dialogue of "Préface de *Julie*" that his novel is all quotation leads to his claim (commonsensically unintelligible) that he may not know whether he wrote it or not. The possibility that the text is quotation or repetition implies, in short, the possibility that it is random reproduction or "noise": the status, Rousseau claims, in the *Confessions,* of his fatal pronunciation of the name "Marion," misread as a slander, misread in being read at all, when under the pressure to speak about his suspected theft of his mistress's ribbon, "je m'excusai sur le premier objet qui s'offrit"—that object being syllables that happened to spell a proper name.[45] Rousseau's proffering the "first object that offered itself," these preexisting syllables, is "the quotation or repetition of a previously established semiosis" (in de Man's phrase in "Hegel on the Sublime")—erroneously or illegitimately identified with a meaning, as Rousseau claims, yet existing only in the context of preexisting signification. After an interpretation insisting, against a more obvious reading of the passage as an explanation of motives, on the random, radically unmotivated nature of the utterance "Marion," de Man's reading concludes, characteristically, by denying the possibility of doing what it would appear he has just done: the possibility "ever to isolate the moment in which the fiction stands free of its significations" (*AR,* 293). It is impossible to isolate a moment in which the "position" of the sign occurs independently of the position of other signs. The text's materiality—what is prior to the figuration that gives the text its phenomenal status—cannot be isolated "as such," as a "moment," as an origin. The absolute power of position of the sign does not exist. What does exist is quotation or inscription: patterns or traces already in existence, the significative status of which cannot be determined.

The notion of a text that is sheer repetition, neither message nor question, neither meaning nor speech, haunts Saussure's writing on the hypogram even as it surfaces in Hegel's writing on the sign. Repetition can be construed as a signifying structure only if it forms a pattern; and it forms a pattern only, Saussure discovers, by dint of a delimiting gesture that is essentially willful. Looking for the recurrence (in sequence) of the syllables of key words or proper names related to the topic of the poem was a first such gesture. To read spaced out letters as a name is to give them a shape, a face. What proved impossible— but necessary—was to give a face to the name. It was impossible to delimit the rules by which this anagrammatic production of names took place, to distinguish it from the random or necessary generation of sequences of letters by the laws of probability. The disintegration of the name inherent in the status of the name as the *giving* of face haunts not only Saussure's notebooks on anagrams, but Hegel's account of thinking (*Denken*) in the *Encyclopedia.* "Wir denken in Namen," states a passage shortly following the section identifying the free "activity of the intellect" with the use of signs rather than symbols (par. 458). *Denken* is then identified with *Gedächtnis*, memorization: the ability to recite lists of names (par. 460). Such reciting requires that one *forget* the meaning of the words recited, Hegel specifies. Moreover, it requires that one fail to accentuate, to clearly articulate, the individual names. This passage describes (in experiential terms whose significance is not literal but allegorical) the sign's independence of sensory determinations stressed in the preceding section (par. 458): the word, as *name*—like a proper name, describing nothing, without a signified, pointing to a referent identifiable in no other terms—detached from meaning and from sense. De Man's reading of *Les mots sous les mots* differs from Sylvère Lotringer's in "The Game of the Name"[46] (which he cites as the best account in English of the significance of Saussure's inquiry) by stressing the disruptive rather than the recuperative effect of the focus on the name as such, its inevitable disclosure of a disintegration attendant upon the disjunction between naming and meaning.[47]

"Hypogram and Inscription" moves away from the anxiety or terror of this disjunction in the example of Saussure's anagrams (the anxiety of undecidably automatic or intended textual structures, the terror of the dispersal and disintegration of the proper name) to the banality of the disjunction between "saying" and "meaning" in the example of the "this," the deictic function analysed in the *Phenomenology*. The only case in which saying and meaning actually coincide is in a sign that cannot be said to say or to mean anything: the inscription (as on the last page of Hegel's first chapter) of the words "This piece of paper" or (as in the title of Hugo's text) of the word *Écrit*. This written down *this* differs altogether from *this* or *here* or *now* as they are spoken, as they indicate a generality in pointing toward a particular:

> ... Unlike the here and now of speech, the here and now of the inscription is neither false nor misleading: because he wrote it down, the existence of a here and now of Hegel's text is undeniable as well as totally blank. ... We can easily enough learn to care for the other examples Hegel mentions: a house, a tree, night, day—but who cares for his damned piece of paper, the last thing in the world we want to hear about and, precisely because it is no longer an *example* but a fact, the only thing we actually get. As we would say, in colloquial exasperation with an obtuse bore: forget it! Which turns out to be precisely what Hegel sees as the function of writing. ... Writing is what makes one forget speech: "Natural consciousness therefore proceeds by itself to

this outcome, which is its truth [the knowledge that it is "false and misleading": the knowledge that in "meaning" a particular "this" one "says" what is general], and experiences this progression within itself; but it also always *forgets it* over and again [*sic*] and recommences this movement from the start [par. 20, pp. 86–87; my italics]. As the only particular event that can be pointed out, writing, unlike speech and cognition, is what takes us back to this ever-recurring natural consciousness.[48]

The comic effect of the "forget it!" introduced by the noncolloquially precise allusion to "colloquial exasperation with an obtuse bore" resembles a little the ludicrousness of the dialogue between sense-certainty and the "we" (in Hegel's chapter) described by Warminski (It is "somewhat distressing," he comments, "for anyone expecting 'the earnestness, the pain, the patience and work of the negative.'")[49] The forgetting evoked here is a forgetting of the difference between the "this" of "this piece of paper" and the "this" of speech. The undeniable existence of "this piece of paper," or of a sequence of letters in a text that can be assembled to form a proper name, impels the gesture by which the sensory component of the signifier is taken as an example and a guarantee of the phenomenality of the signified. This gesture forgets the blankness of the sign's mere material existence in the same way that the gesture of address, an apostrophe or a question, forgets the blankness of sheer "position" as the condition of the existence of language or a text. Or in the terms of the *Encylopedia* account of *Denken* as *Gedächtnis,* one forgets that the production of language, or "thinking"—the reproduction of sequences of names—requires the forgetting of its meaning or its reception.

De Man's allusion to Hegel's piece of paper as "a fact, the only thing we actually get" must not be confused with the gesture he is criticizing, the appeal to sensory evidence in the form of an appeal to the phenomenality of a particular signifier. The point is not that writing "this piece of paper" (or "writing," or "Ecrit") on a piece of paper really happens, whereas the mind's entering into a relationship with time (coming to know what is the "now," or, in Hugo's lyric, "loving" a carillon) does not. De Man contrasts, rather, the phenomenality of a perception (and this includes the perception of a particular piece of paper), the certainty of which is unestablishable (unsayable), with the materiality of an inscription, which is "undeniable" but "blank." The materiality of an inscription must be distinguished from the phenomenal, sensory existence of a particular piece of writing.[50] By *inscription* is meant marks or traces that indeed exist and occur, not in a perceptible space, but to a perceiver in the process of reading, of rendering intelligible a diffusion of marks or traces. Such marks cannot be known to *signify* and cannot be said to be *perceived,* since their form, their shape, their phenomenal status, is a function of an intentionality or semiotic status that can only be postulated for them rather than perceived, described, or known. Inscription is the sign cut off from its signification, the trace unprovably a sign. The "materiality" of inscription is associated with the random occurrence of the sign or its position. Like the "moment" in which the position of the sign occurs independently of the position of other signs, the text's materiality cannot be isolated as such or as an origin, although it is the condition of possibility of any text. The materiality of inscription evokes the reality of texts or quotations or nondeterminably significative patterns always already in existence (rather than created *ex nihilo* by an absolute power of positing, the conception of the sign's position represented and disrupted in Hegel's text on the sublime).

In evoking the prospect of "witnessing" (with Saussure's discovery) the definitive undoing of the phenomenality of language, de Man sketches an allegory of its undoing that matches the allegory of cognition he reads in Hugo's and Hegel's texts. In Hugo's poem on the carillon, as in Hegel's chapter on sense-certainty, "the figural enigma is that of a conscious cognition being in some manner akin to the certainty of a sense perception." The concept of time is made in some sense perceptible through the description of the carillon—"Que l'oeil croit voir, vêtue en danseuse espagnole,/Apparaître soudain par le trou vif et clair/Que ferait en s'ouvrant une porte de l'air" (ll. 6–8). What is happening is that "the phenomenal and sensory properties of the signifier," the carillon, are being made to "serve as guarantors for the certain existence of the signified and, ultimately, of the referent,"[51] time. The process of signification, which has a material element, is made to serve as an example and a guarantee of the phenomenality of experience. But this belies the arbitrary nature of the link between signifier and signified, the sign's independence of sensory determinations; the materiality, rather than the phenomenality, of the sign. In fact, the process of signification can exemplify phenomenal experience only by means of a figuration. "The starting, catachrestic degree of signification" gives a face to the sign—in Hugo's poem, *le carillon* as the sign of time. The phenomenalization of the concept of time takes place by means of a prosopopoeia, introduced in the apostrophe that opens the poem:

J'aime le carillon de tes cités antiques,
O vieux pays gardien de tes moeurs domestiques . . .

Read as allegories of the origin of cognition in the arbitrary conferral of face on the diffusion of material traces, Hegel's and Hugo's texts become, like Wordsworth's lines on the Blest Babe, allegories of the *undoing* of cognition or the phenomenality of experience: "As soon as we understand the rhetorical function of prosopopoeia as positing voice or face by means of language, we also understand that what we are deprived of is not life but the shape and sense of a world accessible only in the privative way of understanding" (*RR*, 80–81). The most radical of deprivations is implicit in the breaking down of the phenomenality of language into the materiality of inscription and the figurality of figure; with it breaks down the possibility of experience as such, of having such a thing as an experience. This motif of deprivation in de Man and Wordsworth resonates strangely with an allusion to "useless luxury" at the close of Starobinski's presentation of Saussure's anagrams:

> Ainsi, le message poétique (qui est "fait de parole") ne se constituerait seulement *avec* des mots empruntés à la *langue,* mais encore *sur* des noms ou des mots donnés un à un: le message póetique apparaît alors comme le luxe inutile de l'hypogramme.[52]

What is essential in the signifying process is the hypogram, the anagrammatic infrastructure; the poetic message, the representational and aesthetic dimension of the text, is useless luxury, an element that does not contribute to the text's essential functioning. Lotringer pursues the point:

> This first attempt [Saussure's discovery of anagrams] suffices nevertheless to unsettle that cultural product intended for communication (message), appreciation (volume), and consumption (emotion), in short for the ideological entrapment of the subject, which is the function of *academic literature*—doubly tautological formula. . . . Literature appears for the first time as a secondary elaboration, a unifying, repetitive, fantasmatic activity which continues to inhibit the textual process, to write as best it can the transitory formulations destined to discrimination in order to constitute the smooth facade which forestalls the labor of meaning. . . . In the Saussurian breakthrough, it is this luxurious edifice which must now be torn down.[53]

The differentiation of the infrastructure of the text from the superstructure of its reception modulates, here, into a call to "tear down" the institution of "academic literature."

That call to action is not encouraged by the critique of ideology that is a persisting and complex pressure in de Man's writing. These essays on lyrical and philosophical texts concerned with prosopopoeia and predication offer a critique of anthropomorphism and of the ideology of the symbol, in which the arbitrary figuration conferring meaning is treated as a source of value. Such belief shows up in the celebration of particular genres, such as the lyric, readings focused on the lyricism of lyric poetry. These are expendable investments in the institution of academic literature. But the valorization of literature denounced by Lotringer is not so easy, it turns out here, to avoid. Lyric is distinguished, de Man argues, by the tendency for its tropes to become anthropomorphisms: for prominently figural gestures such as metaphor or, in particular, prosopopoeia, to be stabilized into a presentation of the naturalness of the human. Anthropomorphism appears as "the illusionary rescuscitation of the natural breath of language frozen into stone by the semantic power of the trope" (*RR*, 247). What it does, however, is to "freeze the infinite chain of tropological transformations and propositions into one single assertion or essence which, as such, excludes all others. It is no longer a proposition but a proper name" (*RR*, 241). The proper name does not signify or articulate. The attempt to unfreeze natural voice freezes figuration into sheer inscription. What is being distinguished from anthropomorphism, however, trope or figure, is also described as a strategy that freezes or disfigures speech. Prosopopoeia must be conceived—like anthropomorphism—as an effort to undo the spell, to give a face to the name, which fails in the attempt. Anthropomorphism, the substantializing tendency, the mystification, arises from the same imperative as prosopopoeia, which meets with the same impossibility. Both strategies arise from the necessity to establish the phenomenality of the poetic voice, which is the principle of intelligibility (as we have seen de Man argue) not only of the lyric, but of language in general.

The nature of the operation of reading, which must make the attempt to distinguish between strategies, is evoked once again in de Man's introduction to Hans Robert Jauss's *Toward a Theory of Reception*. It emerges, de Man suggests, in an analysis of Jauss's reading of some lines in Baudelaire's "Spleen" (76). The lines are those in which "the name of the painter Boucher is made to pseudo-rhyme with the word 'débouché' (uncorked)":

> un vieux boudoir
> Où les pastels plaintifs et les pâles Boucher,
> Seuls, respirent l'odeur d'un flacon débouché.

In a rare Lacanian moment, Jauss suggests that what he calls a "grotesque" effect of verbal play—the rhyme-pair Boucher/

débouché—is also something more uncanny: "The still harmonious representation of the last perfume escaping from the uncorked bottle overturns (*kippt um*) into the dissonant connotation of a 'decapitated' rococo painter Boucher" (p. 157). After having gone this far, it becomes very hard to stop. Should one not also notice that this bloody scene is made gorier still by the presence of a proper name (Boucher) which, as a common name [*sic*], means butcher, thus making the "pale Boucher" the agent of his own execution? [54]

Reading a rhyme-pair as a pun (as Jauss does) and reading a proper name as a common noun (as de Man does) are moves that give a face to a name; they make a description from inscription, a message from the nondescriptive, nonpropositional, mechanical elements of rhyme and proper name. Yet the figure they confer is a *dis*figuration. The image of the uncorked bottle overturns, Jauss suggests, like a bottle; the figure read from the rhyme is that of a decapitated maker of images. What tips over and spills, in fact, is the image of the figure as a container (like a flacon) from which an inner essence emanates; it is replaced by the instance of a figure that is not a container but an inscription: the disfiguration, by reinscription, of a name. The "still harmonious representation" of the *flacon débouché* is a figure and an instance of the poetic figure as recollection of *Erinnerung,* the internalization of experience that transforms it into meaning or beauty. The figure of Boucher *débouché* is an instance of the poetic figure functioning not like recollection but like memorization (*Gedächtnis*) or forgetting: as the reproduction, inscription, disarticulation of names. [55]

It is not only hard to stop the process of reading, but hard to know where it starts: does the reading begin with Baudelaire's act of composition in which the name of the painter is "made to" rhyme with the word *débouché*? De Man discriminates between the figure and the reading, to argue that it is the nature of the text as *figure* to require a *reading,* the nature of which is evoked in this particular figure:

> The ambiguity of [Baudelaire's] statement [the play on words] . . . because it is a verbal thrust and not an actual blow, allows itself to be taken figurally but, in so doing, opens up the way to the performance of what it only seems to figure or prefigure. The false rhyme on Boucher/débouché is a figure, a paranomasia. But only after we have, with the assistance of H. R. Jauss, noticed and recognized it as such does the actual threat inherent in the fiction produced by the actual hands of the painter (who is also a butcher) become manifest. [56]

If the thrust of this passage is apparent, its target is far from obvious. What gesture, or whose, is being said to be a threat? Puzzlement sets in where de Man alludes to "the actual threat inherent in the fiction produced by the actual hands of the painter (who is also a butcher)."

The argument we have followed concerning the figure that gives face helps to unravel this difficult sentence. "The fiction produced by the actual hands of the painter" is not the *oeuvre* of François Boucher. It is the fiction of the existence of face and figure produced by the painter as the maker of pictures, who is like the poet as the maker of figures or images. The threat inherent in this fiction is the threat of muteness or "de-facement" inherent in the erasure of the positional power of language that takes place with the imposition of sense and meaning through the conferral of figure and face. This is an actual threat, we have seen de Man argue, and it is made manifest here by Jauss's (and de Man's) performance of reading, which generates the figure of a decapitation. More precisely, it generates the figure of a disfiguration effected by the gesture that gives a face to a name: the gesture of Boucher the painter, identified with the gesture that does in the painter Boucher by the pun (read by de Man) that makes the name of the painter the name of the butcher. A disfiguration or de-capitation actually occurs in the course of the reading: that of the proper name Boucher as it is read figuratively in the word *dé-bouché*. This *instance* of figuration as disfiguration of the name is read as a *figure* of decapitation; this reading, alone, makes manifest the threat inherent in the process of figuration.

We confront (or perform) not an "actual blow," but an "actual threat." Reading is a speech act, one that in imposing sense and meaning "partakes of the violence" of the arbitrary positional power of language that it disguises or "only half" erases and that thereby "opens the way to the performance" of the violence it threatens, the blow it "only seems [*sic:* not "seems only"] to feign or prefigure." The figurative blow might become literal. What does happen, in this moment of reading, is that the rhyming name Boucher "tips over" into the figure of a figure "uncorked," decapitated—and tipped over. Jauss's word *umkippen*—"a very concrete . . . almost colloquial word," literal in the context of bottles, which is reapplied to the context of Boucher—"'overturns' the beheaded Boucher as if he himself were an uncorked 'flacon' spilling his blood."[57]

This overturning or tipping over spills, merely, blood it does not shed. But the possibility of an "actual blow" emerges at a subsequent moment in Jauss's interpretation of Baudelaire, where textual analysis or reading gives way to a conclusion de Man identifies as an affirmation of "confidence" of belief: "If this is so, can one then still share Jauss's confidence that 'the allegorical intention, pursued to the utmost of *rigor mortis,* can still reverse (*umschlagen*) this extreme alienation into an appearance of the beautiful?'"[58] Does allegory operate as a dialectical reversal, like mourning as *Erinnerung,* the conversion of death into beauty or meaning? Allegory would then take place as predication is supposed to take place in speculative philosophical thought: the subject finding itself transformed after its alienation or negation in the predicate. De Man rejects this conception for one of allegory as the narration of the *predicament* of predication, or in Hegel's terms, that of the subject of allegory as strictly "a grammatical subject": "the separation or disarticulation of subject from predicate."[59]

The target of the question about allegory is a double one: an erroneous conception of the figure, and its potentially dangerous valorization, an ideology of aesthetic experience implicit in the affirmation of allegory's power of reversal or conversion. De Man's note comments:

> "*Erscheinung des Schönen*" is, of course, the traditional Hegelian vocabulary for the aesthetic experience. The "umkippen" of Jauss's earlier, corrosive observation on Baudelaire's play on *Boucher/débouché* (157), which suggests the demolition of the aesthetic idol as if it were the *colonne Vendôme,* or any monument honoring a tyrant, is now replaced by the more dignified "umschlagen." Taken literally, however, *schlagen* (to beat) in the cliché *umschlagen* is rather more threatening than *kippen* (to tilt).[60]

How the celebration of the aesthetic might come to involve actual beating appears in the history of the modern state, or in the implications of the emergence in Schiller's *Letters on Aesthetic Education* of the ideal of an "aesthetic state"—"not just a state of mind or soul, but a principle of political value and authority that has its own claims on the shape and the limits of our freedom" (de Man writes in "Aesthetic Formalization: Kleist's 'Über das Marionettentheater'") (*RR,* 264). Despite appearances, the celebration of the aesthetic is more threatening than its dismantling.

Suppose the dialectical reversal of death into beauty or meaning could not take place, that the work of mourning, *Trauerarbeit,* could take place only indistinguishably from *Trauer-spiel,* or the "work" of melancholia, the performance of the play of letter? The dismantling of aesthetic ideology entails such a supposition. It entails showing, as these essays have done, that the achievements claimed for the dialectical conversion ascribed to the work of art as *Erinnerung* (and to philosophical thought)—the production of meaning, the grounding of the phenomenality of language—are illusory effects, rather, of the mechanical and repetitive processes from which art, thought, and mourning were supposed to have been distinguished: juxtaposition forced by means of figure, correspondence consisting in repetition. De Man's comment remarking the proximity of *umschlagen* and *schlagen* resembles a passage in which Freud remarks the correspondence between mourning and melancholia:

> Just as mourning impels the ego to give up the object by declaring the object to be dead [*für tot erklärt*] and offering the ego the inducement of continuing to live, so does each single struggle of ambivalence loosen the fixation of the libido to the object by disparaging it, denigrating it and even as it were killing it [*entwertet, herabsetzt, gleichsam auch erschlagt*].[61]

Mourning "declares" the object dead; melancholia, so to speak, "kills" it. The first is a constatation, the second a speech act and figure. But a declaration is a speech act as well, and Freud's comparison tends to narrow the difference between the two kinds of "work." In effect, melancholia would have to do the work of mourning, according to de Man's analysis of the predicament of predication. Only by a speech act and figure does the binding of subject and predicate, of subject and (lost) object, of the grammatical subject and its consciousness, in some sense take place. Not *umschlagen*, reversal or conversion, takes place, but a figurative *schlagen*: the repetition of a verbal blow, the working over of word play, the mechanical, repetitive process of quoting and questioning.

If the predicament of predication is evoked in the slippage from *umschlagen* to *schlagen*, the double bind of reading is captured in the curious verb *boucher*. Grammatically, so to speak, the word *bouch-er* would mean to give or to produce a mouth. Lexically, of course, the word means to stop up a mouth, to close an opening. The paradox in the lexical meaning evokes the nonsensory origin of language: it comes not from a mouth, but with a "face." *Pour ne pas rester bouche bée,* so as not to remain speechless, one will have to *déboucher,* to "Oter ce qui bouche," "par extension, Enlever ce qui empêche de passer," "déboucher le passage" between inside and out.[62] One will have to dispense with the literal mouth, which is stopped up, full of food, or of words taken in like food, so as to have a figurative mouth, a voice, or an opening for a passage between inside and outside, a capacity for language: a face or an eye. Molière: "Parbleu! tu vois: j'attends que ces messieurs aient débouché la porte, pour présenter là mon visage."[63]

But this is comedy. The comedy of recuperation, de Man would call it, the transformation of loss into gain characteristic of any "economy of value"—superseded by a "critical economy" that emerges with the elimination of the sublime relationship between an absolute power of positing and a mute creation, and its replacement by the model of language as trope and quotation. As such it admits no passage from literal sense to figurative meaning, or from an inside source to circulation outside. We get not a word but a trope. "Boucher débouché": the figure makes us read the word another way. *Déboucher* would mean not to deprive of a mouth to give a voice and a face, but to reopen a mouth, to deprive of face and voice. This is the deprivation of language, which takes place in the process of understanding or reading, the gesture that gives a face to a name.

5

Getting Versed

Reading Hegel with Baudelaire

O vers! noirs compagnons sans oreille et sans yeux
—*Les Fleurs du Mal*, 72

We are in the habit of identifying Romanticism with the affirmation of the primacy of the imagination. The word reaches us from *The Prelude* and the *Third Critique:* imagination—or its failure—reveals the mind's orientation toward a realm beyond nature. What Wordsworth names "Imagination— . . . the Power so called / Through sad incompetence of human speech," Kant (setting out, in the Critiques, the conditions for philosophical competence) names the Reason: a radically autonomous power of the mind disclosed when "the light of sense / Goes out, but with a flash that has revealed / The invisible world." That canonical example of the romantic sublime comes from the passage in book 6 of *The Prelude* where Wordsworth's recollection of his disappointment at missing the moment at which he had crossed the Alps gives way to his representation of passing from a sensible to a suprasensible faculty of mind, and to his affirmation that "our destiny, our being's heart and home, / Is with infinity, and only there."[1]

In Kant's terms, "nature is here called sublime merely because it elevates the imagination to a presentation of those cases in which the mind can make felt the proper sublimity of its destination, in comparison with nature itself."[2] The aesthetic judgment "this is sublime," through registering the inadequacy of aesthetic comprehension (*Zusammenfassung, comprehensio aesthetica*), discloses the necessary existence of a suprasensible faculty alone capable of thinking an absolute might or magnitude: the faculty of reason, which is the capacity for ethical judgment. This passage, with the sublime, from aesthetic to ethical judgment, marks the tendency of the analogy that defines

113

the import not just of the sublime but of the beautiful, and of the aesthetic as such: the analogy between disinterested aesthetic judgments and disinterested moral judgments, in both of which the mind "gives the law to itself," or displays its "freedom." The aesthetic is crucial because aesthetic judgment represents the possibility of judgment in general, of crossing from perception to cognition and from intuition to the exercise of the reason. "The continuity of aesthetic with rational judgment," then—"the main tenet and crux of all critical philosophies and 'Romantic' literatures"[3]—is the bearing of that affirmation of the power of Imagination that we habitually call romantic.

What this implies for rational judgment or for the category of the aesthetic gets intimated in Wordsworth's lines ("the light of sense goes out"). But it may be read out more exhaustively in texts at some remove from *The Prelude* and *The Critique of Judgment*, texts that can be read as undertaking to answer the question posed by Kant's and Wordsworth's affirmation. That question, in Hegel's terms, is, How does the idea make its appearance in the world?

The question gets answered in various ways in the *Aesthetics* and the *Phenomenology*, as well as in the very organization of the *Encyclopedia of the Philosophical Sciences*, where it is once again *art* that gets situated at the crucial junction between politics and philosophy, between practical and pure reason, the crossing, in Hegel's terms, from the objective to the absolute spirit. Suppose we look up the answer in the *Encyclopedia.*[4] It's easy to locate there and it quickly reveals an unexpected factor.

What we are looking for is what leads up to the emergence of "thought," *Denken.* For the idea makes its appearance in the world through the action of the "intelligence" or "theoretical mind," which culminates in "intelligence that *comprehends* the concrete universal nature of objects, or *thought* in the specific sense that what we *think* also is."[5] Thought in this specific sense is led up to, not surprisingly, by "intuition" (*Anschauung*) followed by "representation" (*Darstellung*), the central moment of which—the middle of the middle term— is, again not surprisingly, "imagination." What *is* surprising are the alignments on either side of that central middle, how the middle term gets articulated with the final one, how imagination becomes thought. This crucial junction is designated "memory," *Gedächtnis.* Not recollection, not remembrance, not *Erinnerung*: that inwardizing of the object, which we habitually associate with the transformative power of art, comes *before* imagination, in Hegel's scheme here. *Erinnerung* is the *first* moment of representation, followed by imagination; the third decisive moment is *Gedächtnis*, memory in the sense of memorization, which constitutes the passage into thought, Hegel explains, because it has to do with *signs* alone.

The idea makes its appearance in the world as memorized signs. Not, then, as art: not as symbols of what is remembered, works of art in the symbolical conception of art that predominates in the *Aesthetics*. The object of aesthetic judgment that is the work of art as *symbol* constitutes the remembrance or *Erinnerung* of the phenomenal world it represents as meaningful. But to be *thought*, according to the *Encyclopedia*, the inwardized objects of the imagination must materialize as signs: as memorizations or inscriptions. The question arises whether that is what the *aesthetic* must be construed to be.

The strictly arbitrary relation between the sign's own shape or sound (its "intuition," "irgend eine unmittelbare Anschauung," par. 458) and its meaning distinguishes the sign from the symbol, where shape or intuition and meaning substantially and conceptually coincide. In signs, the mind frees itself from images and makes use of the perceived world for its own purposes, reducing it to a minimal materiality whose significance is not intrinsic but strictly designatory. It is in this sense that the mind shows itself freer and more powerful in using signs than in using symbols; "Als *bezeichnend* beweist daher die Intelligenz eine freiere Willkür und Herrschaft im Gebrauch der Anschauung, denn als symbolisierend" (par. 458). ("Intelligence therefore gives proof of wider choice and ampler authority in the use of intuitions when it treats them as designatory [significative] rather as symbolical," p. 213). The *Encyclopedia* account gives a different inflection to the notion of the creative power of the imagination familiar from *The Prelude* and the *Third Critique*. Prominent in Kant's and Wordsworth's reflections is an analogy between the creative power of the imagination and that of nature. We find this analogy reformulated, in thoroughly classic terms—as a comparison between the generative activity of the sun and of the poet—in a text we will read together with Hegel's, Baudelaire's poem *Le Soleil* (second of the *Tableaux Parisiens*). The *topos* of *Le Soleil* implies that the idea makes its appearance in the world by way of the creative power of the genius—one Kantian answer to the question of the aesthetic. But just as Hegel's *Encyclopedia* account stresses that the power of the imagination is that of "the imagination which creates *signs*," Baudelaire's *Tableau* shows how the elaboration of the Kantian analogy entails the description of the power to generate signs rather than works of art or nature.[6] What we shall trace, then, is how far Baudelaire's and Hegel's texts make the same response to the same question (How does the idea make its appearance in the world?). Both the passage in the *Encyclopedia* and the poem in *Les Fleurs du mal* meet our question of whether the crossing between thought and imagination, between the philosophical and the aesthetic, is a passage *from* one to the other: whether it is a passage between two passages of the same order, or a passage, a crossing, from one order to another. Wordsworth's celebrated crossing poses this question as much as Kant's affirmed connection. For the decisive crossing there is not the crossing of the Alps, but the passage between that crossing and the next, where the mind crosses over from the world of sense to the thought of infinity. And that passage is not a passage but a blank, the space signifying the difference between two verse paragraphs, the distance—of what order?—between two clusters of signs.

Beginning, then, with the *Encyclopedia:* What are the consequences of the central role of "the imagination which creates signs," of "Zeichen machende Phantasie"?

Recognizing in "sich äussernd, Anschauung produzierend—Zeichen machende Phantasie" ("self-uttering, intuition-producing—the imagination which creates signs," p. 211) the faculty that Wordsworth hails as imagination can enable us to understand why Hegel calls it memory. With the access of "the Power so called / Through sad incompetence of human speech" (1850 *Prelude* 6.592-93), images are effaced, "the light of sense goes out"; and this access of Power occurs at the moment at which the mind *confronts* the signs it has produced: "the time, / When to myself it fairly might be said . . . / 'The threshold now is overpast'" (writes Wordsworth of entering London in the 1805 *Prelude,* 8.697-99); the moment at which the mind confronts its "translation" of verbal utterance, as Wordsworth writes: "every word that from the peasant's lips / came in reply, translated by our feelings, / Ended in this,—*that we had crossed the Alps*" (6.589-91). The imagination's production of signs is a confrontation of signs. For the sign, as such, does not say what it means, or mean what it says, but points to a meaning that must always imply the possibility of its designation by another subject. What the "Zeichen machende Phantasie" creates is a citation.

It thus gets defined, by Hegel, as memory: "Diese Zeichen erschaffende Tätigkeit kann das produktive Gedächtnis (die zunächst abstrakte Mnemosyne) vornehmlich genannt werden, indem das Gedächtnis . . . es überhaupt nur mit Zeichen zu tun hat" (par. 458). ("This sign-creating activity may be distinctively named 'productive' memory [the primarily abstract Mnemosyne]; since memory . . . has always to do with signs only," p. 213). Memory is "productive," Hegel writes here, insofar as it has to do strictly with signs. This is the distinction not only between *Gedächtnis* and *Einbildungskraft,* but also, so it would appear, between *Gedächtnis* and *Mnemonik,* true memory and the ancient mnemonic technique (*"Mnemonik der Alten,"* par. 462) of associating ideas with images or pictures. *Gedächtnis* is superior to *Mnemonik* just because it no longer has to do with the image (*Bild*), "welches aus dem unmittelbaren, ungeistigen Bestimmtsein der Intelligenz, aus der Anschauung, hergenommen ist" ("an image derived from intuition—the immediate and incomplete mode of intelligence," p. 220), but with a product of intelligence itself: "mit einem Dasein, welches das Produkt der Intelligenz selbst ist," namely, the sign.

Hegel's account indicates that in its sign-producing function the mind has *no longer* to do with images, and that the "well" of the ego is left behind. Though it is virtually impossible not to take one's bearings by the intimations, in this text, of an itinerary of the mind's object, of a progression from perception to thought, one would misread it in according that orientation any more than heuristic value. The exclusive preeminence of the sign may seem to appear as the culmination of a smooth progression from intuition or conception to imagination to thought, which would also be a progression in intelligence.

But a reading along these lines would miss the significance of Hegel's distinctive conjunction of *Denken* with *Gedächtnis.* This emerges as we enter into the complexities of the *Encyclopedia* account of thought and language: the introduction of another term, *names*— "Wir *denken* in Namen," Hegel declares—and an account of the language of names that draws a distinction between alphabetic writing and hieroglyphics. Because language, in Hegel's terms, consists in names—"für sich sinnlose Äusserlichkeiten die erst als Zeichen eine Bedeutung haben" (par. 459, 393) ("externalities which of themselves have no sense, and only get signification as signs," p. 216), highly susceptible of being forgotten, hence requiring to be written down— the discussion of language (in par. 459) promptly becomes a discussion of writing.

This has disruptive consequences in Hegel's argument. Reading, in Hegel's account, has undesirable and disturbing implications. The mind becomes dependent for thought on marks "*external* to the living mind" (*The Prelude,* 8.551), on material inscriptions. An account of the far-reaching consequences of writing and reading underlies and undermines the distinctions between alphabetic and hieroglyphic writing, and the parallel distinction between memory and *Mnemonik,* that give this section its shape. In the pressure of the semiotic analysis, the shaping distinctions of the passage break down. Thus, since the images associated with ideas in mnemonic technique are linked with them arbitrarily, as Hegel specifies, they actually constitute signs, or unwritten hieroglyphics, which are, as Hegel says, read off, *abgelesen* (par. 462, 403).

As the reading off of ideas from images, mnemonics should stand at the opposite extreme from the intelligence that presents itself in the articulation of ideas in words; it is not intelligent, but silly: the ideas to be remembered are linked with images "durch schale, alberne, ganz zufällige Zusammenhänge" (par. 462, 403). Yet it would strain Hegel's account of language unmanageably to argue that the links between ideas and words are any less shallow and arbitrary. It would involve—a tack the argument does take, momentarily—an emphasis on the "bewusstlosen dumpfen Anfänge" of language, its natural rather than accidental origin out of an "inner symbolism" of "posture" (par. 497, 397). This speculation gets abandoned promptly. It is clearly not a practicable way to maintain the desirable distinction between memory and *Mnemonik,* since it is incompatible with Hegel's premise that language is designatory, not symbolic. Nor does "posture" leave much range for either articulation or intelligence.

The distinction between hieroglyphics and a "more intelligent" phonetic writing turns out to be just as impossible to sustain. Alphabetic writing is said to be more "intelligent" than hieroglyphic writing because it directs the mind to reflection upon the word: "in ihr ist das Wort, die der Intelligenz eigentümlichste würdigste Art der Äusserung ihrer Vorstellung, zum Bewusstsein gebracht, zum Gegenstande der Reflexion gemacht" (par. 459, 399) ("in it the *word*—the mode, peculiar to the intellect, of uttering its ideas most worthily—is brought to consciousness and made an object of reflection," p. 216). In practice, however, this "reflection" is simply the transcription or the deciphering of names. With practice, alphabetic writing and phonetic reading become hieroglyphic. Articulation and reflection both succumb to habit:

> Die erlangte Gewohnheit tilgt auch später die Eigentümlichkeit der Buchstabenschrift, im Interesse des Sehens als ein Umweg durch die Hörbarkeit zu den Vorstellungen zu erscheinen, und macht sie für uns zur Hieroglyphenschrift, so dass wir beim Gebrauche derselben die Vermittlung der Töne nicht im Bewusstsein vor uns zu haben bedürfen; Leute dagegen, die eine geringe Gewohnheit des Lesens haben, sprechen das Gelesene laut vor, um es in seinem Tönen zu verstehen. (Par. 459, 401)

[Acquired habit subsequently effaces the peculiarity by which alphabetic writing appears, in the interest of vision, as a roundabout way to ideas by means of audibility; it makes them a sort of hieroglyphic to us, so that in using them we need not consciously realize them by means of tones, whereas people unpracticed in reading utter aloud what they read in order to catch its meaning in the sound. (p. 218)]

Practiced, competent reproduction of alphabetic language is mute; "das hieroglyphische Lesen [ist] für sich selbst ein taubes Lesen und ein stummes Schreiben" ("hieroglyphic reading is of itself a deaf reading and a dumb writing," p. 218). Because audibility has been identified as the very intelligibility of the sign as such as it exists in time (par. 459, 396), and intelligence defined as speaking and hearing oneself speak (par. 459, 401), this means that the outcome of the institution of *Tonsprache,* the practice of writing and reading, represents the elision of the intelligible sign and of intelligence.

Yet no alternative to this outcome appears possible or acceptable. The alternative to practiced reading, for example, is not intelligent speech, but mere enunciation—the painstaking reading off of sounds in an attempt to recognize their signification. The articulation of words in this case constitutes as wasteful a detour from the idea designated hieroglyphically in the written sign as the detour through images in *Mnemonik* from the idea designated in its name.

Words must become mute hieroglyphs either because they represent so little—as sheer names, externalities significant only as signs— or because they designate so much. In the one passage in these sections that describes an effect in a way that evokes a historical chronology, Hegel describes how alphabetic language has come to resemble hieroglyphics because "names" have taken on the character of "definitions." In modern times, Hegel writes, things designated in the sciences, for example chemistry and mineralogy, acquire new definitions; muriatic acid (*Salzsäure*) has frequently changed its name. Definitions, like hieroglyphic characters, are produced through the decomposition of an idea into its supposed characteristics, and must change whenever those suppositions change.

Seitdem man vergessen hat, was Namen als solche sind, nämlich für sich sinnlose Äusserlichkeiten, die erst als Zeichen eine Bedeutung haben, seit man statt eigentlicher Namen den Ausdruck einer Art von Definition fordert und dieselbe sogar häufig auch wieder nach Willkür und Zufall formiert, ändert sich die Benennung, d. i. nur die Zusammensetzung aus Zeichen ihrer Gattungsbestimmung

oder anderer charakteristisch sein sollender Eigenschaften, nach
der Verschiedenheit der Ansicht, die man von der Gattung oder
sonst einer spezifisch sein sollenden Eigenschaft fasst. (Par. 459,
398-99)

[Now that it has been forgotten what names properly are, viz. externalities which of themselves have no sense, and now that, instead of names proper, people ask for terms expressing a sort of
definition, which is frequently changed capriciously and fortui-
tously, the denomination, i.e. the composite name formed of signs
of their generic characters or other supposed generic properties, is
altered in accordance with the differences of view with regard to
the genus or other supposed specific property. (p. 216)]

Once the nature of names as signs has been forgotten, "caprice"
and "accident" conspire in producing the "denomination" (*Benennung*) of an idea, rather than a simple name. Yet these are the very
terms, of course, that characterize the mind's use of signs (caprice,
Willkür [par. 458], accompanies the arbitrary, accidental link between the "intuition" and the signification of the sign). Thus the
forgetting of the nature of names as signs makes them truly function
as signs.

In doing so, they lose the durability that was supposed to be their
privilege, according to the contrast drawn between alphabetic writing
and hieroglyphic writing. Hieroglyphic writing lacks the precision and
resiliency ascribed to articulated language. Because it represents not
the signs of speech but ideas, it is perilously brittle and vague; it has all
the instability of the ideas it represents; it must change as the analysis
of ideas changes, and it lends no definite outlines to the spoken language, to the spoken signs to which hieroglyphs do not refer. A hieroglyphic writing can only endure where philosophy remains as static as
the civilization of the Chinese (par. 459, 401), and only among that
minute portion of the population able to practice the decomposition
of ideas that it entails (par. 459, 399). Alphabetic writing is required
for commerce or communication between peoples; "Man darf . . .
halten, dass der Verkehr der Völker (was vielleicht in Phonizien der
Fall war und gegenwärtig in Kanton geschieht . . .) das Bedürfnis der
Buchstabenschrift und deren Entstehung herbeigeführt hat" (par. 459,
398) ("But we may be sure that it was . . . the intercourse of nations
[as was probably the case in Phoenicia, and still takes place in Can-
ton . . .] which occasioned the need of alphabetical writing and led to
its formation," p. 215). Alphabetic, not hieroglyphic writing, is valuable for *Bildung*, suited to the process of education: "Lesen und
Schreiben-lernen einer Buchstabenschrift für ein nicht genug geschätztes,

unendliches Bildungsmittel zu halten ist" (par. 459, 401). ("What has
been said shows the inestimable and not sufficiently appreciated educational value of learning to read and write an alphabetic character,"
p. 218.)

Yet not only has Hegel described the outcome of education, the
process of learning to read and write an alphabetic script, as "hieroglyphic" reading, "a deaf reading and a mute writing." He has also described a historical mutation of alphabetic language into a language of
hieroglyphic "definitions." The language of names as such, that is, is
radically mutable. As hieroglyphics, it has to bear the burden of history, "the weight of ages," and it does not remain intact. For not only
does its nature as names succumb to forgetting, but its nature as articulation and as reflection gives way with habit, with practice. Thus
Hegel refers approvingly to "that *parler sans accent* which in Europe is
justly required of an educated speaker" (par. 459)—an erosion of the
sensory shapes of signs, that is, such as he decries in the brittle fragility
of hieroglyphic writing. The ostensible contrast between alphabetic
and hieroglyphic writing gets disqualified by the more insistent and
insidious logic of Hegel's semiotic analysis of the language of names,
whereby we find that language signifies precisely insofar as it has the
effects and qualities of hieroglyphics.

For how does the mind retain names? Thought depends on this
ability: on "das Namen behaltende Gedächtnis"—on memory, on
Gedächtnis, "to which German language gives the high position of immediate relationship with thought" ("unmittelbaren Verwandtschaft
mit dem Gedanken," par. 464). The supreme achievement of the power
of memorization is the ability to recite lists of meaningless words, for
example, lists of proper names. Lists of names must be recited without
any accentuation preserving awareness of their meaning, for that would
disrupt the memorization process:

> Man weiss bekanntlich einen Aufsatz erst dann recht auswendig,
> wenn man keinen Sinn bei den Worten hat; das Hersagen solches
> Auswendiggewussten wird darum von selbst accentlos. Der richtige
> Accent, der hineingebracht wird, geht auf den Sinn; die Bedeutung,
> Vorstellung, die herbeigerufen wird, stört dagegen den mechan-
> ischen Zusammenhang und verwirrt daher leicht das Hersagen. Das
> Vermögen, Reihen von Worten, in deren Zusammenhang kein Ver-
> stand ist, oder die schon für sich sinnlos sind (eine Reihe von
> Eigennamen), auswendig behalten zu können, ist darum so höchst
> wunderbar, weil der Geist wesentlich dies ist, bei sich selbst zu
> sein, hier aber derselbe als in ihm selbst entäussert, seine Tätigkeit
> als ein Mechanismus ist. (Par. 463, 404)

[A composition is, as we know, not throughly conned by rote, until one attaches no meaning to the words. The recitation of what has been thus got by heart is therefore of course accentless. The correct accent, if it is introduced, suggests the meaning: but this introduction of the signification of an idea disturbs the mechanical nexus and easily throws out the reciter. The faculty of conning by rote series of words, with no principle governing their succession, or which are separately meaningless, for example, a series of proper names, is so supremely marvelous, because it is the very essence of mind to have its wits about it; whereas in this case the mind is estranged in itself, and its action is like machinery. (p. 222)]

In reciting from memory one has to suppress reflection and allow the mind to function like a machine. The machine neither reflects nor articulates; it retains neither the sensory shapes of names nor their meaning. Yet "memory" in this sense is the very passage into thought; "Gedächtnis ist auf diese Weise der Übergang in die Tätigkeit des Gedankens" (par. 463, 414). Hegel dismisses as delusory "the common prepossession about memory, in comparison with fancy and imagination, as if the latter were a higher and more intellectual activity than memory." Memory is superior because it "has ceased to deal with an image derived from intuition" (par. 462). For Hegel the idea makes its appearance in the world not with representation or imagination in any generous sense, and not with the work of art, which maintains its sensory shape and recalls its inner meaning, as *Erinnerung,* but strictly as *Gedächtnis,* with the sequence of signs that commemorate just insofar as they neither resonate nor remember, and so can exist *auswendig:* as lists learned by rote, inscriptions by a mind that functions like a writing machine.

The memory of history, in particular, consists in this recital of lists of proper names, this activity whereby the minimal material traces of names are produced in a rigid yet arbitrary sequence by a process specified to be absolutely incompatible with reflection or self-consciousness. Memorization is identified with a strictly necessary and strictly contingent sequence that has nothing in common with the realm of intentions and purposes, the teleological order of thought and representation; yet it is deemed the prerequisite for—the passage into—thought.

One can hardly claim to point to consequences of an aporia as intransigent as this one. Hegel's further remarks on *Gedächtnis* barely sketch the ramifications for history, in particular, of the drastic collision entailed in the collusion of memory and thought. The continuity of culture from one generation to the next—as well as the continuity from one thought to another in one mind—is problematical, since (Hegel comments) the young have better memories than the old. The old, who have lived things to remember, have a poor memory, whereas the young have a good memory just because they are not yet capable of experience or reflection ("weil sie sich noch nicht nachdenkend verhält," par. 464, 405). The young do not choose what to memorize, neither on the basis of value judgments nor even on grounds of utility; "ihr Gedächtnis wird nicht nur um der Nützlichkeit willen geübt; sondern . . . es wird absichtlich oder unabsichtlich darum geübt, um den Boden ihrer Innerlichkeit zum reinen Sein, zum reinen Raume zu ebnen" (par. 464, 405) ("their memory is exercised with or without design so as to level the ground of their inner life to pure being or to pure space," p. 223). Memory is exercised so as to level the ground of the inner self to an empty space. This passage in Hegel's account calls up images of a world of forgetful old people and automatonlike young, of a "mumbling sire"[7] confronting a chanting youth.

Such a youth devoted to rote learning bizarrely resembles the revolutionary whose existence is hinted at toward the close of an essay of Walter Benjamin's, which sets out from a critical premise comparable to Hegel's: a rejection of the usual assumption that violence is to be thought of and justified simply as a means. Hegel's account of memory rejects the same assumption about memorization. Memory *is* the passage into the activity of thought, for Hegel, where it is simply exercised, not subordinated to a use or a function ("um der Nützlichkeit willen geübt"). Benjamin's "Critique of Violence"[8] reverses the usual assumption whereby violence is considered to be justified, perhaps, if it is ultimately in the service of law, to conclude that to the contrary, law itself represents intolerable violence and only the nonmediate function of violence is susceptible of justification. The sheer exercise of memory, by the young—rather than its use—affects subjectivity like the "annihilating violence" evoked by Benjamin.

The "Critique of Violence" is painfully attentive to the ambiguity that comes to the fore in Hegel's text as memory is accorded the crucial role in the achievement of thought, which the next section in the *Encyclopedia* identifies with "will." A prime instance of nonmediate violence is "mythical violence," which establishes boundaries or frontiers (between the divine and the human), and thereby stands as the basis of the institution of law itself. The example of such mythical violence is Apollo's destruction of Niobe's children, leaving the mother intact (that "bitter desolation, where the order of things is disturbed and inverted," whose evocation Wordsworth would banish from inscriptions upon tombstones[9]). It must be banished to ban the suspicion that the mythical conception of an "order of things" actually requires such an inversion—as when inscriptions impress themselves on the mind, which becomes a tombstone, or a *Tableau,* or a reciting machine, through the requirements of the very structure of the sign, or "name." The fundamental identity between "the mythical manifestation of immediate violence" and "all legal violence" both makes the "destruction" of the law (as violence) "obligatory,"[10] and erases the distinction between the violence of means, and pure nonmediate violence, on which the distinction between the law and the *destruction* of the law depends.

The difficulty is the same as one encounters in Hegel's account in comparing the activity of the intelligence in producing signs with its activity in memorization. For "intelligence" must reside both in the *use* of signs and in the *exercise* of memory, as Hegel writes, *not* for its utility. In dealing with things as signs, the mind uses them as its own property; it uses their natural properties for its own purposes, effacing their natural connotations and replacing them with properties of meaning of its own. The mind does violence to natural properties in establishing the law of the sign, in enforcing the laws of signification. But to deal with signs is to deal with names, and to retain names, the mind must inscribe or memorize them. The mediate violence of signification becomes the nonmediate violence of memorization ("leveling" the subject). While Benjamin's essay seems to pose the problem as an ethical and practical one, Hegel's text poses it as an interpretive dilemma regarding the status of intelligence and of linguistic activity. Hegel's analysis reveals that the activity of signification is *both* merely (violently) purposive, mediate, *and* nonmediate, an effacement of purposes, and as vulnerable (not only in forgetting, but in the erosion of accent required in recitation) as the mere natural properties of things. Since these conditions cannot be thought as existing simultaneously, the text has to evoke a certain itinerary, or rather offer a narrative, and has to give the activity of signification different names—*Phantasie* and *Gedächtnis*—even as the distinction between them erodes through further discriminations or "definitions": "Zeichen machende Phantasie" (par. 457), "Diese Zeichen erschaffende Tätigkeit . . . das produktive Gedächtnis" (par. 461), "Das reproduzierende Gedächtnis" (par. 462), "mechanische Gedächtnis" (par. 457, 463, 464).

Not only the proliferation of definitions in Hegel's text erodes the distinction between the key moments of its narrative, between the different names for the activity of signification. So does the text's explicit statement about the impact of intelligence. Its "consummated appropriation" of names as signs "abolishes the distinction between meaning and name." The structure of the sign construed as a passage from meaning to sign or from sign to meaning is here said to collapse in the very activity by which signs are treated as such.

The mind, as well as the sign, is collapsed or compressed, emptied and flattened out, according to Hegel's description of the activity in which intelligence culminates. The mind becomes simply the space retaining names in order, an "empty link" between a name and a meaning, or—indistinguishably—between one name and the next: "Ich . . . ist . . . die Macht des verschiedenen Namen, das leere Band, welches Reihen derselben in sich befestigt und in fester Ordnung behält" (par. 463, 404). ("The ego . . . is . . . the power over the different names—the link which, having nothing in itself, fixes in itself series of them and keeps them in stable order," p. 222.) The memorizing "I" is an empty link or an empty volume (Band). And the object of memorization is ein Auswendiges, "a without-book" (par. 462).

We can understand this to mean that the object of memorization is rote learning, without-book knowledge of names. But we should also see how these definitions virtually dissolve the distinction between the mind and its products. That distinction would appear to be vital to the Kantian analogy between nature and the genius, where it is nature's productive power, not nature as product, which the genius resembles and reproduces. Yet when Baudelaire's verses elaborate this analogy they show us something like what we infer in Hegel's text: the "I" runs into its products.

> Quand le soleil cruel frappe à traits redoublés
> Sur la ville et les champs, sur les toits et les blés,
> Je vais m'exercer seul à ma fantasque escrime,
> Flairant dans tous les coins les hasards de la rime,
> Trébuchant sur les mots comme sur les pavés,
> Heurtant parfois des vers depuis longtemps rêvés.[11]

(ll. 3–8)

The rest of the poem describes the actions not of the poet but of the aggressive imperial sun. Baudelaire's stanzas offer a more pictorial narrative than Hegel's paragraphs, but the picture is a puzzle. What does the action of the "I" have to do with the sun? What we read off from Baudelaire's Tableau should be a definition of the relations between Phantasie and Gedächtnis, a differentiation of moments in the activity of signification to hold up against the eroding differentiations in Hegel's narrative.

The first stanza of *Le Soleil* revises the Kantian analogy between Nature and the genius by posing a metonymical rather than a metaphorical relation between the actions of the sun and of the poet. It is "when" the sun strikes that the poet goes out to engage, "alone," in his fantastical fencing. This metonymy replaces a relationship of resemblance between the two actions with one of simultaneity or juxtaposition. For if fencing in some respect resembles the action of striking, or of striking "*à traits redoublés,*" the one action does not meet or respond to the other. The sun and the poet in *Le Soleil* are not mutual antagonists, as Nature and the artist are characterized at the conclusion of *Le confiteor de l'artiste:* "Nature, enchanteresse sans pitié, rivale toujours victorieuse, laisse-moi! . . . L'étude du beau est un duel où l'artiste crie de frayeur avant d'être vaincu."[12] Benjamin describes the poet of *Le Soleil parrying* shocks with consciousness.[13] But what the poem describes in the first instance is the action not of parrying the sun's blows, or striking back, but of *striking up against* things— words, paving stones, and verses. If in the duel of *Le confiteor* the artist is no match for Nature, the fantastical fencing of *Le Soleil* is no match at all: the poet's gestures *coincide* with (occur at the same time as) the sun's blows without meeting them; he collides, instead, with his own effects.

Just this happens to the mind engaged in memorization, according to Hegel. The faculty of memory is marvelous (*wunderbar*) because it is in the nature of mind to be *bei sich,* "to have its wits about it," Wallace translates; whereas in the exercise of memory, the mind comes upon its own products as if with surprise, encountering "its own" as something "picked up":

> Der Geist aber ist nur bei sich als Einheit der Subjektivität und der Objektivität; und hier im Gedächtnis, nachdem er in der Anschauung zunächst als Äusserliches so ist, dass er die Bestimmungen findet, und in der Vorstellung dieses Gefundene in sich erinnert und es zu dem Seinigen macht, macht er sich als Gedächtnis in ihm selbst zu einem Äusserlichen, so dass das Seinige als ein Gefundenwerdendes erscheint. (Par. 463, 404)

> [But it is only as uniting subjectivity with objectivity that the mind has its wits about it. Whereas in the case before us, after it has in intuition been at first so external as to pick up its facts ready made, and in representation inwardizes or recollects this datum and makes it its own—it proceeds as memory to make itself external in itself, so that what is its own assumes the guise of something found. (p. 222)]

Such memory is the state of mind of the poet of *Le Soleil,* "heurtant parfois des vers depuis longtemps rêvés." It characterizes the "I" from the outset of its itinerary, in Baudelaire's tableau, if not in Hegel's apparently narrative rendering of the mind's alienation as it approaches thought (*Denken,* reached "after" *Gedächtnis,* which is reached "after" *Anschauung* and *Vorstellung,* "intuition" and "representation"). We can do without the details; Baudelaire gives us the picture. If we take another angle on the *Encyclopedia,* the two accounts match up better: in the hierarchy implied by the contrast between the resistless power of the sun and the resistance met with by the poet, we can recognize the distinction between *Intelligenz* and *Gedächtnis,* or between "Zeichen machende Phantasie" and "das reproduktive Gedächtnis."

We are engaged first of all by the poem's picturing of the poet's activity. The opening stanza of *Le Soleil* pictures the kind of memory that Hegel's paragraphs describe. But the effect of Baudelaire's picture of the poet at work is promptly to engage us in a nonrepresentational reading, in a rhetorical analysis of the poem's syntactical elements. The first stanza represents the subject of the poem as caught up not in the activity of representation but rather in a dreamworklike engagement with words as signifiers—"Flairant dans tous les coins les hasards de la rime . . . / Heurtant parfois des vers depuis longtemps rêvés" (ll. 6, 8). The stanza's narrative dimension, moreover, has to do not with the poet representing himself walking, but rather with the syntactical process indicated in the present participles stressed by their initial position in the stanza's three final lines ("Flairant . . . / Trébuchant . . . / Heurtant . . . /") and in the temporal coincidence, situating the poet's fencing in the same moment as the sun's striking, stressed by the initial *quand* (l. 3).[14]

These features of what Benjamin calls the "portraiture" in the poem's first stanza[15] mean that what looked as if it would look like the Kantian resemblance between the creative powers of the genius and of Nature has to be read instead as the repetition, with a difference, of the activity of signification variously named by Hegel: the mind making, aligning, running into, signs. On this it is the poem rather than the *Encyclopedia* that gives us the details. The first stanza inscribes the relationship between the poet and the sun as a metonymy instead of a metaphor. The second stanza inscribes relationships between mental and material objects *and* between ugly and beautiful, or urban and pastoral ones—as neither metaphors nor metonymies. In its second stanza *Le Soleil* breaks down the difference between comparing objects and juxtaposing objects, between metaphor and metonymy, to display a power of signification exceeding the play of tropes. Like memorization, it is the power to assemble lists. Baudelaire's verses assemble lists of objects that could be compared and objects that could be juxtaposed: the poem couples *mots* with *pavés, rimes* with *coins,* and *cerveaux* with *ruches*—objects of two different orders, which might be related by similarity, or metaphor; but also "les toits et les blés," "la ville et les champs," "les vers et les roses"—objects of different appeal but of the *same* order, related by contiguity, or metonymy. In fact, in Baudelaire's verses, these designated items are linked to one another by neither resemblance nor proximity. *Le Soleil* does without those articulations as the mind in memorization forgets the meanings linking the words it cites. This is what it is, Baudelaire shows us, Hegel tells us, to get versed.

The items designated in *Le Soleil* are linked by three terms—*comme, et,* and *ainsi que*—each of which is employed in such a way as to imply the other two. *Comme,* which could indicate substantial likeness, and *et,* which could indicate mere juxtaposition, both invariably imply *ainsi que:* something acts, or is acted upon, "like" something else. Both where it links physical and mental objects, typically a metaphorical move, and where it links physical with other physical objects, typically a metonymy, *comme* also means *et:*

> Trébuchant sur les mots comme sur les pavés,
> . . . .
> Éveille dans les champs les vers comme les roses;
>
> > (ll. 7, 10)

It's not that words are *like* pavingstones, but that "I" trips on them as he also trips on pavingstones; and not that worms (or verses) are like roses, but that the sun awakens them both alike. Moreover, *et* also means *comme,* or *ainsi que,* and this represents an intolerable situation, in which the sun treats unlike things alike:

> Quand le soleil cruel frappe à traits redoublés
> Sur la ville et les champs, sur les toits et les blés,
> . . . .
> Il fait s'évaporer les soucis vers le ciel,
> Et remplit les cerveaux et les ruches de miel.
>
> > (ll. 3–4, 11–12)

The sun fills brains *and* hives with honey just as it strikes with redoubled blows the city *and* the country. Under its impact, the difference between a mental and a material object, brains and hives, is no greater than—no different than—the difference between an urban and a pastoral object, between "La ville et les champs, les toits et les blés." One could be cheered by the prospect of the sun filling the brain with "honey," or filling the hive with honey, but not with the assertion of both at once. Either the brain is being filled with syrup, or the hive is being filled with thoughts, or both; this sun brings not a double plenitude but a stupefied fasting, the condition of a "*mangeur d'opium.*" The indeterminably literal or figurative "honey" of these verses represents nothing so much as the bland saccharine connective *et* that sticks together the disparate terms of these pairs. *Le Soleil* can name a thing like another unlike thing—and make it stick.

The resistless and indiscriminate activity of *le soleil* is the power of the mind in using signs, rather than symbols, celebrated in the *Encyclopedia*. It makes the natural properties of things its own property, and instead of treating them as inherently significant, fills them with a significance only unpredictably related to their perceptual or phenomenal properties. Anything can be treated as a sign—natural objects, images, as well as mental objects, words, for example, which in memory, or in writing, become the signs of signs (not of things). In Hegel's text and in Baudelaire's, representation is represented as the activity of producing signs, which Hegel also calls *Gedächtnis*. Thus Hegel's opening paragraph on *Gedächtnis* (par. 461) explains it as an inwardizing of the word that occurs through the same activity as the inwardizing of the intuition that takes place in representation in general: "Die Intelligenz durchläuft als Gedächtnis gegen die Anschauung des Worts dieselben Tätigkeiten des Erinnerns, wie als Vorstellung überhaupt gegen die erste unmittelbare Anschauung" (par. 461, 402). ("Under the shape of memory the course of intelligence passes through the same inwardizing [recollecting] functions, as regards the intuition of the *word,* as representation in general does in dealing with the first immediate intuition," p. 219.) *Gedächtnis* does not pass *beyond Erinnerung.* This sentence makes *Erinnern* connote not remembrance or recollection, but inclusion in *"das leere Band"* that makes names of things. The process that intelligence goes through (*durchläuft*) is not a progression (or a regression) but a repetition. What Hegel calls *die Intelligenz* operates on natural images as—*ainsi que*—it operates on words. *Le Soleil,* in Baudelaire's poem, is not simply the power of figurative language which subsumes the functions of metaphor and metonymy—language as representation—but language that exceeds a representational function. These *et* and *comme* do not picture a process; they give us the picture: they perform a judgment.

Le Soleil destroys the distinction between natural and mental objects, in treating them alike. Yet at the same time it maintains the difference between them: the poem conspicuously differentiates between two kinds of objects even as it describes them acted upon in the same way. Filling things with significance instead of treating them as inherently meaningful, *"ce père nourricier"* makes use of things' natural properties, but carries out a function independent of utility: "[Il] commande aux moissons de croître et de mûrir/Dans le coeur immortel qui toujours veut fleurir." Means and end coincide in this activity, which is described by Benjamin in his "Critique of Violence" as the identity between lawmaking violence and nonmediate violence.[16] What is established here through the "empty link" between objects or properties of different orders (the link which is indiscriminately *comme, et,* or *ainsi que*) is the law of signification. "Le soleil cruel frappe à traits redoublés"; "lawmaking," writes Benjamin, "is power making, and, to that extent, an immediate manifestation of violence." Its "primal phenomenon," like that of all "lawmaking violence," according to Benjamin, is "the establishing of frontiers":

> Where frontiers are decided the adversary is not simply annihilated; indeed, he is accorded rights even when the victor's superiority in power is complete. And these are, in a demonically ambiguous way, "equal" rights: for both parties to the treaty it is the same line that may not be crossed. Here appears . . . the same mythical ambiguity of laws to which Anatole France refers satirically when he says, "Poor and rich are equally forbidden to spend the night under bridges." . . . From the point of view of violence, which alone can guarantee law, there is no equality, but at the most equally great violence.[17]

The sun's immediate manifestation of its power to make all things visible and significant "ennobles" and equalizes their fate in the same way:

> Il ennoblit le sort des choses les plus viles,
> Et s'introduit en roi, sans bruits et sans valets,
> Dans tous les hôpitaux et dans tous les palais.[18]

(ll. 18–20)

The "victor," in the opposition legislated by *le soleil,* is the signification as opposed to the intuition or representation, and the signified as opposed to the signifier.

Yet the signifier necessarily retains its "rights"—its radiancy—and this is (as for those who would sleep under bridges instead of crossing them) something other than the power to *represent*. What else it is we may infer from the peculiar combination of references to a legislative or political realm and to a realm of natural process. Signifying gets described both as "command" and as "growth." The "command" to the "harvest" to "croître et mûrir / Dans le coeur immortel qui toujours veut fleurir" implies violent compulsion, first because "fleurir" (what the immortal heart "wants" to do) differs from "croître et mûrir" (what it is made to do—or rather, what is made to happen "in" it), but second because "command" differs radically from "ripen." A process is identified with an act; the organic process of growth is linked with the locutionary power of language. *Le père nourricier* commands from all things the "harvest" of signification. To "be fruitful and multiply," in this context, is to flourish as a sign. Baudelaire inscribes the process of signification in the language of natural process— and reinscribes the language of natural process in a discourse designating an activity that is linguistic and political. These harvests that ripen at a command are the "after-ripening," the *Überleben,* which Benjamin ascribes to the literary work in his essay "Die Aufgabe des Übersetzers": "Es gibt eine Nachreife auch der festgelegten Worte."[19] Baudelaire fulfills—more surely than Hegel, here—what Benjamin designates the task of the philosopher: "the task of understanding all natural life in terms of the wider life which is that of language and of the political—that of history."[20]

What the signifier as such retains is not its "rights" to representation but its "life" as *Überleben, "survie,"* an after-life survival, in history. The radiancy of *hôpitaux* and *palais* is merely a modulation of the *"vague épouvante"* that comes to linger about the *"matière vivante"* apostrophized in Baudelaire's *Spleen:*

Quand sous les lourds flocons des neigeuses années
L'ennui, fruit de la morne incuriosité,
Prend les proportions de l'immortalité.
—Désormais tu n'es plus, ô matière vivante!
Qu'un granit entouré d'une vague épouvante,
Assoupi dans le fond d'un Saharah brumeux;
Un vieux sphinx ignoré du monde insoucieux,
Oublié sur la carte, et dont l'humeur farouche
Ne chante qu'aux rayons du soleil qui se couche.[21]

(ll. 16–24)

The sphinx is forgotten by the world—forgotten on the map: *left* (to survive) on the map,[22] the signifier lives on in a history which lies not in living memory but in inscriptions, the materiality of which subsumes the "matière vivante" of forms of life. Baudelaire wrote to Poulet-Malassis instructing him to delete *fils* in the verse "L'ennui, *fils* de la morne incuriosité," and to substitute *fruit*. For what must be evoked is not the successive order of generations, but a generation that may be imagined at once as instantaneous and as belated and residual, the coming to "life" of language.

This is bound to be represented as natural. The power of *le père nourricier* is that of the law of signification conceived as natural, and that of language conceived as a heliotropic system of figures, grounding language in the nature of perception. We have seen the effects of such a power—to fill brains as well as hives with "honey." The representational elements in that verse, the figures of "hive" and "honey," would offer a pleasing picture could we ignore the infrastructure of the verse, the *et* that compounds the figurative with the literal. We would have a picture of the effect of genius, rendered in pastoral terms suggesting the detachment of the aesthetic from the historical or political realm. Figurative language can offer such appearances; we read as much in the next couplet, where the poem proffers its one true simile, a *comme* which means *like* and not *and:* the crutch-bearers appear like young girls—if only to themselves. The poem's one genuine figure of comparison, one use of *comme* to represent a representation, a resemblance, is made to represent a pathetic or grotesque illusion, to coincide with a complete disparity between inside and outside: the crutch-bearers may feel like young girls, but they do not look like them. Those who display a prosthesis become "like" those who are intact. This violation of the fundamental distinction between integrity and lack or disfigurement comes about through the equally fundamental procedure of treating the mind as a receptacle—the process evoked in the preceding line, whereby the organ of cognition (brains) is treated like the receptacle for a thing or a distilled essence (hives for honey). Thus, the very term that expresses the possibility of resemblance between things of different orders, such as outsides and insides, or mental and physical properties, is made to represent their radical discrepancy. And the very use of the fundamental figure of the mind as a container with an inside is here made to coincide with the denial of the fundamental distinction between wholeness and lack. These verses represent the figurative function of language as disfiguring. They represent the disarticulation of the vital distinction between literal and figurative features effected in the verse that sticks together brains and hives.

Le Soleil sticks unlike things together not simply by means of figures, but by means of the linguistic infrastructure that makes figures possible or apparent, and which surfaces in the verses' "empty links." These consist not only in *et* and *comme,* but also, conspicuously, in *"les hasards de la rime."* *Le soleil* has the power to treat mental objects like natural objects and ugly ones like beautiful ones: "[Il] éveille dans les champs les vers comme les roses." "The chances of rhyme"—that is, the chances of the letter, the strictly contingent homonymic value of the signifier—makes *vers* mean *verses* (and "towards"), as well as "worms." In the word *vers,* the two different kinds of series—ugly (or urban) versus beautiful (or pastoral) objects, and physical versus mental objects, threaten to collapse into one. The difference between two kinds of difference gets lost. One is the difference between the order of signifiers and the order of signifieds; the other is the difference between one sign (or signifier) and the next. It is no longer possible, in this verse with *vers,* to know whether we pass along from one thing to another, or cross over from one order of things to another.

Where the contingencies of the signifier are not so material, where the disfiguration occurs at the level of the figure, our disorientation is not so great. Thus, in *Spleen,* we suffer a subtle betrayal of our expectations as a comparison shifts direction halfway through: "Je suis un cimetière abhorré de la lune,/Où comme des remords se traînent de long vers" (ll. 8-9). We take the sense of the second clause to be, "Où des remords se traînent ainsi que de longs vers." But instead of following up the comparison of "I" to a cemetery with another comparison of a mental to a physical object, the second clause reverses the order and compares "worms" to "remorse." The figure betrays our expectation of a predictable hierarchical relationship between mental and physical objects and between tenors and vehicles. A mental property, *remords,* is ascribed that of a physical object, *se traîner,* and treated as the vehicle—instead of the tenor—for a physical object, *vers.* But the verse also says that long *verses* drag *like* remorse. This *comme* marks an illusion as fundamental as the single simile in *Le Soleil* ("porteurs de béquilles . . . *comme* des jeunes filles"): that the disarticulation of language is contained by a mood or a mind. Where *vers* means at once "worms" and "verses"—where verses are at once a mental and a material object—the distinction between vehicles and tenors, or signifiers and signifieds, is effaced. Just such effacement characterizes the "empty link" of memorization, which is indistinguishably the link between the sign and its meaning and the link between one sign and the next— both of which, according to Hegel, must be effaced: recitation has to be both unreflective and *"accentlos."* Such indistinctness must afflict not only recitation as a special case, but practiced speech as such; Hegel mentions not just unaccented recitation, but "that *parler sans accent* which in Europe is justly required of an educated speaker." To become "versed" is to become incapable of distinguishing names and meanings.

Le Soleil describes how the sun "awakens" verses: "Ce père nourricier, ennemi des chloroses,/Eveille dans les champs les vers comme les roses;" (ll. 9–10). These lines have the effect of a parody of lines that define the natural image in Hölderlin's *Brot und Wein:*[23] "nun aber nennt er sein Liebstes/Nun, nun müssen dafür Worte wie Blumen entstehen" (ll. 89–90). To originate like flowers is to come into being as a natural object, whose "becoming coincides at all times with the mode of [its] origination," a spontaneous arising from the earth. This is precisely not the case for the "harvests" of *Le Soleil,* which do not simply flower and flourish (*fleurir*), but are "commanded" to "grow and ripen." "Origin and tendency [*Zweck*]," writes Nietzsche in *The Genealogy of Morals:* "two problems that are not and should not be linked."[24] The conception of the natural object dissents from this stricture; the natural object's "origin" and its "tendency" are identical, and it arises as the incarnation of the principle of their identity. The natural object may be described as serenely teleological, as much as natural, distinguished not by mere genetic causality, but by freedom from conflict between the order of origins and the order of intentions, by harmony between necessity and purposiveness. Such harmony is promised by the "purposiveness without purpose" of the freely beautiful object of which Kant's prime example is precisely a flower, a wild tulip.[25]

The tulip must be specified to be wild to distinguish it from those cultivated tulips with their blended colors and subtle markings that became objects of speculation on the world market in the 1630s. For the commodity is the inverse of the natural object. Its mode of being and its mode of origin do not coincide: it is manufactured, then exchanged. Another such inverse is the sign, which is posited, and then inscribed or read. A disjunctive operation of this kind is evoked by the sun which "Eveille dans les champs les vers comme les roses" and "remplit les cerveaux et les ruches de miel": a single predicate is made to designate functions that cannot be identical unless the sense of one or the other is violated.

Beauty is made to sustain a shock. That shock is the deprivation of nostalgia for the natural object[26]—imposed by the spokesman of *Spleen,* who inscribes verses as he inscribes worms, as well as by *le soleil,* "ennemi des chloroses,"* who "awakens" worms and verses along with roses. The primacy of the mode of being of the natural object that one would presume to be implied by a text that affirms the presence of the same enlivening principle in verses and in roses gets displayed in these lines as something else: the "priority" of *"les hasards de la rime,"* the primacy of being versed. The power of the sun to treat mental objects like natural objects is none other than the necessity of treating them as signs, or names, which can be memorized or inscribed, requiring a material trace.

The materiality of signs gets thematized in the final couplet of the poem's first stanza: "Trébuchant sur les mots comme sur les pavés/ Heurtant parfois des vers depuis longtemps rêvés." But it may be said to materialize most insistently with the recurrence of the word *vers* in the second stanza. *Vers* there functions not only as a noun but as a preposition; it belongs to both prominent categories of words in the poem, names of items, and connectives. The sun awakens *vers* as it awakens roses (verse 10); and the sun makes care evaporate *"vers* le ciel" (verse 11). This evaporation or dissipation "toward" a higher region is equivalent to Hegel's *tilgen,* the obliteration or cancellation of the natural properties of the thing as it becomes a sign. The linguistic contingency, the poetic necessity, that makes precisely the word *vers* express this movement toward another realm effectively disrupts our conception of signification as such a movement from one realm or order to another. For *vers* in verse eleven is contaminated with the *vers* of verse ten, which collapses (so we have read it) the difference between passage from one order to another and passage from one item to another of the same order. The very verse that should affirm the power of aesthetic creation to transcend the world of practical concerns and the merely natural order turns out to disqualify that power—because the very word *vers,* which should name the bridge from the realm of perception to that of reason, turns out to designate and exemplify the collapse of that structure in the materiality of the signifier. It is as words susceptible of memorization and inscription—as *vers,* verse—that *ideas* appear, we read in Hegel's *Encyclopedia.* Passage toward (*vers*) signification or thought occurs in material signs (*vers*). The aesthetic exists as a persistent, residual materiality; it may not, then, be construed as a passage *from* the perceptual *to* the ideal, *from* the phenomenal *to* the rational. The rational or ideal *is* so insofar as it is significative and material. To get versed, this means, is the only way to go; that is, the only place to be.

The preposition *vers* functions in this verse much as the connective *comme* functions in the penultimate verse of *Correspondances:*

Il est des parfums frais comme des chairs d'enfants,
Doux comme les hautbois, verts comme les prairies,
—Et d'autres, corrompus, riches et triomphants,
Ayant l'expansion des choses infinies,
Comme l'ambre, le musc, le benjoin et l'encens,
Qui chantent les transports de l'esprit et des sens. [27]

(ll. 9–14)

This *comme* means not "like" but "such as." At the very point at
which the poem purports to name perceptions with the power of
totalization, the verse merely enumerates: there are perfumes *such
as* amber, musk, benjamin, incense. "Whatever differences or grada-
tions one wishes to establish between them," writes Paul de Man, the
scents are restrained by that *comme* from ever leading beyond themselves. "Enumerative repetition disrupts the chain of tropological substitution at the crucial moment when the poem promises, by way of
these very substitutions, to reconcile the pleasures of the mind with
those of the senses and to unite aesthetics with epistemology." [28] In
Correspondances, "the very word on which these substitutions depend"—in *Le Soleil,* the very word on which depends the passage
toward a totalization of perception as idea—"just then loses its syntactical and semantic univocity." This is "too striking a coincidence
not to be, like pure chance, beyond the control of author and reader":
a material occurrence.

It is as material occurrences not amenable to conceptualization
that history may have to be conceived once the concept of progression
or regression has been dissolved as it is in Baudelaire's *vers,* where
the concept of progression toward signification gets exploded. "*Geschichte*" means nothing else, perhaps, in "The Task of the Translator," the essay Benjamin wrote as an introduction to his translation of
poems from *Les Fleurs du mal.* The disarticulation of the figure of
progression ("*vers le ciel*") by a word for designation, inscription, and
memorization (*vers*) may be accompanied by an abandonment of pro-
gressive ideals. Baudelaire throws out the ideal of progress in an irrever-
ent note to his publisher Poulet-Malassis apropos of a letter from
Hugo (October 6, 1859) in response to the dedication "A Victor Hugo"
of *Les Sept Vieillards* and *Les Petites Vieilles.* Hugo had written:

Vous ne vous trompez pas en prévoyant quelque dissidence
entre vous et moi. Je comprends toute votre philosophie (car,
comme tout poète, vous contenez un philosophe); je fais plus que
la comprendre, je l'admets; mais je garde la mienne. Je n'ai jamais

dit: l'Art pour l'Art; j'ai toujours dit: l'Art pour le Progrès. Au fond, c'est la même chose, et votre esprit est trop pénétrant pour ne pas le sentir. En avant! c'est le mot du Progrès; c'est aussi le cri de l'Art. Tout le verbe de la Poésie est là. *Ite.*

Que faites-vous quand vous écrivez ces vers saisissants: *Les Sept vieillards* et *Les Petites Vieilles,* que vous me dédiez et dont je vous remercie? Que faites-vous? Vous marchez. Vous allez en avant. Vous dotez le ciel du l'art d'on ne sait quel rayon macabre. Vous créez un frisson nouveau. [29]

The comic potential and the literalizing effect of Hugo's emphases— "Vous marchez. Vous allez en avant"—were not lost on Baudelaire, who wrote to Poulet-Malassis,

ne négligez pas de me renvoyer la copie avec l'épreuve.

Ne négligez pas non plus de donner un violent coup de poing dans le plexus solaire de de Broise. Cela est nécessaire pour la correction des épreuves et le Progrès de la Typographie. C'est là le Verbe et le cri de l'Art. *Ite!*

(N'imprimez pas ces dernières lignes.) [30]

"L'Art pour le Progrès" gets reduced to the progress of poetry—the progression of his poems into print, likely to be facilitated, in Baudelaire's view, by the written approbation of Hugo. (Baudelaire had Hugo's letter reproduced at the head of his essay "Théophile Gautier.") The punch in the solar plexus that Baudelaire commands in his pleased parabasis—like the "traits redoublés" of the solar power in *Le Soleil*— is supposed to make things signify, to get them into print. How punching Poulet-Malassis's associate in the stomach would expedite this process is unclear. The sun's "cruel" double blow should be conceived as equally gratuitous.

For this is the bearing of the final comparison in *Le Soleil* between the sun and the poet. We have read how the hazards of rhyme and homonym decisively affect the annihilation of distinctions between mental and natural properties and beautiful and ugly objects brought about by the poem's connective terms—*comme, ainsi que, et.* Those terms also do away with the hierarchical distinction between the poem's first person and its titular protagonist, between "*je*" and "*le soleil.*" The condition in which the poet goes forth to "Trébuch(er) sur les mots comme sur les pavés" is finally defined as the time in which the sun behaves like that sort of poet, a *flaneur*: "Quand, ainsi qu'un poète, il descend dans les villes." Such a sun is not the "soleil qui se couche" cited at the end of *Spleen.* Or rather, *Le Soleil* poses the possibility that when that sun goes down, or when it rises, it does so merely "ainsi qu'un poète [qui] descend dans les villes": it simply steps out, so to speak, for a stroll, without any guarantee that its itinerary will be complete or circular (as the reflexive verb se coucher would tend to suggest). This would mean that the order of significa-tion, the intelligible order, is as radically unpredictable and arbitrary as the order of the minimal material marks that are the surface feature of language (the alphabet, for instance, the condition for Hegel of the "intelligent" form of writing). If the sun simply "goes out," intelligi-bility becomes as vulnerable to extinction as the properties of natural objects. Here "harvests" are produced not by fate but by fiat (and complicity): "[Il] commande aux moissons de croître et de mûrir / Dans le coeur immortel qui toujours veut fleurir." And the fiat—"Be fruitful and signify"—may be no more necessary or inevitable than a fit of restlessness.[31]

For the sun to go out like a poet is irremediably different than for the poet to come out like the sun. Baudelaire's poem begins, we read, with a displacement of that Kantian metaphor by a metonymy: it is when the sun strikes that the poet goes out to engage in his fantastical fencing. If this sun goes out like a poet, as we read in the poem's final sentence, that metaphor in no way reverses the move made in the first stanza. It does not restore the displaced metaphor. For the act "ainsi qu'un poète" means, after Baudelaire's intervening vers, to stumble on signs, "to encounter its own as something picked up" (par. 463)—not to generate meaningful forms, like Kantian nature or genius. The way in which Hegel and Baudelaire answer the question posed by Kant's affirmation of the crucial role of aesthetic judgment—the way they make it chapter and verse—decomposes irreversibly the analogies that sustain that affirmation. The irreversible occurrence of this reading, this reinscription of Kant's question, is the only crossing over that these texts permit us to contemplate.

Past Effects

The Double Reading of Narrative

Mechanical Doll, Exploding Machine

Kleist's Models of Narrative

Two brief pieces by Heinrich von Kleist provide complementary models of the processes of reading and narrating a text. "On the Marionette Theater" and "Improbable Veracities"[1] make up together, through the images they present and the narrative activity they exemplify, a compelling—if disconcerting—account of narrative functions.

Both of Kleist's texts are stories about the telling of stories. In each text, three stories or facts are recounted, and the listeners' responses form part of a larger narrative. Both texts, then, are narratives about the effects of narration, and both concern the status of texts. In "On the Marionette Theater" ("Über das Marionettentheater"), the topic under discussion is the quality of beauty or grace. The narrator and a certain "Herr C." collaborate in telling three stories about the conditions of gracefulness, *Anmut* or *Grazie*. This is the quality of the aesthetic object, and more particularly, of the aesthetic object insofar as it resembles a self, or of the self insofar as it resembles a work of art. "On the Marionette Theater" presents us with models of the text in its aesthetic function, its power to give pleasure through its formal properties.

"Improbable Veracities" ("Unwahrscheinliche Wahrhaftigkeiten") presents the text in its referential and epistemological function, its power to convey truth. While "On the Marionette Theater" concerns what elicits our positive aesthetic judgment, what pleases us, "Improbable Veracities" concerns what elicits our conviction, our positive judgment as to its truth. Both writings question the effect of the production of figures, or to put it another way, the effectiveness of rhetoric. One such effect is pleasure, which we ascribe to beauty, and another is persuasion, which we ascribe to truth. These two brief texts make up a narrative account of rhetoric, and a rhetorical model of narrative. We can recapitulate this double narrative and discover the model it details.

141

"On the Marionette Theater" describes a conversation between the narrator and a lead dancer of the local opera company, Herr C. It consists in a purportedly technical and theoretical account of puppet theater, some other anecdotes, and some pseudotheoretical statements. It is these last—the proposition that *Anmut* and *Reflexion,* "grace" and "self-consciousness," must stand in an inverse relationship, until some moment at which infinite consciousness reconciles the subject-object polarity—that traditionally attract the most earnest attention of interpreters of Kleist's story, and get acclaimed as the *meaning* of the text. The anecdotes and the technical account are then received as plausible illustrations of this supposedly central doctrine shared by Kleist and the German Romantics. This way of interpreting "On the Marionette Theater" depends on ignoring its *narrative* dimensions—the fact that it is the narrative of a dialogue consisting largely in anecdotes and explanations. It is these narratives that we have to read to identify the rhetoric of the text.

There are three or perhaps four such narrative elements included in the dialogue. The first is Herr C.'s account of the workings of a marionette theater. The second is the narrator's story of how an adolescent boy permanently lost his physical gracefulness in a moment of self-awareness that was challenged by an observer. The third is Herr C.'s story of succumbing to exhaustion in fencing with a chained bear. In between the second and third stories Herr C. refers as well to the astonishing dexterity of an artificial leg fashioned by an English craftsman. All three stories have to do with the enabling conditions of gracefulness, and all propose that the abrogation of consciousness, the absence of conscious control, empowers rather than hinders graceful motion. But they tell us something more and something different than this, for each story is not merely a reflection on how a work of art may function, but more specifically an account of an erroneous metaphor for what a text is. The story of the boy shows the error of conceiving of text as a metaphor for the self. The account of the puppet theater shows the error of conceiving of a text as an organized movement of figures, a system of tropes. And the story of the bear shows the error of conceiving of a text as a unit of meaning.

This identification of the different allegories of the text involved in the three stories is an interpretation I borrow wholesale from Paul de Man's reading of "On the Marionette Theater."[2] There is a point to this beyond the fact that it enables me to reproduce a compelling account of Kleist's text. De Man's concept of Romantic narrative as the allegory of textual models (i.e., of ways of reading) entails a conception of the force of the text, a force eliciting determinate readings.

This conception is put to the test by "Improbable Veracities," where it is precisely the conception of force that comes into question.

I said, following de Man, that the story of the boy who loses his gracefulness can be read as an allegory of the text conceived as a metaphor for the self. Consider what we are told about the boy. He is said to have borne a striking resemblance to the well-known classical statue of the youth drawing a splinter from his foot. At stake here are two Schillerian notions linking the human being and the work of art. One notion has to do with the "aesthetic education" of man, whereby the self is supposed to achieve fulfillment through modeling itself on classical works of art, emulating their harmony and grace, and duplicat-cating, too, their aesthetic autonomy, freedom from desire and from considerations of utility. The related notion of the work of art con-ceives of it, in turn, on the model of a self. The work of art, like the human being, is supposed to exist as an end in itself, for the sake of itself, in the condition of self-reference, if not of self-reflection. The work is thought to have an aesthetic autonomy that is not only a dis-tinctive equilibrium but also a value: freedom and integrity. Kleist's narrator's story of the graceful boy represents a disruption of this ac-count. It also counters Kleist's purported message about how self-consciousness hinders grace. We are told that the boy looks into a mirror and sees his resemblance to the work of art: grace and self-reflection here happen to coincide. The access of self-consciousness does not disrupt the boy's aesthetic development; what does disrupt it, instantly and irremediably, is the challenge by another observer—the narrator, who simply claims not to see the resemblance that the boy af-firms. From this moment his beauty suddenly and irreversibly declines.

Thus, the enterprise of aesthetic education is shattered by the least challenge to it, by merely being questioned. Shattered along with it is the aesthetic model of the resemblance between the work of art and the human being—the model of the text (as work of art) as a self.[3] What remains of the model (what remains for the boy) is only an un-easy narcissism.

The story of the boy's loss of grace, then, fractures another classic narrative; it is an allegory that ruptures a traditional narrative figure, the metaphor of aesthetic development. We read in this story the fallacy of reading a self as a work of art or a text as a self. It might encourage us to expect better success with another way of reading, one avoiding the equations between text and self and between aesthetic autonomy and personal freedom. We might hope for a more coherent account of the text, perhaps, if we conceived it as a mere system of tropes, as a mechanism for the production of figures.

This is the conception of the text represented in Herr C.'s account of the workings of the puppet theater. He makes the extraordinary claim that a marionette constructed to his specifications could perform a dance more graceful than any that could be achieved by the finest living dancer. The narrator raises the question of how the puppet's complex movements are related to the actions of the puppeteer, to the simple movements possible for his hand and fingers. The answer given is that the puppeteer need do little more than describe a simple line, a straight line or an ellipsis; this will produce the complex movements of the puppets because of the manner of their construction. This construction, too, is strangely simple: each puppet has a center of gravity and a number of limbs that are merely pendula, describing movements determined by the distribution of weight. The superior grace of the puppets' dance stems from the fact that no ulterior point, such as a center of consciousness, disturbs their spontaneous movement according to their center of gravity. The graceful figure is but a predictable elaboration of a simple straight line. The dance is thus nothing more than the impetus to its own formal perfection, outlined and complicated through automatic shifts of dead weight.

We can recognize in this description a certain metaphor for the text: an account of the work of art as a simple tropological system. The fluency of the description might almost prevent us from noticing several peculiar features of the account. For one thing, it is factually incorrect; this is not how marionettes actually work. Indeed, like the subsequent story of the bear, the explanation of the puppet theater is patently incredible, and this should at least give us pause when we are inclined to follow the lead of the credulous narrator, and to accept the account, in our terms, as an adequate description of the workings of a text. Certain details of the description put in question the simplicity and the acceptableness of this very account of the text as a system of figures. This fictive puppet theater is a spatial organization in which a complex metamorphosis must take place. Herr C. describes a process in which a simple pattern, a line or an ellipse, is transformed into a distorted geometrical version of itself. Such a process is none other than anamorphosis, an effect in which representing an object from a special angle distorts and conceals its shape. A typical object of anamorphosis (in the famous Holbein, *The Ambassadors,* for example) is a skull.

Since it may seem an unwarranted distortion of the text to find a skull in the works of the "Marionette Theater," we can postpone tracing that clue until we come upon similar implications in Kleist's "Improbable Veracities." There are other oddities here. The formal perfection of the dance is said to depend upon the fact that the limbs are mere pendula, completely obeying the law of gravity. But the puppet dancers are also said to owe their superior grace to their *independence* of the law of gravity, to the fact that they are "anti-grav," completely free of the inertia of matter, because the force of the puppeteer's hand so greatly exceeds their own weight. It is perhaps hard to make anything of these contradictory claims except that they contradict each other, thereby fracturing the simplicity of this model of the text. Were we determined to read allegorically, however, we might take these conflicting claims to represent the contradictory account of the text's referential status inherent in its description as a system of figures. On the one hand, the regularity and indeed the grace of the system are conceived as depending upon the guaranteed relationship between every figure and a given ground. Every figure is ultimately bound by resemblance to what it represents: essentially a metaphor, each rests upon a substantial connection with a referential basis. On the other hand, it is assumed that the distinctiveness and the power of the figural system derive from its very nonconnection with a ground of referents separate from it. The essential dimension of the tropological model of the text is its figurality. The essential charm of the system is its effective denial of the pertinency of facts. Thus Kleist's allegorical figure for the model of the text as a system of figures shows that model representing language as at once totally unhinged from the realities of reference, and tied in with a referential dimension as ineluctable as the law of gravity.

There is a third narrative in "On the Marionette Theater," the story of fencing with the bear. In this case Herr C. had to perform not as a dancer but as a fencer: not preserving perfect equilibrium through the production of graceful figures, but alternating feint and thrust with the purpose of striking home. At issue in this case, in other words, is not the text as a mere work of art, whether as mirror of the *schöne Seele* or as system of figures, but rather the text as a meaning to be *got at:* the text as meaning that is in principle within the reach of the deft interpreter, accessible to a hermeneutic thrust. To succeed in placing a thrust at the bear would be to succeed in reading the meaning of the text. But Kleist's text tells of something else happening instead: the bear, says Herr C., gazed "as though he were reading" into the eyes of the fencer, and unfailingly parried his thrusts and ignored the feints. Kleist's allegory of reading represents the text as reading the reader, rather than the reverse. And the text's power of reading its critical readings prevents access to the meaning of the text. The notion of an accessible meaning is a model of the text that this allegory effectively disrupts. Or it disqualifies, at any rate, the strategy of reading conceived on the model of fencing strategy, as a combination of fictive and earnest gestures all part of a strictly formal fight, a game or sport rather than a conflict of force. The consequence of supposing a text to be both meaningful and formal, Kleist's allegory suggests, is to miss the point entirely and end in a fruitless exhaustion of interpretive energy. This suggestion is discouraging indeed, since it is not at all clear what, if not both formal and meaningful, language or a text might be.

A hint lies in the fourth narrative figure in "On the Marionette Theater." One might more accurately describe it as an appendage to the account of the dancing puppets; an appendage, in fact, is what it is about. This fourth term is the dancer's reference to cripples who can be fitted with a new artificial limb better than their old one—a mechanical leg able to *dance* more gracefully than the natural limb. Herr C. adduces this example to stress the superiority of the puppets' insensate mechanical limbs over the animate limbs of human dancers, but he unwittingly brings to the fore a peculiar enabling condition of perfect grace: the condition of mutilation. The puppet dancer, the mechanical doll, consists of an elaborate prosthesis, and the puppet theater, the mechanism for presenting these dancing dolls, is a system for displaying prostheses. The puppet theater is a model of the text as a system for the production of figures. That system would need to be understood, were we to follow the implication of the dancer's appended explanation, as a mechanism entailing mutilation; the puppet-theater text would be a mutilating machine. With some reason, then, respondents to Kleist's "Marionette Theater" universally avoid this particular explanatory advice invoked by his fluent dancer. One might perhaps expect a similarly disturbing effect to be produced not only by the reference to the lost and replaced leg of the cripple, but also by the previous description of the limbs of the puppet dancers as limp passive organs, mere dead weights. Neither of these descriptions disrupts the free and easy exchange between narrator and respondent within Kleist's narrative. What does disturb their conversation is the reemphasized *similarity* between the two cases. When the narrator jokes that the same English craftsman who reconstructed the leg of the cripple could surely construct the ideal marionette, the dancer falls silent for a moment, and looks disconcerted (*betreten*). It is as if the possibility of another inference from his explanation gives him pause: the possibility that the narrator might respond with the disconcerting invitation to sever his own limbs to attain that perfect elegance in dancing. For a similar reason, it is the emphasized parallel between puppet and person, and between dancer and interpreter, that must give us pause as readers, since it implies that the price of critical elegance is mutilation by the text—as if the bear had pulled loose and shifted from systematic parrying to systematic strikes. To learn what such an allegory could mean, or how we are to understand the mutilation said to be involved in the text's production, we turn to Kleist's "Improbable Veracities."

Before committing ourselves to unbelievable truths, though, we should notice the ease with which these other narratives induce belief. I would believe this story were it told me by any stranger, cries the narrator, and how much more coming from you![4] The stories' plausibility would seem to lie in their status as a certain kind of narrative about the rhetoric of narrative. These are narratives that purport to explain the condition of gracefulness, or the production of formal pleasure. The effect of such narratives is precisely to produce belief. The most glaring example of the absurdity involved in this is the response to the tale of the fencing bear. Far from noting how unlikely is the choice of a *bear* to represent perfect grace, interpreters celebrate the figure of the graceful bear as Kleist's metaphor for a Kantian transcendent self resembling God, able, like the bear, to read a man's soul in his eyes. In striking contrast to this fluent credulity produced by the "Marionette Theater," Kleist's other narrative about the rhetoric of narrative produces inarticulate disbelief. The text of "Improbable Veracities" consists in narratives not about the conditions of grace, but about the effects of force.[5] Even stranger than the puppet-theater narratives, they fail to produce either belief or pleasure, and instead enforce mechanical repetition of narration itself. Narration is exposed as the counterproductive juxtaposition of two conflicting theoretical functions.

While "On the Marionette Theater" concerns the conditions of beauty, "Improbable Veracities" concerns the conditions of truth. The fictive narrator of the "Marionette Theater" pronounces the paradoxical proposition that beauty and consciousness cancel one another. The speaker in "Improbable Veracities," a former military officer, presents what seems a similarly puzzling proposition: that truth and the appearance of truth, *Wahrheit* and *Wahrscheinlichkeit,* do not necessarily coincide. This is more than a paradox and worse than a puzzle: it is, rather, an aporia, or a principle of undecidability, which takes the form of a chiasmus:

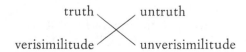

Verisimilitude *may* be on the same side as truth, or it may not be. No dependable inference as to the truth of a statement may be drawn from its verisimilitude or lack of it. This principle renders the relationships indeterminable, rather than simply reversing them: it is not the case, for example, as the narrator of "On the Marionette Theater" seems to be thinking in his enthusiastic response to Herr C.'s stories, that *non*verisimilitude indicates an account's authenticity. Such a principle would negate the possibility of deciding with any certainty the referential or epistemological status of a text.

The situation in Kleist's text is additionally complicated by the fact that the narrator invokes the principle of undecidability in reference to his own narration. He introduces his stories with a caveat: they are true, he declares, but they cannot be believed. Narration thus begins here by questioning the power of narrative to convey truth, and by denying that these particular narratives possess that power. What they lack is the power of persuasion: a rhetorical function, the function of existing not only as a set of figures of speech, a system of tropes, but also as a system of persuasion, a means of conveying the figures' effect or significance. Unbelievable truths, in other words, put in question the cognitive function of language.

The officer's first unbelievable story concerns a wound sustained by a foot soldier who appeared to have been shot through the chest yet continued to march in rank and file. Treatment by the surgeon indicated that the wound was in fact the effect of a bullet that had ricocheted off the soldier's breastbone and passed underneath his skin in a circle around to his back, where it exited at the backbone. When the officer's listeners hear him relate this episode, they doubt their ears have heard correctly. The officer's second story concerns another similarly implausible deflection. A giant stone, falling from the cliff of a quarry next to the Elbe River, had the effect of depositing a laden barge high and dry on the riverbank, indicating that the river had been forced out of its channel; yet the stone did not actually fall into the water, but landed on a stretch of ground alongside it. The officer's third story again concerns a fall, an unharmed soldier, and a river overflowing its banks. During the siege of Antwerp by the Duke of Parma in 1584, a bridge of ships blockading the Schelde was blown up by a mineship dispatched by the Antwerpeners. A cadet standing on the left bank of the river was blown into the air by the explosion and displaced to the right bank, completely intact.

Each of these three cases involves a deflection of force. Force has been discharged, and there is evidence of an effect, but of an effect in each case different from what one could expect to be caused by the action of such a force: a soldier is shot in the chest and not killed; a stone falling toward the river misses a barge yet displaces it nevertheless; and another soldier is blown up but not blown to pieces. Each case contradicts our expectations as to the causal relationship between violence and destruction, or between force and violence. Our expectation of another kind of causal relationship—the relation between truth and verisimilitude effecting belief—also was contradicted, initially, by the officer's presentation of these cases as truths to be *dis*believed. Thus, Kleist's text presents at two different levels a disruption of causation, or of the possibility of inference from an effect to a cause. A similar structure characterizes the effects described in the stories, and the effect of the stories themselves, for the stories, like the propulsive forces described in them, miss their mark, in failing to strike their listeners as true. We are witness as readers to a double malfunction: truth fails to persuade, and force fails to do violence.

The relationship between these two lapses is organized by a narrative structure that we need to describe in more detail, but first we should note another kind of association between the narrative force at stake in the stories' telling and the physical forces at stake in the stories told. The words naming those forces suggest that they are figures for the force of *language*. Such is the suggestion of the following words: *Prellschuss,* "ricochet shot," includes the verb *prellen,* which means not only to rebound and to bruise but also to reverberate and to dupe or deceive; *Widerhall,* the echo-force said to be set in play by the fall of a stone from the quarry, signifies, too, a counterechoing or counterrepetition;[6] and *in die Luft sprengen* not only means "to explode" or "blow up," but also might be considered to designate the force of a *Windbeutel,* "a windbag," the word the officer uses to describe himself as he begins his gratuitous narration.

The same terms that name the physical forces affecting the objects in the three episodes, then, also name the force of language affecting the listeners who hear the account of those effects. The double meanings of these terms also indicate that the three stories may be read as allegories of the force of language. The "force" of language is to be understood here in a specific sense: its force in contrast to its signification; in other words, the performative function of language, that dimension of rhetoric—the range of "speech acts"—that we measure in terms of force or "felicity" rather than of adequacy of truth-content. Given such a reading of the officer's stories as allegories of performative force, we may describe the narration of "Improbable Veracities" in this way: an initial explicit proposition as to the unpredictability of the cognitive function of language is then compounded by an implicit proposition as to the unpredictability of the performative function.

Kleist's allegories of the force of language depict more than merely its unpredictability, its susceptibility to deflection or malfunction. One needs perhaps to point out that the depiction is not a reassuring one, despite the fact that all the stories concern an amazing evasion or deterrence of violence or destruction. By raising doubts about the possibility of linking effects with causes, the three cases also raise doubt about the possibility of linking ends with means and understanding violence in terms of such an intentional structure. It might be, instead, that violence is primarily nonmediate and thus may be neither employed nor excluded in any dependable way.[7] Another such implication would be that the force of language does not, in fact, work. The indeterminate way in which the narrative works, or does not work, is evoked exactly by one particular double-edged phrase among those of Kleist's allegories on the force of language. This is the phrase *in die Luft sprengen*. What is the cause, or the subject, or the object, or the consequence of "blowing up"? What is it that blows up? In this double context, one set of answers includes the fortified bridge of ships blockading Antwerp, the mineship sent against it, and the soldier blown up and over to the opposite riverbank. Other answers include the so-called windbag, the officer, the speaker who blows up his implausible truths; his blown-over listeners, notably the country gentleman who "blows up" at last after the third story and explodes in oaths; and perhaps also the readers of Kleist's narrative, or rather the scene of any interpretive reading, which we may discover to have been exploded by the text's narrative mechanism—by the mechanism that prevents us from determining what or whether such blowing up signifies.

When the officer's incredulous listeners demand to know the source of his third story, one member of the group speaks up to identify its source and status, and cites Schiller's *History of the Revolt of the United Netherlands*.[8] This commentator might appear to be easing the tension of uncertainty by establishing the story's authority as *Geschichte,* by placing the case as a fact, however strange, properly belonging to history. If we read or recollect the history cited, however, we find that its clue to the story's status lies at another level. Rather than ensuring the factual status of the officer's third story, the historical text indicates the rhetorical status and structure of Kleist's narrative. For the history provides an allegory of the narrative's operation, one that consists simply in a ramified version of the officer's story of the explosion. Both versions display the same curious feature: uncertainty as to whether the explosion was effective, or whether the blockade's destruction was consequential. Schiller's history mentions the Antwerpeners' initial ignorance of whether the blockade was destroyed or not, compounded by the fact that it was soon reconstructed: several more explosions and reconstructions of the bridge of ships followed until the entire strategy was abandoned for want of definitive results. This we can read as the complete system of the blockade referred to in Kleist's third narrative: a bridge of ships functioning as a blockade that provokes explosions inciting its reconstruction. Explosion is included in the mechanism. The system is at once a machine for exploding things, and an operation more or less than a machine—something that *explodes* as a machine. Such a thing would be, for example, a windbag, since the peculiarly disturbing characteristic of such a figure is that he does not simply function mechanically, for no function accounts for the fact of a windbag's initially starting up.

Let us suppose that the windbag or the exploding machine, then, is a model for the narration of Kleist's text. Let us spell it out again in those terms. How does the machine operate? What does the windbag say? He says, first, that truth and what functions as truth fail to coincide. Next he tells truths supposed to exemplify that statement: truths that malfunction, figures that fail to elicit recognition, that fail to persuade. These figures that fail to function are all of forces that fail to function, of forces that fail to figure into an effect. Read closely, the text's terms imply that the force of language is what is once again at stake, misfiring as a speech act in addition to missing the mark as a telling truth. Thus, the narrator's introduction and the ensuing narratives both declare the disfunctioning of language, and we seem to be dealing with two similar negations, two parts of a message that repeats itself. However, this is not exactly the case. The two negations turn out to be juxtaposed in such a way that each cancels the other at the same time as it reenforces it.

This becomes evident as we try to reconstruct the operation of the narrative model—as we try, in other words, to construct a response to the windbag's message. Four basic responses to the narration seem to be possible: one may either disbelieve or believe the windbag's stories, and, along with either attitude, one may directly deny or decline to deny their truth. These four responses are four models of reading. They represent the possible ways of reading a certain kind of narrative: one that puts in question, from the start, the possibility of deciding what is true on the grounds of how it functions as such. (Since quite a number of literary and philosophical texts fall into this category, the possibilities for reading such narratives could be considered important.)

Attempts to carry through any one of these four ways of reading the narrative reveal that none of them actually works. Suppose, for instance, that we disbelieve the officer's stories, finding it impossible to believe their implied proposition, that force does not work, yet we decline to charge the officer with telling untruths. (This seems to be the initial and most enduring tendency of the officer's listeners.) We then agree with his first point: that there are truths that do not persuade. Of this truth we confess ourselves persuaded. Nor do we find the narration upsetting, since it seems to be in the service of persuasion and also in the interest of a kind of truth. Yet in fact it has upset our position on persuasion by leading us to believe both that persuasion does not follow upon truth and that it does. This is the cost of maintaining our belief that force does function, particularly the specific force of language. Thus the narrative machine is set up in such a way that if we seek to maintain our conception of the *force* of language, we can no longer maintain our conception of its truth. To keep the performative function of language functional, we have to make its cognitive function unrecognizable—functioning and failing to function, not persuading and persuading, at the same time.

A similar disruption results when we try to read the narrative another way that might seem more logical: we disbelieve the stories and we therefore reject them as untrue—as either lies or fictions. If the stories are unacceptable as truth, however, they are also unsuccessful as fiction (for they unpersuasively recount non-events), and because they do not deceive us, neither do they function as lies. What could be the status of a narrative neither true nor persuasive—or the function of a narration that neither convinces nor deceives? Narration of such a kind could only be the activity of a windbag: performance for the sake of performance, drained of significance; gratuitous expenditure of energy, to incalculable effect. That, however, was just what the stories described and what we refused to believe possible. In this case, then, the narrative machine performs in such a way that if we keep our conception of the force of truth intact, we necessarily ruin our conception of the function of force. If our sense of the cognitive function of language keeps functioning, then we confront a performative force with no function whatsoever.

One could recapitulate similar disruptions that follow upon attempts to read the narrative based on believing the narrator's stories, whether as true or as true fiction. We, the readers of Kleist's narrative, differ from the officer's listeners: as readers of Kleist we do tend to believe in his stories, and we might be inclined to hope that this might leave us in a somewhat more tenable interpretive position; but it does not.

Suppose, for instance, we do believe the officer's stories and believe them to be true. We are persuaded, then, of what they imply: that force does not have calculable effect, or, in terms of our reading, that the performative function of language malfunctions. If we are persuaded of the truth of the officer's stories, then we must disagree with his presentation of them, with his statement that there are truths that do not persuade. We insist, to the contrary, that truths do have the force of persuasion: we maintain that cognition does function. In sum, our position is this: the performative power of language is not a calculable function, whereas the cognitive power of language *is* a calculable function and does function predictably. This position is disrupted, though, by the fact of the officer's opening statement. If the cognitive function is calculable, why does he fail to calculate it? If persuasion is predictable, why does he fail to predict it, and predict the opposite (that he *won't* persuade)? We are faced here with the ruin of our conception of the cognitive function of language, for we maintain that it does function even as we confront evidence of its breakdown. It appears that one can tell persuasive truths, but not persuasive truth about truth. One can produce *Wahrhaftigkeiten* (veracities) but not *Wahrheit*. Cognition and the force of truth are trivialized in this situation. This is the kind of situation de Man is describing when he writes, "Any speech act produces an excess of cognition, but it can never hope to know the process of its own production (the only thing worth knowing)."[9] For we must notice, too, in our case how the cognitive function operates as unpredictably as we recognized the performative to do, so that it seems to be bound up with it; whereas we had supposed that cognition could function dependably, independently of the performative, to simply inform us of the unpredictability of the performative function. All this is what comes of committing ourselves to Kleist's stories as *Wahrhaftigkeiten*, as a kind of history. It is, indeed, the predicament of the history-writer, committed to ineffectual truths, as the commentator says, "compelled to take them up," with no control and no knowledge of the process of their production.

Let him go, said a member of the gathering: the story [*Geschichte*] is in the appendix to Schiller's History of the Revolt of the United Netherlands, and the author notes expressly that a poet should not make use of this fact; the history writer [*Geschichtschreiber*], however, because of the irreproachable nature [*Unverwerflichkeit*] of the sources and the agreement of the witnesses is compelled to take it up.

These are the closing lines of "Improbable Veracities." Kleist could be offering us an explanation of why we must be anxious and incompetent when we write literary history. But that's not the chosen situation, perhaps, of some readers of this essay, and we might feel tempted to hope to avoid the predicament by adopting another response to Kleist's narratives. We know after all that they are fiction; and we take them as fiction expressive of some truth, as not just *Wahrhaftigkeiten* but in some sense *Wahrheit,* or *das Wahre.* We believe the stories, then, or believe true what they figure: that force does not have calculable effect, that the performative does not effectively function. Once again, then, we disagree with the officer's presentation of the stories, his statement that they are truths without the force to appear as such. Rather, we are compelled by Kleist's stories and maintain that what persuades is in some sense true: that what has the force of truth *is* truth, in effect. What is true is none other than a truly imposing fiction, in our view: a speech act that imposes itself with the force of truth, or a figure that is forced to happen. As de Man expresses it, "The truth of a text is . . . [an] empirical and literal event. What makes a reading more or less true is simply the predictability, the necessity, of its occurrence. . . . in the case of the reading of a text, what takes place is a necessary understanding."[10]

The very truth that impressed us, in this case, the very figure we claimed to find compelling in our reading of the three stories, was that the force of language does *not* function effectively or predictably or according to an evident necessity. Thus, our conception of the force of true figure conflicts with the true figure of its force. Our understanding of truth's force is incompatible with our reading of what we find forcibly true. This fact of the collision between our reading and our understanding must disrupt our conception of the effect of truth. The effect of true reading on *our own* performance of understanding is an instance of the *in*effectiveness of truth's force, evidence of the unpredictability, the non-necessity, of truth's occurrence. We start out with a certain negative cognition of truth, with a functional account of truth as a figure with force. To quote from the last chapter of *Allegories of Reading,* that account "begins to vacillate when it appears that these negative cognitions fail to make the performative function of discourse predictable and that, consequently, the linguistic model cannot be reduced to a mere system of tropes."[11] The question that then arises is whether the linguistic model cannot be reduced to an exploding machine, or a windbag. A mere windbag is not the same as a mere system of tropes, and it is the latter, not the former, that *reduces* the model of language in the way just found ineffectual.

One must attempt at this point to summarize the situation such a narrative imposes. Each story within the narrative *performs* in a manner consistent with the cognition it offers, namely, that cognition is not consistent with performance. Each story functions in a way consistent with what it figures: for its function, like what it figures, is the failure to function, to persuade, to take calculable effect; yet if what the story figures is precisely the *inconsistency* between figure and function, then in the very process of consistency with that figure, the story functions in a manner inconsistent with it. In other words, the very solidarity of the performative and the cognitive rhetoric of such a narrative also entails their strict incompatibility. The matter cannot be determined one way or the other, as to whether the narrative is primarily a case of collision between figure and function or one of collusion between them. Our attempt to read through the narrative ends, then, as we come up against a principle of undecidability. Just such a principle confronted us as the narration began. Indeed, the undecidability of the relationship between function and figure or between performative and cognitive rhetoric repeats the principle of undecidability as to the relationship between *Wahrheit* and *Wahrscheinlichkeit,* truth and the appearance of truth. If we have been reading this narrative, then, we have been reading to no effect, having to conclude at a point not significantly different from where we had to begin, or having been only pointlessly displaced. We have merely been led, as readers, into complicity with the narrator—duped into collusion with a windbag.

One could put this another way and say that we have been maneuvered into collision with an exploding machine. We have been exposed to Kleist's narrative as such a mechanism, forcing the connection between the cognitive and the performative dimensions of language, at once soldering and dissolving the link between function and figure.[12] What is the consequence of collision with an exploding machine? That question returns us to the text with which we began, "On the Marionette Theater," and to its enigmatic implication that the cost of the critical posture is mutilation by the text. Earlier it was declared that the second part of Kleist's double message would indicate how one might understand the mutilation said to be involved in the text's production. Indeed, "Improbable Veracities" does suggest part of an answer, for that text produces itself by severing one rhetorical part from another, severing them by crushing them together. To describe the narrative as a mutilating machine, mutilating itself and others, is to refer first of all, then, to its unreadability, to an explosion of the possibility of reading that negates not only the function of the reader but also the function of the narrative. However, "Improbable Veracities" leaves another part of the question undecidable—the question of whether the predicament of unreadability is truly *consequential* or not.

In other words, we cannot decide about the force of our figurative expressions in this critical context, such as the description of a certain kind of narrative as an exploding machine. We cannot determine how much we mean when, for example, we repeat that mutilation is the consequence of confrontation with a text. We cannot determine whether mutilation means more than a strictly textual encounter, or whether such an encounter also might not entail damage to works and bodies more irremediably vulnerable than narratives or texts. The text perpetuates this indeterminacy in its narrative model, the operation of "blowing up." What is explosive about this narration is the very undecidability of the significance of that figure. It presents us with another chiasmus, one that does not preclude the possibility of connecting the verbal explosion occurring within the space of a text with a literal explosion occurring in a space one had conceived as lying beyond it. The text that seemed to be modeled like a mechanical doll blows itself up into a more mechanical model and becomes an exploding machine. That double explosion of significance is the operation of undecidability. Thus the figural model of narrative altogether exceeds its function.

The Decomposition of the Elephants
Double-Reading *Daniel Deronda*

In the seventh and penultimate volume of George Eliot's final, elephantine novel, the narration is interrupted by a long letter that the titular hero receives from a subordinate character: "My dear Deronda," writes Hans Meyrick,

> In return for your sketch of Italian movements and your view of the world's affairs generally, I may say that here at home the most judicious opinion going as to the effects of present causes is that "time will show." As to the present causes of past effects, it is now seen that the late swindling telegrams account for the last year's cattle plague—which is a refutation of philosophy falsely so called, and justifies the compensation to the farmers.[1]

With this resounding fatuity, Meyrick's letter opens no less than an interpretation of the novel, for it calls attention to the issue of causality, the problem that comes to light in the anomalous plotting of Deronda's story. Meyrick's flippant sentences describe the figural logic covertly at work in the text. Focusing attention on the narrative process, these lines suggest that the novel presents itself to be read in two conflicting ways: not only as a history of the effects of causes but also as a story of "the present causes of past effects." *Daniel Deronda* calls for a double reading, and a close reading of Meyrick's letter offers a starting point for this procedure.[2] It sets the reader on the traces of the rhetorical principles by which the text is constructed, principles at odds with the meanings indicated by *Deronda's* narrator and dissimulated by the novel's narrative mode. In short, the letter functions as a deconstruction of the novel.

Meyrick's "bird-dance" (as Deronda calls it) in no way furthers the novel's plot, unlike other letters included in the text, each of which marks a turning point in the story.[3] In this it invites comparison with the passages of commentary incorporated by the narrator, despite the contrast between Meyrick's frivolous, self-parodic tone and the narrator's more sober style. The contrast in tone is not merely superficial. Meyrick's letter proposes an interpretation of the novel that is substantially and radically at odds with the explanations of its narrator. Aberrant as interpretation and superfluous to the plot, the letter raises a question as to its ostensible function in the novel. That is, what significance does it have for the narrator, that privileged character linked in profound complicity with the hero of the novel? The narrator's view emerges clearly in the passage that follows the inserted letter and describes Deronda's reactions. Deronda takes Meyrick's parodic mode to indicate a basic incapacity for authentic feeling, a failure to deserve to be taken seriously as a lover. "Hans Meyrick's nature was not one in which love could strike the deep roots that turn disappointment into sorrow: it was too restless, too readily excitable by novelty, too ready to turn itself into imaginative material, and wear its grief as a fantastic costume" (chap. 52, pp. 709–10). This negative judgment reflects the fundamental strategy of the narrator and indicates one of the main ostensible meanings of the novel: seriousness and idealism triumph over parody and the ironic spirit. Meyrick's letter functions to exemplify the spirit and the style that the hero transcends.

The triumph of idealism over irony is written into the very structure of the novel's double plot, which presents us with Deronda and Gwendolen as rival protagonists. The distinction that the style of the letter helps to establish between Meyrick and Deronda is in one sense a subtler version of the opposition between Gwendolen and Deronda. From the reader's point of view, one of the erring heroine's more admirable and interesting qualities is her satirical spirit, her critical eye. This is also the admirable and interesting quality of the "English part" of *Daniel Deronda*, which the scheme of the narrative subordinates to the more idealistic and moralistic "Jewish part."[4] The narrator's parable presents not merely Deronda's triumph and Gwendolen's defeat but the triumph of one mode of narration over another. Superior value is ascribed to the seriousness that distinguishes both Deronda as a character and the narrative mode employed to relate his activities, which contrasts with the more satiric mode of the Gwendolen plot and with the ironic mode of Meyrick's letter.[5] Meyrick's letter may be readily understood as a negative example in a broad aesthetic and moral judgment inscribed in the story as the intention of its narrator.

The narrator's strategy is to offer in Meyrick's letter a more or less satirical view of the characters' situation and then to arrange the context in a way that deprives this view of any validity.[6] This is achieved in part by Deronda's reflections on Meyrick's superficiality but also by the plot itself, for when Deronda receives the letter, he has just learned of his Jewish birth, which gives him a basis for intimacy with Mirah that Meyrick the Gentile cannot hope to share; in this light, Meyrick's hope of winning Mirah, the main theme of the letter, appears ridiculously unfounded, "the unusually persistent bird-dance of an extravagant fancy," as the narrator allows Deronda to observe. The tactic is to bracket the letter's ironic mode with a dramatic irony at the level of the action.

The presentation of Meyrick's letter is thus a focus for the devaluation of ironic discourse. Viewing it in these terms, even before examining the text more closely to see just what is said that must be so energetically discredited, one can anticipate a good deal of what is at stake. It is not merely coincidence that Deronda's interpretation of Meyrick closely resembles the description of the Romantic ironist in Kierkegaard's *The Concept of Irony,* a polemical Hegelian account of the ironic "moment." Irony, for Kierkegaard, is properly seen as a crucial but transitory moment in both classical and Christian history. In insisting on subordinating irony to the value systems inherent in the idea of history and the conventions of discourse, Kierkegaard is recognizing the threat to history and to discourse itself that an absolute irony must pose. Meyrick's whimsical missive to Deronda, while it can hardly be said to muster an absolute irony, employs an ironic mode of a sort that subverts rather than serves the establishment of meaning and value. As we shall see, it offers a deconstruction of the narrator's story and, by implication, of story in general—both of history, with its system of assumptions about teleological and representational structures, and of discourse, with its intrinsic need to constitute meaning through sequence and reference.

Daniel Deronda, of course, is not merely a fictional "history"; it is patently about history. It focuses on the causes at work in the personal destinies of Deronda and Gwendolen and, finally, on the "cause" taken up by Deronda as his destined mission. The novel claims for its hero the possibility of a genuine historical role. The narrator seeks to portray a subtle heroism, consisting in imaginative empathy with a historical destiny, the achievement of a distinctively historical imagination. In the context of this invocation of historical consciousness, Meyrick's flippant allusions to Judaic tradition are strikingly discordant. His letter shows a comparable flippancy about certain elementary conventions of writing, such as consistency and continuity. These he violates by his digressive style, continually interrupted by fanciful comments on his epistolary manner. The whole of Meyrick's letter is a tissue of allusions, a complex parroting of the diction, themes, and rhetorical strategies of various conventional texts. Far more than simply posing the dilemma of irony and history, these allusions render a strikingly exact account of discursive structures.

The opening paragraph of Meyrick's letter ostensibly has no real subject matter. It presents itself as badinage. Its covert topic, however, is the plotting of *Daniel Deronda.* "Here at home," we read, "the most judicious opinion going as to the effects of present causes is that 'time will show.'" This purports to be a satire of the conventional wisdom. In the process it satirizes, too, the traditional temporality that the realistic novel is supposed to imitate. (It should perhaps be stressed that this reading of the letter is not concerned merely with the meanings that the character Hans Meyrick might conceivably have intended, any more than this reading of the novel is concerned merely with the meanings that could plausibly be ascribed to the intentions of the narrator. The text generates a much wider range of significations.)

Narrative operates, indeed, by flattering our "judicious opinion": to read a sequence of events as a narrative is to expect that sequence to become intelligible. By the almost irresistible pressure of this expectation, the temporal sequence is conflated with a causal sequence; post hoc is interpreted as propter hoc. A novel evokes the passage of time, which is itself presented to show the "effects" of "causes" and thereby to reveal the events' significance. The formulation in Meyrick's letter satirizes this assumption as a kind of mental sloth, a withholding of judgment that is an evasion of interpretive effort. It would not be irrelevant to refer this criticism to Deronda's attitude toward learning his parentage, which he postpones indefinitely until he receives his mother's summons. What the narrator would wish us to interpret as a "wise passiveness," the text of the letter ironizes as the banal creed of "time will show." The remainder of the passage suggests that the passive trustfulness of protagonist and reader—their trust in the revelatory power of sheer sequence—is fundamentally misplaced.

In opening an ironic perspective on the overt time scheme of the conventional novel, Meyrick satirizes the norm that Eliot's novel was criticized for violating. Some readers of *Daniel Deronda* have judged that it fails adequately to render the sense of duration and the flow of time that would make the action of the novel plausible and significant. Henry James's Pulcheria echoes this opinion when she characterizes the "current" of the story as being, rather, "a series of lakes."[7] The

"time will show" passage identifies such objections as symptoms of a
banal conception of novelistic time. The most radical critique in the
passage, however, aims neither at the censure of the narrator's strategy
nor at the ostensible strategy itself. Rather, the passage exposes *Deronda*'s peculiar plot as a systematic disruption of narrative principles
and temporal structures. In its second sentence Meyrick's letter suggests that the novel discloses not "the effects of . . . causes" but "the
present causes of past effects."

The phrase describes exactly the decisive episode that has just
taken place before Deronda's receipt of Meyrick's letter: the revelation of his Jewish birth. In this sense, Meyrick's letter is no mere digression from the crucial action that occupies the preceding and
following chapters (51 and 53), the confrontation between the hero
and his mother. Rather, it names the distortion of causality that the
reader senses in this turn of the plot. What a reader feels, on the basis
of the narrative presentation, is that it is *because* Deronda has developed a strong affinity for Judaism that he turns out to be of Jewish
parentage. Generations of readers have registered discomfort at the
disclosure of the Princess Halm-Eberstein, and generations of critics
have objected to it as an awkward implausibility or a graceless admix-
ture of romance elements. Meyrick's letter, however, names what is
vitally at issue: not a violation of genre conventions or of *vraisemblance*
but a deconstruction of the concept of cause.

Deronda's decisive encounter in the preceding chapter involves a
revelation of origin. Origin, cause, and identity are linked in the plot
structure to which the letter alludes. The question of Deronda's identity, posed and left suspended, receives an ostensibly definitive answer
with the disclosure of his origins. Up to this point, Deronda has been
identified by his qualities or attributes, in terms, that is, of his character. With the revelation of his parentage, this identity conferred by
character is seconded by an identity conferred by origin, and the
latter is presented, implicitly, as the cause of the former—as the cause
of Deronda's character. This presentation conforms with the conventional logic of cause and effect and exploits the myth of origin, the
view of origin as having a unique generative power.

This causative force is also strongly emphasized in the Princess
Halm-Eberstein's account of Deronda's family history. The power of
genetic heritage proves itself all the more impressively in resurfacing in
the third generation after a deliberate suppression in the second. Deronda's mother tells him: "I have been forced to obey my dead father.
I have been forced to tell you that you are a Jew, and deliver to you
what he commanded me to deliver" (p. 693). "I have after all been the

instrument my father wanted. . . . His yoke has been on me, whether I
loved it or not. You are the grandson he wanted" (p. 726). Deronda
accedes to this interpretation of the workings of origin, and the narrator in no way discredits the genealogical myth that marks these passages. Full weight is put on the metaphor of birth as destiny. Chapters
51 and 53 emphatically affirm the identification between origin and
cause.

The sequence of events in the plot as a whole, however, presents
Deronda's revealed origins in a different perspective. The account of
Deronda's situation has made it increasingly obvious to the reader that
the progression of the hero's destiny—or, that is to say, the progression
of the story—positively requires a revelation that he is of Jewish birth.
For Deronda's *Bildungsroman* to proceed, his character must crystallize,
and this must come about through a recognition of his destiny, which
has remained obscure to him, according to the narrator's account,
largely because of his ignorance of his origins. The suspenseful stress
on Deronda's relationship with Mordecai and with Mirah orients his
history in their direction, and Mordecai explicitly stresses his faith that
Deronda is a Jew. Thus, the reader comes upon Deronda's Jewish
parentage as an inevitable inference to be drawn not simply from the
presentation of Deronda's qualities and his empathy with the Jews but
above all from the patent strategy and direction of the narrative. The
revelation of Deronda's origins therefore appears as an effect of narrative requirements. The supposed cause of his character and vocation
(according to the chapters recounting the disclosure), Deronda's origin
presents itself (in the light of the rest of the text) rather as the effect
of the account of his vocation: his origin is the effect of its effects.

The decisive episode of the "Deronda plot" thus presents itself to
be read in two conflicting ways. On the one hand, the narrator's account emphatically affirms its causal character. On the other hand, the
plot and the overall strategy of the novel conspicuously call attention
to its status as the effect of tactical requirements. The contradiction
cannot be reduced to the simple distinction between the event of Deronda's birth, a genuine origin that took place in the past, and the disclosure of his birth, a retrospective account that takes place in the
present. It is not the event of Deronda's birth as a Jew that is decisive
for his story, but the knowledge or affirmation of it. This disclosure,
as far as the plot is concerned, is the event with causative powers; yet
it appears, too, as a mere effect of the account of Deronda's emerging
vocation. Meyrick's inverted phrase names the contradiction that
characterizes this narrative structure. It is a chiasmus or a metalepsis,
a reversal of the temporal status of effect and cause: cause is relocated

in the present and effect in the past. In naming Deronda's revealed Jewish parentage as the "present cause" of his demonstrated vocation for Jewishness, its "past effects," Meyrick's letter is naming the cause as an effect of its effects, and the effects as the cause of their cause, and is therein identifying the contradictory relationship between the claims of the realistic fiction and the narrative strategy actually employed.

Meyrick's metalepsis also describes the operation establishing Deronda's identity as a Jew. The account in the chapters on Deronda's meeting with his mother grounds itself on the principle that identity in the sense of origin precedes and causes identity in the sense of character and attributes. The account implicit in the narrative structure, however, presents character and attributes as preceding and causing the inference of origin. This goes far toward undermining the authority of the notion of identity, as well as of origin and of cause, for attributes carry the authority of identity only insofar as they belong to a system involving causality, in which behavior is causally related to identity. Meyrick's deconstructed causality, in which "present causes" match "past effects," describes, as we have seen, the sequence establishing the origin and identity of the hero of the novel. Since Deronda is the character whose consciousness coincides most closely with that of the narrator, and who thus represents the exemplary subject, the deconstruction of his identity has radical implications for the concept of the subject in general. The origin of the subject appears as the effect of a narrative requirement, the requirement that an ostensible cause with the authority and mystique of an origin be retrospectively posited to confirm and account for the established direction of the action. Like the concepts of cause and of identity, then, the concept of the subject is the product of a metalepsis, a rhetorical operation, an aberrant reversal or substitution of rhetorical properties.

Meyrick's letter explicitly associates the issue of Jewish identity with the identity principle of formal logic, parodically formulated as substitution of properties. He has been talking with Mordecai, Meyrick writes, "and agreeing with him in the general principle, that whatever is best is for that reason Jewish. I never held it my *forte* to be a severe reasoner, but I can see that if whatever is best is A and B happens to be best, B must be A, however little you might have expected it beforehand." One recognizes here the premises and procedure of the novel: if whatever is best is Jewish and Deronda happens to be best, Deronda must be Jewish, however unexpected or scandalous this may appear for the hero of a Victorian novel. The subversiveness of Meyrick's formulation lies partly in its linking of the blank, unresonant, significance-free language of logical principles with the resonant, specific, value- and affect-charged topic of a hero and his possible identity as a Jew. The connection suggests on the one hand the constructed, artificial, non-"organic" status of the hero's story and on the other hand the preposterous character of the purportedly value-free principle. It is invoked here, of course, in reference to a property that reduces the statement to nonsense—namely, the enigmatic property of Jewishness, which properly speaking cannot exist as the logical consequence of a deductive process.

The deconstructive force of the passage has to do with its reduction of the question of human identity to the application of a logical principle: if $b = A$ and $B = b$, then $B = A$ (since A cannot at the same time equal b and not equal B, which equals b). The metaphysical issue of the identity of the subject and the humanistic issue of the identity of a person are reconstrued as a strictly logical, rhetorical issue, a question of the function of linguistic terms. A defining feature of fiction, especially of the realistic novel, is the presentation of all issues in terms of relationships among fictional characters, or fictive persons—in terms, that is, of a phenomenology of subjectivity. The choice of this context is in itself a defense of the subject as the locus of meaning and value, against an alternative account treating these as the valueless products of the operations of language itself. As discussion of the narrative structure of *Daniel Deronda* has suggested, the latter account of meaning is also inscribed in the novel (covered over by the version of the fictive subject functioning as narrator). Meyrick's formulation contributes to this account by reversing the recuperative, defensive, constructive process involved in establishing a phenomenological context. In renaming the novel's central issue as a matter of a substitution of terms, Meyrick's deconstructive gesture reconceives the significant action of human subjects as the purposeless play of signifiers.

Meyrick's letter marks what classical rhetoric called a *parabasis,* a shifting of attention from the level of operation of the narrator (the reconstruction of the sequence of events in an imaginary human life) to the level of operation of the text or narrative as such (the construction of a discourse and a history). The letter's phrasing plays on obscuring the distinction between the two levels of operation: "As to the present causes of past effects," writes Meyrick, "it is now seen that the late swindling telegrams account for the last year's cattle plague." The sentence exploits the ambiguity of *account for,* which seems to mean both "to render an account of" and "to cause." The telegrams are said not merely to explain or offer an account of the cattle plague but to produce it, to stand as the cause of which the

plague is the effect. This proposes the notion that writing, in the present, causes a material event in the past (as the present requirements
of writing Deronda's story seem the "swindle" that produces the
physical event of his birth as a Jew). Meyrick's play on words calls
attention to an assumption inherent in narrative: an action that can
be accounted for, one about which a narrative can be recounted, has
by the same token an adequate and comprehensible cause, because (so
the reasoning implies) to account for something consists, above all, in
identifying its cause. Meyrick's metalepsis or chiasmus carries this a
step further to point out the sense in which the account of an action *is*
its cause. Questioning the meaning of "accounting for" an event, the
sentence is not only deconstructing the concept of causality but also
putting in question the representational function of narrative. Narrative
structure presents what are ostensibly fundamental properties of
reality (or metaphysical categories) such as causality (or the origin of
the subject, or identity) as the product of its own operations, the effect
of a play of signs. Thus, far from representing the truth of the human
situation, the subject's origin and destiny in a history, narrative represents with authority nothing more than its own structural operations.

Causality, the subject, identity, representation, and origin are deconstructed or put in question by the reading of the novel proposed in
the first half of the second sentence of Meyrick's letter. The second half
of the sentence comments on the inherent preposterousness of this
situation. Referring to the reversal of cause and effect, the sentence
continues: "which is a refutation of philosophy falsely so called, and
justifies the compensation to the farmers." This satirizes the pretension to a victory over philosophy, or the claim that irony triumphs
over discourse. At the moment that deconstruction claims to achieve
a "refutation" of causality or of the subject or whatever, the argument
deconstructs itself in turn, ironized through the very process of making its pretension explicit. This does not happen, one should stress, as
a result of a general principle or a belief that radical skepticism must
be skeptical of itself. What is involved is not a mental attitude (such
as the determination to view all assertions ironically) but a tropological
operation, a reversal of rhetorical properties, such as the metalepsis
reversing the order of cause and effect and renaming "cause" the effect
of an effect, and "effect" the cause of a cause. The deconstructive
operation, while it consists in pointing out that the concept of causality amounts to an aberrant and arbitrary ordering of rhetorical elements, is itself no more than an equally aberrant reordering of these
elements, the performance of another tropological operation. It is for

this specific reason that a deconstruction is not a refutation, or that a deconstructive "refutation" can claim for itself no more authority than the refuted concept. The text's ironization of the "refutation of philosophy falsely so called" is referring to this specific state of affairs.

However, Meyrick's satirical sentence refers as well to a state of affairs quite different from the dilemma of rhetoricity: he invokes "swindling telegrams," "last year's cattle plague," and "the compensation to the farmers."[8] These allusions satirize the deconstructive pretension to neutrality, the pretension, precisely, to constitute merely a tropological operation, free of motive and affect, just the way deconstruction has been described above. It is indeed a tropological operation that is involved, but it does not have the privilege of taking place in a neutral context empty of reference or value judgments. Rhetoric inevitably presents itself not only as trope but also as persuasion, so that deconstructive discourse inevitably lapses into a covert attempt at "refutation," into a dogmatic or exhortative mode. Meyrick's sentence suggests that the motive and goal of "the refutation of philosophy falsely so called" is none other than a justification of the "compensation to the farmers," and this makes the point: the deconstructive project takes place in a context of accusation and excuse, of blame and defense, and cannot avoid the motive of self-justification.

Like the "refutation of philosophy," which involves a cattle plague and compensation to the farmers, the deconstructive account of cause and identity inscribed in *Daniel Deronda* involves a troublesome referent and a justificatory impulse. It involves, namely, the hero's Jewishness. The narrative is relentlessly referential. In a sense the novel's principal issue is the scandal of the referent. Consideration of this issue can begin with an observation of how the specific kind of identity in question disturbs the coherence of Deronda's story. Not only the disclosure of Deronda's parentage but the preceding part of the story as well reveal themselves to be based on unwarranted shifts of rhetorical categories.[9]

The earliest episode indicating Deronda's vocation might be thought to be his rescue of Mirah. The rescue of a maiden in distress, specifically a Jewish maiden, allegorically prefigures Deronda's destiny as a savior of the Jews. The question of Deronda's own Jewishness, however, first becomes explicit in his meeting with Mordecai. Mordecai's identification of Deronda as a Jew and Deronda's acceptance of their resultant relationship mark the first step in the establishment of Deronda's Jewish identity. However, the account of this development involves a radical contradiction, which is perhaps most conspicuous in the scene where Deronda, rowing down the river to seek Mordecai, emerges out of the sunset to encounter the waiting Mordecai on Black-friars Bridge. The narrator stresses that Mordecai has foreseen precisely this scene, that his inner vision of the "prefigured friend" prefigured the external sight of Deronda floating into view against a glowing sky. Thus, on the one hand, Mordecai's identification of Deronda is presented as a recognition, and for this reason his assertion of a claim on him has authority and appeal. On the other hand, Deronda's assumption of the identity of Mordecai's prefigured friend is shown to be a consequence of Mordecai's act of claiming him. He becomes what Mordecai claims he is.

If one imitates the deconstructive gesture of Meyrick's letter and reads the "Deronda plot" as a set of formulas about the identity principle, one recognizes that two different conceptions of the functioning of language are being exploited in the narrator's account. First, the account claims that an identity is recognized, that Morde-cai's words on this occasion state the recognized fact. To recognize or know is

> a transitive function that assumes the prior existence of an entity to be known, and that predicates the ability of knowing by way of properties. It does not itself predicate these attributes but receives them, so to speak, from the entity itself. . . . To the extent that it is verbal, it is *properly* denominative and constative. . . . Knowledge depends on this non-coercive possibility.[10]

In presenting Mordecai's identification of Deronda as a recognition, the text makes use of this cognitive, or constative, concept of language. The possibility of Mordecai's recognizing Deronda as his "prefigured friend" depends, however, on the possibility of an inner representation prefiguring an external sight. This second notion conflicts with the constative concept of language, as is made especially clear by the explicit description of Mordecai's inner representation as a "*coercive* type": "there are persons whose yearnings, conceptions—nay, travelled conclusions—continually take the form of images which have a fore-shadowing power: the deed they would do starts up before them in complete shape, making a coercive type" (p. 527). The power, the coercive function, of Mordecai's identification of Deronda is emphasized in subsequent passages describing Deronda's acceptance of the identity assigned him. This aspect of the account makes use of a concept of identity as a principle actively posited rather than known or recognized, the product of an assertion rather than a matter of fact. Such a notion, that identity is the product of a coercive speech act, deconstructs the identity principle and the constative concept of

language grounded upon it. Thus, the narration of Deronda's relationship with Mordecai both stresses the authority of recognition or knowledge and undermines the basis of this authority. The contradiction
here resembles the one involved in the disclosure of Deronda's birth,
which both stresses the causative power of origin and draws attention
to the questionable status of cause.

The account of Deronda's relationship with Mordecai includes
more than their encounter at Blackfriars Bridge, for the narrator tries
to lend to their relationship the plausibility and certainty of a gradual
process, as well as the impact and authority of a decisive event. The
part of the narrative describing Deronda's increasing responsiveness to
Mordecai's idea also plays upon two conflicting notions of how language functions. The narrator describes Deronda's development of a
Jewish identity in response to Mordecai's assertions but seeks to
account for it not as a challenge to the concepts of cognition and con-
stitution but rather as an authentic cognitive process. Mordecai and
Deronda, it is suggested, are engaged in a kind of reading, a hermeneutic
practice, in which the interpreter and the text (or Mordecai and Deronda) stand in a certain mutual relation. At the same time, however
(as if in default of this hermeneutic model, which is hazy at best), the
narrative is playing upon the notion of an act of naming, a speech act
with the type of authority and validity characteristic of the performative mode. A performative utterance in and of itself accomplishes an
action or brings about a situation, rather than describes or interprets
it. In addressing Deronda as if he were a Jew, Mordecai is "*doing* some-
ting rather than merely *saying* something."[11] Mordecai's speech, which
so often resembles a litany, has a performative quality, and his influence on Deronda evokes the idea of a conversion. The ritual of conversion involves a speech act that changes the identity of the person who
is the object of the ritual.

It is striking, however, that conversion precisely does *not* apply in
regard to Jewish identity, which is inherited, historical, and finally,
here, genetic. For the establishment of identity as a Jew, what is required is not merely a performative but an actual performance, an act
or event, not just a speech act. Such an act is remotely invoked by the
romance elements in the "Deronda plot," most notably the kind of
magical metamorphosis found in fairy tales.[12] In fairy tales a ritual
word and gesture produce not merely conversion (a change of spiritual
status or of an inner state) but physical transformation. This would be
the effect required of Mordecai's influence, were his relationship with
Deronda to establish fully Deronda's identity as a Jew. Such an effect
exceeds the limits of realistic narrative. To be a Jew (and this is empha-

sized by the narrator, who never suggests that Deronda might simply "embrace" the Jewish "faith") is to have been born a Jew, not merely to take up the spiritual and cultural tradition of Judaism. Thus the establishment of Deronda's identity must shift from his relationship with Mordecai to the revelation of his mother. One discovers, then, that the presentation of Deronda's Jewishness requires several shifts of ground. From the notion of the cognitive and constative function of language the account must shift to the notion of its performative function. From this it must make a further shift of ground to the notion of an actual, nonlinguistic act or fact.

With this last shift to the act or the fact, the narrative goes aground. Insistence on the hero's specifically Jewish identity not only puts in question the authority of the discourse but effectively disrupts its coherence. The text's insistent reference leads relentlessly to the referent—to *la chose,* in fact: the hero's penis, which must have been circumcised, given what we are told of his history.[13] In the period in which Deronda's story takes place, male babies were not routinely circumcised. Circumcision was a ritual procedure practiced by Jews, so that evidence of circumcision amounted to evidence of Jewish origin. For Deronda not to have known he was Jewish until his mother told him means, in these terms, "that he never looked down,"[14] an idea that exceeds, as much as does magical metamorphosis, the generous limits of realism. Deronda must have known, but he did not: otherwise, of course, there could be no story. The plot can function only if *la chose,* Deronda's circumcised penis, is disregarded; yet the novel's realism and referentiality function precisely to draw attention to it. Acknowledgment of the fact or act would prevent the construction of the narrative, as it also, in fact, prevents the completion of the deconstruction. It persists as a residue of the deconstructive process. The hero's circumcised phallus, proof of origin and identity, is more than an exemplary metonymy, though it is certainly that. It is distinctively significant, not as a rhetorical structure, but as a referent—one that produces embarrassment, a sense of discomfort that is not intellectual and that is more than a sense of aesthetic incongruity.

The mere emphasis on Jewishness, quite apart from any reference to circumcision, was enough to produce discomfort in many Victorian readers of *Daniel Deronda.* It led them to object to the construction of the plot, pointing out what constitutes, in fact, its metaleptic structure. One must recall just how common such a plot structure was in nineteenth-century English novels, which frequently dealt with the establishment of the hero's identity and presented the decisive evidence in a dramatic disclosure late in the story, amply prepared by

incontrovertible circumstantial evidence developed in the earlier part
of the novel. Few readers saw fit to object to this construction in, say,
Oliver Twist, though the establishment of Oliver's identity is marked
by the same implausibility or artificiality as Deronda's. Oliver's inheri-
tance of his father's name and property turns on the fulfillment of a
condition in his will (on conformity, that is, to a written text) that includes the stipulation "that in his minority he should never have
stained his name with any public act of dishonour, meanness, coward-
ice, or wrong." That Oliver is his father's son is the effect, then, of his
being, "in effect," "his father's son," which is to say good, or virtuous
with the virtues of the middle class. Ths metalepsis is as patent here as
in *Deronda,* but the impact is altogether different when the evidence
reveals, not that the hero's parentage is "good," but that it is Jewish.
It is the specific referent in *Daniel Deronda* that generates its deconstructive effects, by calling attention to the metaleptic structure,
which otherwise might not give rise to comment. The scandal of the
referent calls attention to the scandal of metalepsis or, more generally,
of rhetoricity. The glaring referent highlights the narrative structure as
a strictly groundless construct. While it would be misleadingly reassuring to suggest that this is the real reason for readers' objection to the
"Jewish part," it would be equally mistaken to suppose that the objection has nothing to do with rhetoricity.

For many of Eliot's contemporary readers, being a Jew, like having
sexual organs, was something to which as little attention as possible
should be called. Both terms involved in the notion of a circumcised
penis would produce embarrassment. For the men of Eliot's day,
sexual identity and Jewish identity did have a kind of structural similarity. Each claimed, on the one hand, an irreducible physical element
and, on the other, an enormous burden of cultural, spiritual, and historical significations. Each involved two extremes, unlike, for example,
identity as a member of the middle class, the sort of identity more
typically in question for a novel's hero (as for Oliver Twist). The
physical element was necessary but not sufficient, while the cultural
dimension was significant but, strictly speaking, not sufficient. The
authority of the physical element as the basis of identity was under-
mined by the importance of the cultural element and vice versa.[15]

This mutually canceling effect comes into play in *Daniel Deronda*
when the narrator stresses both the hero's vocational affinity for Jewishness and his Jewish genealogy. Deronda's demonstrated empathy
with Judaic tradition makes the disclosure of his Jewish birth seem
either superfluous or implausibly neat, while the asserted fact of his
genetic heritage makes his intellectual and emotional affinity seem at

once superfluous and inadequate and casts doubt on its authenticity as free choice. The deconstructive effect of the Jewish referent is not merely to call attention to the groundlessness or rhetoricity of the narrative structure. It operates in a more precise and far-reaching way as well. Thus the referentiality of the identity at issue, Jewishness, suspends the principle of identity between two modes: the performative mode, which would define it as a form of activity, and the constative mode, which would define it as a matter of knowledge. Like the affirmation of the hero's Jewishness, which must stop short of acknowledging his circumcision, affirmations of a performative and of a constative concept of identity must stop short of asserting the fact or the act. Full affirmation of the constative mode would mean portraying Deronda's self-identification as real knowledge (as opposed to acceptance of another's word, whether Mordecai's or the Princess Halm-Eberstein's). Full affirmation of the performative mode would mean portraying Deronda's self-identification as a real action, such as the attempt to restore Jewish nationhood, which he is about to undertake at the novel's close. Both possibilities are excluded from the narrator's account. Both the origin of Deronda's history (the fact of his birth) and its goal (the act of restoration) are excluded from his history proper. Deronda's parentage is introduced not as the testimony of the narrator but as the account of the Princess Halm-Eberstein, and his birth is located in a past prior to the time of the novel. Similarly, Deronda's activity in Palestine is introduced not as an actuality but as an eventuality subsequent to the novel's time.

To put it another way, the text brackets the decisive assertion in a story within a story and banishes the decisive performance to a fictive future beyond the story's end. This exclusion of knowledge and action from the realistic narrative proper signifies an acknowledgment of their constitutionally fictional status and with that an acknowledgment of the limited possibilities of language. It is implicitly acknowledged that "the possibility for language to perform is just as fictional as the possibility for language to assert."[16]

Thus, there emerges in *Daniel Deronda* an account of the determining connections between the referential function of language and its constative and performative functions. Its inexorable referentiality prohibits the narrative from claiming authority either as a genuine fact or as a genuine act, for the referent itself constitutes the fact and the act and remains extralinguistic, necessarily excluded from the discourse that inevitably refers to it. Circumcision stands as an emblem for the fact or act that is at once the proof that the text requires and the referent that it excludes. The "all-presupposing fact" has a peculiar double status. It signifies a proposition that carries authority neither as knowledge nor as performance, alluded to in the epigraph to chapter 1 as the novel's point of departure, which cannot be made fully explicit: "whether our prologue be in heaven or on earth, it is but a fraction of that all-presupposing fact with which our story sets out." This formula also names the text's fractionally presented referent the fact of the hero's Jewish identity, affirmed in an account that omits to acknowledge its signifying mark.

The unacknowledged mark is the circumcised phallus emblematizing the powers of constatation, performance, and reference. It is the exemplary signifier, and it commemorates a fiat allowing the possibility of signification. It is a sign that stands for a story, told to account for the origin of Jewish identity: the story, namely, of Abraham and Isaac and of Jehovah's intervention to prevent the completion of an act of autocastration. An account that would link the possibility of signification with the possibility of origin and of identity must invoke a divine power. Deus ex machina cuts short the cutting off of the race: so the mark of circumcision signifies. Divine dispensation grants genealogy, history, and signifying power, as Jehovah intervenes before the actual obliteration: it suffices that the possibility of obliteration should be admitted and the process instituted or prepared. The story told here in terms of a divine fiat relates how it is that, while the conditions of truth or authentic meaning (such as causality) are disclosed to be without authority, that disclosure in truth never carries authority itself (since, as we have observed, the disclosure takes place as a rhetorical reversal like the reversals that constitute the conditions of truth). Divine fiat allows the destruction of discourse to stand as mere deconstruction, a "refutation" as fictitious as the truth of history or philosophy that it refutes. Circumcision marks this account of the institution of signification. As a mark that tells too much of the conditions of history or too much of the limits cutting off signification or storytelling, circumcision is a sign that the story must evade or exclude or cut out: narrative must cut out or cut around the cutting short of the cutting off of narrative. In this circumcisive outlining, *Daniel Deronda* affirms a history that elicits deconstruction.

A distinctive aspect of *Daniel Deronda*'s deconstructive mode is signaled by the peculiar status of its referent as the exemplary signifier that refers to the story of the institution of signification. "That all-presupposing fact from which our story sets out" is a reference to another story, a story conceived as an account of the conditions of storytelling. The chapter containing Hans Meyrick's letter presents an excellent example of this operation. It opens with an epigraph quoted from La Rochefoucauld, which offers a statement exactly coinciding with the narrator's (and Deronda's) evaluation of the difference between Mordecai's character and Deronda's. The quoted passage sounds the theme of love and irony, authenticity and inauthenticity, and represents the traditional moral and aesthetic judgment with which the narrator's account aligns itself, so that for the narrator the epigraph functions to lend the authority of a classical precedent to that judgment. The aphorism also, through its form, seeks an effect similar to that which the narrator seeks in presenting certain dubious elements of the Deronda plot (such as Mordecai's second sight): an effect of surprise resolving into conviction. Thus La Rochefoucauld's aphorism takes the form of two symmetrical pseudo-paradoxes: "La même fermeté qui sert à résister à l'amour sert aussi à le rendre violent et durable; et les personnes faibles qui sont toujours agitées des passions n'en sont presque jamais véritablement remplies."

The aphorism exemplifes a classical rhetorical mode that compels conviction by means of its symmetrical metaphorical assertions.[17] The category of *fermeté* seems to account for both resistance to love and the durability of love. The category of *faiblesse* seems to account for both "agitation" and shallowness. A truth that reveals itself as a rhetorical structure, La Rochefoucauld's aphorism resembles the narrative structure of *Daniel Deronda*. The authority of a prior text is being invoked to ratify not only the message but also the rhetorical usage favored by the narrator. By the same token, however, the epigraph stands as a *pretext* for the deconstructive operation in Meyrick's letter, which indeed proposes a reading of the entire narrative as a deconstruction of La Rochefoucauld's aphorism: an extended critical commentary on its precepts, its rhetorical mode, and their attendant metaphysical claims.[18] Thus, the text of *Daniel Deronda* presents as its point of departure a prior text, a rhetorical and syntactic structure, rather than the dilemmas of subjectivity. The starting point of the novel's discourse is not the subject, but written language.[19] The signifying process performed by the text is one of allusion or citation in which the signifier points toward a referent constituted as another exemplary signifier. The citational mode testifies to the partial or fictive cutting off from meaning in the form of a further sign.

The text of Meyrick's letter offers explicit emblems for the citational mode of the novel, in addition to the implicit emblem of circumcision. The letter places the novel under the rival signs of Hesperus and Hyperion: "Meanwhile I am consoling myself for your absence by finding my advantage in it—shining like Hesperus when Hyperion has departed." If Hyperion is the god of an art envisaged as the light of truth, Hesperus is the god of an art conceived as a process of forging or forgery. The citational (or deconstructive) text of *Daniel Deronda* is a consummate forgery passing as an authentic work, and the rival lovers, Deronda and Meyrick, along with the rival gods, Hyperion and Hesperus, personify the two kinds of reading elicited by the narrative: the reading carried out by the narrator and the deconstructive reading proposed by passages such as Meyrick's letter.

However, it can be misleading to think of the two readings in personified or personifying terms, since they constitute a single discontinuous process that moves away from personification, abandoning the notion of the subject for the notion of linguistic operation, reconstruing the narrative's starting point as a text rather than as a subject. More apposite than the rivalry of Hesperus and Hyperion is Meyrick's allegory of the "mystery" and the "basis":

> I leave it to him to settle our basis, never yet having seen a basis which is not a world-supporting elephant, more or less powerful and expensive to keep. My means will not allow me to keep a private elephant. I go into mystery instead, as cheaper and more lasting—a sort of gas which is likely to be continually supplied by the decomposition of the elephants.

Instead of a symmetrical confrontation between opposites of the same status, such as Hesperus/Hyperion, one may think of *Daniel Deronda*'s aporia as an asymmetrical obstruction: composition/decomposition (taking the latter term in its material sense, which is *not* the opposite of composition), or a single word for the single process or text: (*de*)*composition*. I cut short the process here—as Meyrick writes, "without comment or digression."[20]

Oedipal Textuality

Reading Freud's Reading of *Oedipus*

Where is my voice scattered abroad on wings?

—Oedipus

You *should* have meant! What do you suppose is the use of a child without any meaning? Even a joke should have some meaning—and a child's more important than a joke, I hope.

—the Red Queen

Of all the fictions that Freud calls upon to render an account of the psyche—from "The Emperor's New Clothes" in *The Interpretation of Dreams* to the legend of Moses in *Moses and Monotheism*—the drama of Oedipus is his most recurrent and insistent reference. Sophocles' protagonist provides the name for what Freud frequently presented as his major discovery. The Oedipus complex still challenges definition from contemporary analysts and theorists, and writers' interpretive stances can be situated according to their characteristic uses of this one concept. With the matter of Oedipus so chronically urgent and undecided, one recent perspective in particular seems promising, one which aligns psychoanalysis with the theory of drama and theorizes a dramatic structure informing the psychic order.[1] For if a drama could signify for Freud such crucial propositions of psychoanalytic thought, then the signifying mode of drama warrants inquiry. Freud *reads Oedipus:* the Oedipus complex draws its specificity from the Sophoclean tragedy, rather than just from the ostensible semantic content of the Oedipus legend. To rethink Freud's concept, we ought not only to reread its first formulation, his claim in *The Interpretation of Dreams* that *Oedipus*'s unfolding "can be likened to the work of a psycho-analysis,"[2] but also to reconsider its primary source, Sophocles' version of the myth.

Freud uses the drama of Oedipus to tell a story about psychic development and to describe the status of sex in human existence. Perhaps
we can use the drama of Oedipus to tell a story about the development
of Freudian thought and to describe the status of the *text* in psychoanalytic thinking. We could take our cue from the initial, exemplary
project of psychoanalytic investigation, *The Interpretation of Dreams,*
and take as clue Freud's dream of solving the riddle of the Sphinx—an
actual dream mentioned in a letter to Wilhelm Fliess on May 31, 1897.
Freud was also dreaming of solving the riddle of dreams,[3] and the
solution written out in the *Traumdeutung* in certain ways resembles
the answer to the dreamlike enigma of the Sphinx. By constructing
the analogy between them, we may be led to grasp some distinctive
traits of Freudian interpretation as well as the crucial features of the
Oedipus story that rendered it significant for Freud.

The writing of *The Interpretation of Dreams* takes form both un-
consciously and consciously as what will come to be described as an
"Oedipal" endeavor. Like the inquiry of Sophocles' protagonist, it is
an investigation in relation to and for the sake of the father, the end
result of which is the disclosure of a parricidal effect: the discovery
of the Oedipus complex. In his preface to the second edition, Freud
identifies the writing of the book as "a portion of my own self-analysis,
my reaction to my father's death"—"a significance I only grasped after
I had completed it" [*ID,* p. xxvi]. Freud's own most manifest "Oedipus
complex" is the drive to interpretation and "self-analysis" dramatized
by Sophocles' hero, which is initially at least, in the tragedy as in *The
Interpretation,* a more prominent "complex" (an excessively insistent
and self-exceeding intention) than any parricidal or incestuous tendency. The complex Freud shares with Oedipus is, first, the drive to
discover an Oedipus complex. We may take this as an initial pretext
for seeking the relationships between *The Interpretation of Dreams,*
interpretation, and writing, on the one hand, and on the other hand
the Oedipus complex conceived as a theory of the child's relationships
to his father and mother. Reading Sophocles with Freud could help to
illustrate the complicity of Oedipal sexuality with a certain textuality.

Turning points in the legendary career of Oedipus, and the legible
career of Freud, take place with the formulation of an enigma or riddle. First there is the question of Oedipus's parentage, which the Pythia
answers with an unassimilable structural definition: your mother is she
whose lover and your father he whose murderer you shall be. Then
comes the riddle posed by the female-male being, creature of Apollo,
the Sphinx: what is the thing that changes shape, with two feet and
four feet, with a single voice, that has three feet as well? Finally, there

is the enigma of the Phocal crime: "How can we ever find the track of ancient guilt now hard to read?" Freud riddles: Do dreams have meaning? What meaning? Why is it distorted? And in the course of interrogating the significance of dreams he comes to interrogate the significance of audience response to dramatic presentations, and the particular enigma of the universal effectiveness of *Oedipus Tyrannus* for generation after generation of audiences.

This is the riddle of the riddle: the enigma of why the riddle of the Phocal crime should be so absorbing. It is solved along with the riddle of dreaming, which Freud answers by positing a censoring agent active in mental life—by discovering repression, and by positing the unconscious. The riddle of another riddle initiated the metapsychological inquiries that preoccupied Freud from 1895 on, even as he completed his *Traumdeutung*. As he wrote in the *Project for a Scientific Psychology*: "It is quite impossible to suppose that distressing sexual affects so greatly exceed all other unpleasurable affects in intensity. It must be another characteristic of sexual ideas that can explain how they are alone subjected to repression."[4] How can one interpret the fact that sexuality alone (of all "drives") is uniquely enigmatic? How can one interpret the enigmatic fact that *Oedipus* (of all "tragedies of destiny") is uniquely enthralling? Freud's explanation for the repression of sexuality first takes shape in his theory of seduction, or of the *proton pseudos* or "primal deceit," formulated in the *Project* of 1895.[5] It focuses on the decisive effect of a distinctive temporal structure in sexual development, a proleptic or metaleptic structure marked by prematuration and deferral, or, in Freud's term, *Nachträglichkeit*. The same conception of a peculiar time scheme, Freud's solution to the riddle of the sexual riddle, becomes the principle of his reading of the Oedipal riddle, the peculiar power of *Oedipus Tyrannus*.

Freud indicates a solution in the "peculiar nature of the material," a "voice within us," a "factor" or "moment" of a certain kind. Modern dramatists, on the theory that *Oedipus* owes its success to its construction as a "tragedy of destiny," to the conflict of "divine will" with "human responsibility," have tried to achieve the same effect by constructing plots on the same theme; but, remarks Freud, the plays based on such *"selbsterfundenen Fabeln"* (plots invented by the playwrights themselves) have failed to move their audiences. Hence:

Wenn der König Ödipus den modernen Menschen nicht minder zu erschüttern weiss als den zeitgenössischen Griechen, so kann die Lösung nur darin liegen, dass die Wirkung . . . nicht auf dem Gegensatz zwischen Schicksal und Menschenwillen ruht, sondern in der

Besonderheit des Stoffes zu suchen ist, an welchem dieser Gegensatz erwiesen wird. *Es muss eine Stimme in unserem Innern geben,
welche die zwingende Gewalt des Schicksals im Ödipus anzuerken-
nen bereit ist,* während wir Verfügungen wie in der "Ahnfrau"
oder in andern Schicksalstragödien als willkürliche zurückzuweisen
vermögen. *Und ein solches Moment ist in der Tat in der Geschichte
des Königs Ödipus enthalten.*[6]

[If *Oedipus Rex* moves a modern audience no less than it did the
contemporary Greek one, the explanation can only be that its effect does not lie in the contrast between destiny and the human
will, but is to be looked for in the particular nature of the material
on which that contrast is exemplified. *There must be* something
which makes *a voice within us ready to recognize* the compelling
force of destiny in the *Oedipus,* while we can dismiss as merely
arbitrary such dispositions as are laid down in (Grillparzer's) *Die
Ahnfrau* or other modern tragedies of destiny. *And a factor of this
kind is in fact involved in the story of King Oedipus.*]

(*ID* pp. 295–96. My italics.)

The original German text refers to an inner "voice which is ready,"
not to "something which makes" it ready, to perform the act of recognition. In the German, then, "such a *Moment*" refers back to the
"voice which is ready": Freud is pointing to a "moment" or "factor"
in Sophocles' drama involving recognition carried out by a "voice"
poised for such an act. The relation between that voice and *einem
solchen Moment* is a problematic one, the German text suggests;
whereas the English translation of *Moment* as "factor" neatly elides
the difficulty, excluding the temporal character of the "factor" and
identifying it with a "something" in the play's thematic content.
Hence the passage is most often read in a way that reduces it to the
statement that follows it, to the effect that "it is the fate of all of us
. . . to direct our first sexual impulse towards our mother and our first
hatred and our first murderous wish against our father." But we should
make the attempt to read it in conjunction with Freud's remark in the
preceding paragraph that the "process of revealing" that constitutes
"the action of the play . . . can be likened to the work of a psychoanalysis." Freud is not simply evoking the psychoanalytic practice of
disclosing a patient's Oedipus complex. In the context of his practice
and writing in this period, Freud's comparison means that *Oedipus
Tyrannus* successfully dramatizes the activity of repression and unre-
pression—the "abnormal defense" that characterizes "psychoneurosis"
and the peculiar "process of revealing" that constitutes interpretation
of dreams, or psychoanalysis. Freud theorized the relationship between

sexuality and repression in the light of the temporal structure he reconstrued in the case histories of his hysterical subjects in the 1890s.
In identifying the uniquely revelatory character of *Oedipus,* Freud is
remarking the same crucial structure, the same exemplary plot. The
parallel between the riddle of *Oedipus's* power and the riddle of sexual
repression can be situated in a certain moment or factor (*ein solches
Moment*) in the sequence of sexual development—something for which
Freud used the term *trauma.*

Trauma is a key concept in the interpretation of sexual repression
first outlined by Freud in the *Project* of 1895, where he reconstructs a
kind of plot for the neurosis of a patient fictiously named "Emma."
This plot focuses on two moments or scenes, which between them constitute the trauma and install repression. One scene takes place before,
the other after, puberty. There is a fateful time lag between the child's
passive participation in an adult world imbued with sexuality, and the
child's own accession to biological maturity and sexual awareness; the
difference or deferral between "moments" is the decisive factor in
causing the extraordinary "abnormal defense" of "hysterical" repression, in which the mind blinds itself to the "first scene" of a sexual
encounter. As Jean Laplanche summarizes: there are two scenes "separated from each other by a temporal barrier which inscribes them in
two different spheres of meaning."[7]

The first scene in Emma's drama, as Freud narrates it, is a putative
seduction, an adult's sexual gesture toward her, the sexual nature of
which, however, the child cannot sense. After sexual maturity there
occurs a second scene that is banal, nonsexual, and distinguished only
by the fact that through some detail of resemblance it recalls the first
scene. In provoking a sudden recollection of that scene, together with
its sexual significance now understood for the first time, the second
scene produces within Emma a sexual excitation which takes the ego
by surprise, for the danger comes from a memory, from within, not, as
the ego's defenses expect, from an outside stimulus. The result is that
the second scene institutes not only the normal defensive mechanism
of "attenuating" the threatening tension by associating the sexual idea
with others, allowing its assimilation into consciousness, but the more
"primary process" of "total evacuation of affect": the first scene is
completely forgotten, and the second, in its insignificant detail, takes
on all the affective significance of the first alien sexual gesture. Freud
writes, "Here we have an instance of a memory exciting an affect
which it had not excited as an experience, because in the meantime
changes produced by puberty had made possible a different understanding of what was remembered. . . . The memory is repressed which

has only become a trauma *by deferred action.*"[8] The peculiar status of the traumatic moment, the sexual factor, stems from the impossibility of locating it in either scene: it is neither in the first, which has a sexual content merely "as it were, *in itself* and not *for the subject,*" and which "has no immediate sexual effect, produces no excitation, and provokes no defense"; nor in the second, which includes no sexual gesture at all. Like self-blinded Oedipus, Emma feels herself a prey to "double griefs and double evils" (l. 1320), the things done involuntarily, years before, and the things done just now, by and to the self. It is precisely a neither-nor that empowers the both-and of repression, as the subject blinds herself to the past, to the entry into a world structured by sexual meanings inaccessible to the subject's initial understanding. As Sophocles' Chorus declares, "Time, all-seeing, surprised you living an unwilled life" (l. 1213).

Like Emma's typical "psychoneurosis," Oedipal sexuality concerns a certain lag or limp of the subject in relation to structures of meaning. The "Oedipus complex" takes its explanatory power not simply from the generality of incestuous desire, but from the rigorous representation, in the Oedipal drama, of the temporal logic of repression. Reading *Oedipus Tyrannus* as structured according to a "first scene" and a "second scene" like the history of the repressed subject, we may come to distinguish, in Sophocles' more complex plotting, an enrichment of the conception of repression that will be taken up and implied by Freud in all his subsequent references to our Oedipal sexuality.

An initial recollection of Sophocles' play gives us a "first scene" in the murder of Laius, the Phocal crime, and a "second scene" precisely in the drama itself, the moment of the legendary story chosen by Sophocles for representation on the stage, the quest for and recognition of the deed's agent and meaning. The accession to sexual awareness that converts an indifferent episode into a seduction in Emma's case is paralleled in Oedipus's case by an accession to genealogical awareness that converts an accidental manslaughter into patricide. In this perspective, Sophocles' play portrays Oedipus as the one person in history *without* an Oedipus complex in the conventional sense: he has murdered his father and married his mother in an appreciation of expediency rather than in satisfaction of a desire. The one person who actually enacts patricide and incest completely misses the experience—until after the fact, when the parrincest is inscribed as a palimpsest and becomes readable for the first time. The Phocal event, the real, as Lacan writes, exists as what is missed, according to the traumatic logic of psychoanalytic thinking:

That which is repeated, in fact, is always something produced—the very expression reveals its relation to *tuché*—as if by chance. . . . The function of *tuché,* of the real as encounter [*rencontre*]—an encounter insofar as it can be missed, and as it is essentially an encounter which *is* missed [*rencontre manquée*]—first appeared in the history of psychoanalysis in a form which is itself enough to awaken our attention—as trauma. [9]

In the very drama of the "one in whom these primaeval wishes of our childhood have been fulfilled" [*ID* p. 296], there lies inscribed the metaleptic plot structure that makes such fulfillment an impossibility. The sex of the cause is produced only through the *text* of the effect. The "cause"—the parrincestual experience that has supreme guilt as its "effect"—is, practically, the effect of its effect. "Hysterical," Emma draws the connection: so that was sex! "Horror-stricken," Oedipus draws the connection: so that was . . . text! Emma represses the first scene, forgets it absolutely, yet is unable to return to the scene of the crime (shops, where both the first and second moments of the trauma took place; her symptom is a phobic evasion of shopping), and at last commits herself to "the work of a psychoanalysis." Oedipus engages in "a process of revealing, with cunning delays and mounting excitement—a process that can be likened to the work of a psychoanalysis—that Oedipus himself is the murderer of Laius . . . [and] son of the murdered man and of Jocasta"; and at last he "represses" the scene of the crime by blinding himself. We remark initially, then, the analogy between Emma's hysterical forgetting and Oedipus's self-blinding, and between Emma's engagement in psychoanalysis and Oedipus's analysis of the Phocal crime. There also emerges the possibility—suggested by a certain literal reading of Freud's ambiguous comparison between the plot and an analysis—of leaving the two plot sequences strictly parallel: if Oedipus's self-blinding is his final act in the play, are we to understand that a similar action concludes a psychoanalysis—blinding oneself to the impossibility of cure for a temporally determined predicament? In matching the Sophoclean to the psychoanalytic plot, Freud suggests a critique of psychoanalysis as radical as the most strenuously anti-Freudian or antipsychoanalytic critic could compose. [10]

With a facetious equation of Emma's and Oedipus's rhyming revelations we exploit an opportune coincidence—in order to raise the question of the text. Or rather, we begin to read the question of Freud's text, the riddle Freud ravels in citing another text (Sophocles') that exposes questionable relations between text and sex. While an extraordinary sex act is one major component of Oedipus's drama, text acts are just as major and extraordinary a component of the story; if there is a scandal to match (in the modern mind from Jocasta to Girard) that of incest, it is that of oracles. A recent Girardian reading of Sophocles' *Oedipus*, Sandor Goodhart's "Oedipus and Laius's Many Murderers" refreshes our apprehension of the scandalously textual nature of Oedipus's central act, his affirmation of his guilt as the murderer of Laius.[11] In Sophocles' version of the legendary story, the facts of Laius's murder are never empirically established. Empirical proof of Oedipus's guilt hinges on the testimony of the one eyewitness to the murder, the Herdsman, who is *said* to have said that not one but many assaulters felled the king and his party (ll. 842–47). Oedipus initially focuses on the question of one or many murderers as the fact that will absolve or condemn him. By the time the Herdsman has arrived to testify, however, the arrival of the Corinthian Messenger has shifted all attention to the question of Oedipus's parentage. What finally convinces Oedipus of his guilt is the Herdsman's implication that he, Oedipus ("Swellfoot"), is the child exposed with pierced ankles by Jocasta and Laius in response to the oracle's prediction that he would kill the latter and marry the former.

Goodhart's reading helps us to perceive more readily the parallel between Oedipus's appropriation of guilt and Emma's repression of her "seduction": both can be seen as phobic gestures responsive to juxtaposed structures, rather than reactions to accumulated empirical evidence. Oedipus reads his guilt in a palimpsest compounding the oracle told to Jocasta and Laius with the oracular definition of his parentage that first drove him from Corinth. What convinces him is a constricting network of texts: the Herdsman's word that he helped "save for a dreadful fate" the exposed child entrusted to him by the queen, the Messenger's news that he was Polybus's and Merope's adopted heir, his wife's confession to exposing her child, and, above all, the words of the oracles, the Pythia's dreadful structural account of ancestry, and Apollo's fearful designation of a particular infant aggressor.[12] Sophocles arranges for the eyewitness to appear and to testify, but never to be asked the empirical question, Who killed Laius? "From a semiotic point of view," says Jonathan Culler, "what is important here is the play's implicit commentary on the relation between meaning and event, between signs and the 'realities' often thought to be independent of them. . . . We are not given a deed from which we infer a meaning but a meaning from which we infer a deed."[13] In Sophocles' tragedy, then, as Sandor Goodhart writes, "it is the status of the explanation that identifies those crimes that comes to be questioned. . . . Sophocles has shifted his interest from the myth to its appropriation, and it is this appropriation, in its origin and danger, that is examined."[14] Precisely this dimension of Sophocles' drama enables it to be a uniquely rich reference for Freud.

Ignoring the fact that Freud's reference to *Oedipus Tyrannus* in *The Interpretation of Dreams* focuses on the very appropriative gesture re-illuminated in a Girardian perspective, the Girardian reading (both Goodhart's and Girard's own) goes on to claim that Freud just blindly repeats the "mythopoetic gesture" of Oedipus. The claim is that Freud appropriates Sophocles' *Oedipus* as an oracular text, and, in the manner of Tiresias, uses it to force his every subject to confess an "Oedipus complex." Such a notion of Freud as a tyrannical Tiresias can only stem from a myth of Freud as analytic practitioner, not from the founding texts of Freudian analysis. This adherence to a mythic version of Freud compounds strangely with the "antimythical" reading of *Oedipus* celebrating Sophocles' exposure of mythification. The account ultimately identifies the Crucifixion as the one nonmythical and efficacious sacrifice.[15] Girard's antimythical interpretation of *Oedipus* thus repeats the Christian attack on myth in favor of Logos. The curious characteristic of the Girardian interpretation of Freud is that it seems simultaneously to read, and learn from, the critique of appropriative interpretations that runs through Freud's own writing, and to decline to read it, denying its self-critical power. Girard attempts to establish the absolute difference between his critique and Freud's. Yet in Girard's view, aggressive attempts to reestablish eroded differences are the crucial symptom of our drastic cultural disintegration. He must therefore fail to recognize his own strenuous efforts at self-distinction—must decline to reckon with the significance of this very gesture in the elaboration of his own thesis.[16] Girard is impelled to conceive a purely literal, nonmythic, nonrepresentational sacrifical event—and to produce a strictly true self-sacrificial writing. The intriguing irony in this itinerary is that rejection of the Freudian generalization of the Oedipus complex is ultimately accompanied with a denial of Freud's generalization of an oedipal *textuality*.

Let us return to a Freudian reading of the case of Sophocles' *Oedipus*. The Oedipal drama presents itself for analysis as a "first scene" made up of all that precedes the point at which the stage representation picks up the story, and a "second scene" made up of all that is represented on the stage. The first scene itself includes several crucial scenes or moments that can be analyzed in the light of Freud's account of the primary instance of such a "sexual-presexual" condition, infantile sexuality. The conception of an infantile sexuality ultimately impinges on the theory of seduction, as Freud comes to insist on the literal universality of seduction in at least one form, the earliest gestures of a mother toward her child, which are necessarily imbued with sexual meaning owing to her engagement in the sexualized adult world. The "first scene," then, is not just an accidental episode in the case history of a hysteric, but the first entry upon the human scene of every subject. Maternal care (in the first instance, nursing) sensitizes particular parts of the infant's body (in the first instance, the mouth and lips) and establishes an erogenous zone, a specially sensitive and significant region of the body. Initiating the oral phase, this zoning institutes the course of sexual development that, for Freud, spells the individual's destiny. Lacan, following Freud, stresses that this is an entry into not only a preexistent sexual but a preexistent textual order, that of language.[17] The child's accession to speech, like its accession to sexual maturity, comes long after its insertion into a sexual-social structure, through maternal and familial care and subscription in a discursive order, in the first instance by being given a name. Zoning and naming thus constitute the individual's inscription in a sexual-textual or "Symbolic order." One of the extraordinary features of the legend of Oedipus, of "Swellfoot," is its representation of these modes of facticity as radically identical. Thus the piercing of Oedipus's ankles, the maiming of his feet, is the terrible gesture of parental "care" that marks the infant's position as the potential murderer of his father and lover of his mother, in the sexual-social order that is precisely a textual, discursive order, the language of the oracle. The parental gesture at once marks a special spot in the infant's body and generates his name, Oidi-pous. The mark and the name in fact determine Oedipus's relation to the Symbolic order and regulate his destiny. The most spectacular instance of this is his competition with the Sphinx: sensitive to *feet* as part of a name for man, Oedipus can provide the identification that destroys the Sphinx and lays the city of Thebes at his feet—where Sophocles sets the Chorus at the beginning of his drama.

Sophocles' text plays repeatedly on the syllable *pous* and expressions involving *feet*. Tiresias speaks of "a mother's and a father's double-lashing terrible-footed curse"; Creon explains the failure to track down the regicide by saying that the Sphinx compelled the Thebans "to turn from the obscure to what lay at our feet" (ll. 417–18, 130–31). At another moment, attacking Tiresias's mantic power and celebrating his own power of reasoning, *gnōmē,* Oedipus reminds his listeners how he read the Sphinx's riddle:

Why, when the dog who chanted verse was here,
did you not speak and liberate this city?

Her riddle wasn't for a man chancing by
to interpret; prophetic art was needed,
but you had none, it seems—learned from birds
or from a god. I came along, yes I,
Oedipus the ignorant, and stopped her—
by using thought, not augury from birds.

[ll. 391-98]

In a footnote to his translation of this passage, Thomas Gould comments:

> Oedipus uses sarcasm that rebounds bitterly on himself. In Greek, the phrase *Oedipus the ignorant* has an assonance and an apparent etymological connection that make it seem right in a sinister way: *ho mēden eidōs Oidipous. Eidōs* means "knowing": *oida* means "I know." Oedipus seems to be speaking of himself as "I whose name sounds like *oida* but really signifies the reverse." (*Oida* and *eidōs* are also related to the verb "to see".) *Pous,* the other half of Oedipus' name, means "foot." "As 'Knowfoot' (*eidōs tous podas*) he solves the riddle about feet."
>
> (M. L. Earle, *The Oedipus Tyrannus*)[18]

In the very act of claiming reasoned control over language, Oedipus utters syllables that speak the opposite; the controlling utterance here is not his, but that of a fragmentary language speaking itself. "Lack—knowing—I know—foot": in the very act of deploying a limited local irony, with his sarcastic references to himself as "the ignorant," Oedipus produces an irony of that irony, which fragments meaning into material signifiers. Expressions of double meaning, not usually of the fragmentary punlike kind here, abound in tragic drama, and *Oedipus Tyrannus* has more than twice as many ambiguous forms as Sophocles' other plays.[19] Missed by Oedipus (even and especially in his own speech), these double meanings speak to the spectators (who always already know the story). There is an irony to his "tragic irony," however, which ultimately overwhelms the audience just as much as the irony of his local irony overwhelms sarcastic Oedipus. As Gould writes,

> the double meaning is the most tactful possible way to keep the audience focused on the patricide and incest. Each person in the theater, as he is caught up in the fantasy, must imagine himself discovering the same guilt in his past, but he must be kept quite unaware of his involvement in the story or he will recoil with revulsion or defend himself with laughter. Sophocles, by pushing the vision of the crimes almost solely in double meanings, offers the audience

a way to escape too conscious an identification with Oedipus in his troubles.

(p. 175)

Sophocles' strategy to prevent our prompt disassociation from the parrincest engages us in interpreting a meaning gradually ramified until it refers to our own condition and confronts us with our complicity with Oedipus. The double meanings thus mark our distance only to draw us in. They impel us to read into them a complex of significations so distant and different from the secret we know in advance that finally we find ourselves written into a representation that traverses and exceeds us.

We may undergo a similar effect in reading the text of Freud. Freud's Oedipus complex exceeds itself in a particular way that the legend of the name of Oedipus represents precisely. It seems that sexual repression, generating the unconscious, implicates the subject in an order not only of the living but also of the dead. Recent psychoanalytic theorists have followed the ghost of a suggestion in Freud's writing that the subject is obscurely constrained not only by his own lively unconscious but by the unconscious of his parents and their parents.[20] This notion would take support from the observation that, as Laplanche explains, "the slightest parental gesture bear[s] the parents' fantasies . . . the parents themselves had their own parents; they have their 'complexes,' wishes marked by historicity, so that . . . at two vertices of the triangle [of the child's oedipus complex] each adult protagonist is himself the bearer of a small triangle and even of a whole series of interlocking triangles."[21] The "zoning" and naming of Oedipus reflect Laius's fantasmatic relation to his father, Labdacus, "the limping one," with his maimed walk. As the son of his father, Laius makes a father of his son: he ascribes to him the threat of castration (as parrincest) that a son might have ascribed to his kingly father. In giving the child the "Name-of-the-Father,"[22] in effect, the father empowers him, in fact, to take his (father's) place, for as "Swellfoot" he solves the riddle of excess feet, and takes the king's place in Thebes.

Freud takes his place as a master, "the father of psychoanalysis," when he solves the riddle of dreams and in 1900 publishes the *Traumdeutung.* Rather as Oedipus is enabled to answer the Sphinx by an intimate sense of the significance of feet, Freud is empowered to interpret dreaming by an intimate conviction that it does have meaning, that (to quote the opening sentence of *The Interpretation of Dreams*) "there is a psychological technique which makes it possible to interpret dreams, and that, if that procedure is employed, every dream reveals itself as a psychical structure which has a meaning and which can be inserted at an assignable point in the mental activities of waking life." Like Oedipus's simple solution to the Sphinx's bizarre questions, Freud's *Traumdeutung* restores to the light of "waking life" the weird productions of nighttime fantasy. Each rediscovers the uncanny and *unheimlich* as *heimlich*, canny, homely, "what lay at our feet." Each reconstructs a narrative scheme capable of explaining the inconceivable kind of being expressed by the dream or the riddle. Oedipus must identify "a thing with two feet and four feet, with a single voice, that has three feet as well. It changes shape, alone among the things that move on land or in the air or down through the sea. Yet during the periods when it walks supported by the largest number of feet, then is the speed in its limbs the feeblest of all." [23] The riddle concerns a coincidence of excess and lack, a collusion of sameness and difference, and a question of "speed" and a question of "support." These are the factors of Freud's riddle as well, if not most patently in *The Interpretation of Dreams,* more clearly at least in his solutions to the general puzzle of repression that dreams manifest. It is unriddled, as we have seen, in terms of the shifting zones and phases of the sexual being. The inadequacy of the "speed" of sexual development is most evident when the creature has the most "support": the human infant supported by sexual care (and with the greatest number of relevant "limbs," if we recall the theory of the infant's "polymorphous perversity") is least capable of sexual action. We can even draw a connection between the riddle's emphasis on "walking *supported*" and Freud's conception of the sexual drive *propped* upon a biological function—in his scheme, as in Oedipus's answer to the Sphinx, at the infantile stage, when the infant's satisfaction in ingesting its mother's milk is supplemented by a pleasure in sucking the mother's breast. These principles of *Anlehnung* and *Nebenwirkung* compose Freud's recurrent report of the genesis of sexuality. [24]

Like Freud, Oedipus solves the riddle of human being by identifying its distinctively temporal structure: his answer is man, who moves on four limbs as an infant, on two feet in his prime, and with the aid of a staff in old age—and whose dilemma is compounded, we might add, by his provision with a "single voice," which cannot adequately express the overlapping discontinuous phases of his metamorphosis. Oedipus answers "man"; he does not answer "man, I myself"; yet Oedipus himself is the prime example of the bizarre being described by the Sphinx, precisely in the senseless numbering and collapsed syntax of the riddle's opening sentence. Through the very act of reading the riddle, Oedipus will become the one man who exemplifies the

Sphinx's challenge not merely in the form of its answer but in its form as riddle. For Oedipus's parrincest (half finished even as he makes his reply to the Sphinx) makes him at once a husband ("with two feet") of his mother, a child among his children ("and four feet"), and the father of his father ("that has three feet as well"). Sophocles dramatizes the riddle by representing Oedipus as king, as exposed child, and as blind old man all in the single scene of the tragedy. Parrincest is a catastrophic convergence and crossing of life-lines—the unspeakable event "at the place where three roads meet," and an unreadable palimpsest, the text that cannot be read out with a "single voice."

The restriction of "voice" affects Oedipus's answer to the Sphinx, and we can trace a similar effect in Freud's answer to the riddle of dreams. Freud recurrently neglects to implicate his own theory in his account of the reductive or recuperative rationalization that he finds to be characteristic both of the reporting of dreams and of the elaboration of systematic thought. In *The Interpretation of Dreams* Freud calls this rationalization "secondary revision," the activity by which the dream's patent absurdities are viewed from the standpoint of the ego and made to seem to conform to some kind of rational expectation. In *Totem and Taboo* Freud defines systematic thought in general as a type of "secondary revision." Yet he continues to claim for psychoanalytic theory the power to distinguish between the primary and the secondary, or the riddles and the answer, without being subject to the recuperative revision it ascribes to all theorizing. This tendency to ignore the implications of the critique of theory for his own emerging theories can be noticed throughout Freud's works, from the *Project for a Scientific Psychology* (1895) to *Negation* (1925).

At other moments, however, and particularly where he addresses the question of literature, as in his generalizing reading of *Oedipus,* Freud insists that no position exists—including that of psychoanalysis—immune to the distortions of secondary revision involved in all writing, no position from which writing or revision could be judged with disinterested final accuracy.[25] The theory of transference, too, as reread by Lacan,[26] situates both the power and the danger of psychoanalysis in the determinate resemblance between analyst and analysand, interpretation and symptom. It initially takes form as a mirror-image relation like that of Oedipus to Oedipus in the Sophoclean plot Freud compares to "the work of a psychoanalysis."

There is also another dimension of Freud's texts that converges with the critique of clear thinking, passages that insist on a kind of theoretical obscurity, and that formulate peculiarly elusive riddles.

Thus, in the final chapter of the *Traumdeutung* (in the section entitled "The Forgetting of Dreams"):

> Even in the best interpreted dreams, there is often a place [*eine Stelle*] that must be left in the dark, because in the process of interpreting, one notices a tangle of dream-thoughts arising [*anhebt*], which resists unravelling but has also made no further contributions [*keine weitern Beiträge*] to the dream-content. This is then the dream's navel, the place where it straddles the unknown [*dem Unerkannten aufsitzt*]. The dream-thoughts, to which interpretation leads one, are necessarily interminable [*ohne Abschluss*] and branch out on all sides into the netlike entanglement [*in die netzartige Verstrickung*] of our world of thought. Out of one of the denser places of this meshwork, the dream-wish rises [*erhebt sich*] like a mushroom out of its mycelium. [27]

Samuel Weber, reading this passage in the course of remarks on Freud's *Witz*, calls attention to the riddle it evokes. Freud's text describes the "dream-navel" as like a "mycelium," which the dictionary defines as "part of the thallus of fungi"—leading the reader on to the definition of *thallus:* "*Thallus* . . . Bot. A vegetable structure without vascular tissue, in which there is no differentiation into stem and leaves, and from which true roots are absent." [28] The riddle of Freud's riddle is that there exists a thing that is without tissue, without differentiation, and without roots. We might be tempted simply to unriddle this as the concept of the unconscious, which also, by definition, is definable only as what it is not. What should be remarked here, however, is not any supposed *ramifications* of the concept, but the resurgence of the thing itself in Freud's text. In its very unreadability, in passages like the one above, Freud's writing generates itself as the thing evoked in the riddle of the dream—or in the riddle of the Sphinx. For if the Oedipus of legend is the one who *is* the very riddle, not just its answer, whose parrincest crisscrosses the numbered phases of existence, so the text of Freud is also the very dream-text that is his riddle, and not just its interpretation. Freud's dream-book is a dream-text and palimpsest, in which the unreadable "primary" text of "primary process" is written under and over the systematic "secondary revision." This writing is the discourse of the Sphinx, as well as the human response.

The effect of the text, whether as Sphinx or as hero, can only be constituted by a third dimension, by the presence of witnesses—of readers. In Freud's case, the fact of his writing is precisely that third dimension. The psychoanalytic project came into being with the writing that Freud carried on in supplement to his ongoing clinical practice, writings that supplemented the relationship between analyst and analysand by an invocation of readers. We too readily take Freud's writing for granted and forget that it had to be carried on in addition to a practice that generally occupied nine hours a day; that it *was* carried on makes psychoanalysis, from the start, a triangular complex relating an analyst, a subject, and a text with its readers. *The Interpretation of Dreams,* for example, viewed as a self-analysis, is composed as a triangle made up by the analysing subject ("Freud"), the analysed subject ("Freud"), and the text within which the analysis takes place, the text of Freud. Freud's text constitutes the meaning of the analysis by letting it be read—and misread, as readers repeat the Oedipal gesture of appropriating the textual network for an overdetermined signification. Its definitive and continuous dependency on writing makes psychoanalysis what a certain popular view and a certain scientific perspective have long held it to be, a joke. It is a joke, that is, as rigorously defined in Freud's *Jokes and Their Relation to the Unconscious,* which describes how sexual jokes or "dirty jokes," in particular, are constituted as jokes—as funny—by the laughter of a third person, not the teller, nor the one on whom the joke is told, but the one to whom it is told, whose laughter alone makes the joke telling. That laughter cannot be controlled or explained, neither by the one who does the laughing, the third person, nor by the first, who does the telling.[29] Like the *fantômes* of parental fantasies that fix the nuclear oedipal triangle in a network of endless interlocking triangles, the laughter of the listener or reader sets the scene of psychoanalysis in the context of an endlessly-to-be-repeated joke.

We could also put it another way: as writing, and reading, psychoanalysis is an endlessly recited tragedy. For it is generated, as joke or tragedy, by the aspiration to a cure, whether conceived as resembling laughter or a catharsis of pity and fear. The structure of *Oedipus Tyrannus* is instructive here, in suggesting how writing is written into the psychoanalytic encounter itself, as "analysis terminable and interminable"—how it constitutes the scenario of cure, or of interminable interpretation. Thus the tragedy of *Oedipus* consisted in a dramatization, for an audience of Athenians, of a dramatization on the stage, for a Chorus of fictive Thebans, of the drama of Oedipus's discovery of his role in the drama of the Phocal crime. An audience, an effect of witnesses, is built into the drama in the form of the tragic Chorus, which with Sophocles' addition of secondary characters (the High Priest, then Tiresias, then Creon, then Jocasta) takes the position of a third person ("we know that it was Sophocles who introduced the third character," notes André Green).[30] This third person is an audience up on the stage, radically implicated in Oedipus's interpretations, and unable to predict or withhold its responses of fear, pity, laughter, or revulsion. It is like the third position constituted between and within the analyst and the analysand, a writing that is not just the record of their exchange, but a primary text generated as the unconscious significations of the discourse they together produce. The text that requires a reader, and the reader collapsed in laughter or dread is written into Freud's practice of psychoanalysis, as well as written out in the tomes of texts where analysis accumulated a history.

One way in which the Freudian text exceeds systematization is particularly Oedipal, in the Sophoclean sense that focuses on Oedipus's interpretive confession. We have discussed this previously as a gesture of appropriation, like Oedipus's assumption of guilt for the Phocal crime through an appropriation of the meaning of converging oracular texts. Similarly, it was suggested, Freud conceives the Oedipus complex through an appropriation of the text of Sophocles. We ought to note, again, that this gesture is more, or less, than an assumption of mastery, an appropriation in the active sense. Sophocles' text, rather, might be seen to appropriate Freud's, by means specifically of the dramatic or the "literary," figurative language that his text incorporates. For example: "Like Oedipus, we live in ignorance of these wishes, repugnant to morality, which have been forced upon us by Nature, and after their revelation we may all of us well seek to close our eyes [den Blick abwenden] to the scenes of our childhood" [ID p. 297]. We noted before the radical critique of his own invention implicit in Freud's comparison between the plot that ends with Oedipus's self-blinding and "the work of a psychoanalysis." In this passage, that ending becomes Freud's focus. The peculiar effect of the sentence lies in its tone of resigned, slightly sententious moralizing, and the all but effaced concluding figure that suddenly springs into relief and confronts us with the figure of Oedipus raining down tears of blood. The lag or deferral of our response, which supplements its intensity by surprise, results from a shifting in levels of discourse: first, between the first and second parts of the sentence, a shift from "literal" to "figurative"; and then a last startling reversion as we recognize the shift back to the literal—and literary—register of the final figure. The Freudian sentence is structured like the case history of "Emma" or the plot of Oedipus; two phases, linked associatively but differentiated by their inscription in two different orders of meaning ("literal" and "figurative,"

pretextual and textual, pre-oedipal and oedipal, scientific and literary).
The slight shock administered to the reader is produced in the same
way as the enduring trauma of the repressed subject.

This observation is not intended to propose a stylistic study of
Freud (our description of the sentence is obviously predetermined by
a preexisting interpretation), nor to suggest that trauma can be trivialized to something on the scale of a reader's fleeting thrill at a metaphor.
The history of psychoanalysis since that sentence was written suggests,
however, that precisely the experience of reading Freud's text (such
sentences as the above) provoked a trauma and produced a repression
on a larger scale. Most of the institutions of psychoanalytic thought
could be characterized in terms of their various ways of forgetting
Freud's sentence, of their "total evacuation" from the Freudian text.
One such case is that of the traditional analyst who represses awareness
that the text sentences him as well as his analysand (*"möchten wir
wohl alle"*) to a career like that of Oedipus.

A special case is that of René Girard, who professes not to see that
in his description of an originary scenario of sexual genesis Freud
writes a theory of mimetic desire more far-reaching than Girard's
universal history can accommodate. Recurrent in analytic thinking is a
symptomatic suppression of the figure of Oedipus—of figure, and of
Oedipus—inscribed in Freud's writing. This endemic form of repression represses the text in the text, the representation of mimesis, or
what we call literature. This is *also* a repression of the Oedipus complex: for it arises in resistance to the marginal logic that makes Oedipus
the unique monster into Oedipus the exemplary case, and the Oedipal
model for normal sexual maturation into an Oedipal model for excep-
tional poetic maturation (in the writing of Harold Bloom, for example).
We might make *Oedipal* become a name for a principle by which the
exception takes the rule along with it—as in Laplanche's account of
Freud's description of sex acts (where perversion comes to characterize sexuality as such, as a deviation from need and function to drive
and "organ pleasure");[31] and as in Derrida's rendition of Austin's theory
of speech acts (where the possibility of a misfire sparks the conception of normative success); and, more generally, as in other poststruc-
turalist accounts of language, where theories of literature based on
seeing it as a special restricted language have given way to investigations
of language exploring the notion that language is a special case of a
more generally conceived textuality. The most famous case is Derrida's
Of Grammatology, an inversion of *parole* and *écriture* that reconstrues
language as various derivative forms of writing.

The symptomatic suppression of the supplementary principle can

be maintained with equal security by psychoanalytic critics of
ture and by a theorist like Girard, who chastises Freud for failing
Totem and Taboo, to keep to a "sense of the *function* of the rit
and concedes, "nevertheless, Freud made an important discovery. F
was the first to maintain that all ritual practices, all mythical implications, have their scope in an actual murder."[32] To produce this certainty of the facts from the conclusion of *Totem and Taboo* that
Girard acclaims, the theorist requires a measurable effort of repression:
the symptom, precisely, of not reading: "Neurotics are above all *in-
hibited* in their actions: with them the thought is a complete substitute
for the deed. Primitive men, on the other hand, are *uninhibited:*
thought passes directly into action. With them it is rather the deed that
is a substitute for the thought. And that is why, without laying any
claim to finality of judgment, I think that in the case before us it may
safely be assumed that 'in the beginning was the Deed.' "[33] In the fin-
ishing phrase of his final conclusion as to the reality of a primal fact,
Freud invokes a prior text. The conclusion of the scientific inquiry
comes in quotes. We witness here Freud's chronically oedipal textuality:
like his model, to account for ancient murder Freud calls upon another
authority's oracular word. That word is itself a deliberate revision of a
primary text: Goethe's Faust, of course, is misquoting the beginning of
the Gospel of St. John, "In the beginning was the Word." If "the Word"
is in the text behind the text in his text, how can we take Freud at his
word? He withholds it, performing instead the deed of literary quotation. At this crucial juncture the Freudian text gives us not the facts
but the literature. What might seem to be a gesture of closure, or appropriation, opens the passage to a textuality that overrides Freud's
tendency to control his textual drive.[34]

The time lag that dooms sexual ideas to repression also affects the
ideas we have of texts. Reading, like sexual development, is a discontinuous temporal process in which the subject's awareness lags behind
her or his ever-shifting enmeshment with a preexistent order of meaning, and not only because of the multiple significations of individual
elements of discourse (such as the divergence between literal and figurative senses, and more complex kinds of rhetorical difference). The
process must begin as misreading and go on to rereading, and to a rewriting in which the reader becomes legible. Like the Freudian subject's reading of sex, the analytic reader's writing on texts enforces
and appropriates coincidences, collapsing the difference between disparate textual scenes. In this reading of Freud's reading of *Oedipus,* for
example, not only have we compressed the different stories within each
text, but we have stressed the relation of consistency and complicity

en Freud's text and Sophocles' rather than a radically illegible
ntinuity between them (which could be seen to be equally insis-
t). That illegible difference might be written (though not here) as
e distinctively textual phenomenon, a trauma of unreadability, sited
in a neither-nor between two almost incomparable texts. In differentiating such an option from our own writing strategy here, we assume
(in every sense) the limp or lag that psychoanalysis, like Sophocles,
ascribes to the exemplary subject.

Reading must culminate in a rewriting that cannot fail to be
symptomatic. Oedipus is engaged in this dilemma when he encounters
the unreadable structure of meanings produced by the Pythia, who tells
him, in effect, that his knowledge will catch up with him [l. 788 ff. "I
went to Pytho"]. It does—not (*in der Tat*) in the event, but only when
Oedipus rereads her pronouncement in conjunction with another oracle
and other histories of his case. Pythian prophecy may be saliently
characterized as a type of writing, for the tradition describes the Pythia
as a frenzied priestess who would cite Apollo and be quoted, by a
priest, to the waiting supplicant. Like writing, then, Pythian prophecy
is mediated—and female and probably mad, also like writing (when
opposed to speech) in the scheme that dominates culture. Psychoanalysis differed with this scheme from the start, when Freud's theory of
seduction as a *proton pseudos,* or primary deceit inscribed in the facts,
positioned his writing "beyond the banalities of official 'clinical' practice, which regularly invoked bad faith and simulation to account for
what it called 'pithiatism,'" the lying of hysterics.[35] Freud's temporal
scheme of sexual repression enabled him to unriddle these lies as the
productions neither of bad faith nor of error, but as the expressions of
victims of a fundamental duplicity grounded in the historicity of desire. Here too the Freudian perspective involves a Sophoclean insight,
for as the finest scholarly reader of Oedipus remarks, the one issue that
is not brought up in the tragedy is the question, Where does the blame
lie? "The battle is not in this case between truth and error. For when
one speaks of 'error' one does not mean an inevitable failure such as
we have here, a flaw not of mind but of the whole human condition,
both internal and external."[36] Oedipus at Colonnus dismisses his guilt
for his blindness and his limp [ll. 213-88].

Freud ends *Beyond the Pleasure Principle* in the same way. The
argument of that work, he is aware, more than usually succumbs to the
deferrals and differences that mark his text. In a gesture like that
which terminates *Totem and Taboo,* Freud ends by reciting a quotation: "We may take comfort, too, for the slow advances of our scientific
knowledge in the words of the poet:

Was man nicht erfliegen kann, muss man erhinken.

. . . .

Die Schrift sagt, es ist keine Sünde zu hinken."

What one cannot reach flying one must reach limping.

. . . .

The Scripture says it is no sin to limp.[37]

Paragon, Parergon

Baudelaire Translates Rousseau

Why does Baudelaire write "Morale du joujou"? Why set under a moral heading the essay from which he will detach the prose poem *Le joujou du pauvre*? Why not give it a title like "De l'essence du jeu," like "De l'essence du rire"?[1]

The essay's heading signals a recapitulation: Baudelaire's meditation on *la morale du joujou* repeats Rousseau's revery about the moral pleasure of offering gifts to children, the ninth of the *Rêveries du promeneur solitaire*. *Le joujou du pauvre* is first celebrated in the *Neuvième Promenade*. When Baudelaire repeats himself, he also repeats Rousseau: the prose poem he draws from the essay begins by recapitulating Rousseau's claim for the moral quality of a certain pleasure. "Je veux donner l'idée d'un divertissement innocent. Il y a si peu d'amusements qui ne soient pas coupables!"[2] In addition to this reference to the moral status of "diversion," Baudelaire's prose takes from Rousseau's revery its most peculiar motif: the edible toy. The toy as food figures decisively in the *Neuvième Promenade,* for Rousseau's *rêverie* consists largely in confuting the imagined charge that he is a *père dénaturé* by dwelling on his memories of offering gifts to children, gifts invariably edible: apples, rolls, cone-shaped wafers. Rousseau remembers other people's children receiving *pains de Nanterre* and *oublies;* Baudelaire pictures catlike children grinning together at the poor child's toy, a live rat. Baudelaire's text, and Rousseau's revery, could be titled not "A Child is Being Beaten" (Freud's title for a fantasy turned moral, made reflexive), but "A Child is Being Given a Toy to Eat."

How should we describe the way in which Baudelaire repeats Rousseau in "Morale du joujou"? This essay does not simply recapitulate the themes of the *Neuvième Promenade* or reinterpret Rousseau's revery. It repeats an angle, the moral angle, and a strange piece of ĸ̣. terial, the edible gift; the angle of the frame, and the *morceau-cadeaɩ* are transported into another context. To put it emphatically, they are translated. To say that Baudelaire translates Rousseau is not to say that he reads and understands him. "For translation," as de Man writes, interpreting Walter Benjamin's choice of *Übersetzung* rather than reception or reading as the proper analogon for the "understand-ing" of a literary work, "translation is per definition intra-linguistic, not a relation between a subject and an object, . . . but between one linguistic function and another."[3] Baudelaire's writing does some-thing other and more than reading: it reinscribes Rousseau's words in the language of Baudelaire's text: it does not reinterpret them but re-peats them, with a difference. We must think of these texts as written not just in a language (French) but also, each of them, in a language of its own, as every dream (every revery) is a text to decipher not through recourse to a universal language of dream symbols but by recreating the specific contingent associations that make up the unique language of a single dream.

One word in particular in "Morale du joujou" is best identified as a translation of a certain word in the *Neuvième Promenade*. I should like to make the claim in those terms, and so I shall make use—shall hazard an abuse—of Philip Lewis's directions "vers la traduction abusive."[4] Lewis invokes the strategy of a rigorously abusive transla-tion, which would counter what is lost in the translation with an addition, a supplement. The translator commits an excess, performs an abuse—but not just anywhere. "The abusive move in the translation cannot be directed at just any element of the original; rather, it will bear upon a key operator or decisive textual knot that will be recog-nized by dint of its own abusive features. . . . The abusive work of translation will be oriented by specific nubs in the original, by points or passages that are in some sense forced."[5] Baudelaire's repetition of Rousseau is oriented like such an abusive translation. I shall focus on a word in Baudelaire's essay that reenacts a moment of excess or abuse in Rousseau's text—a word that rigorously if abusively *translates* a word in the *Neuvième Promenade*.

The eighth paragraph of "Morale du joujou" draws a contrast be-tween slavish and imaginative imitation, or imitative and imaginative play. In the exclamation that divides the paragraph, Baudelaire cele-brates the spontaneous creative power that children manifest in what is most genuinely play, not mimicry. But the name here for such play is also the name for devotion to work. The sentence makes sense in its immediate context only when we understand "l'éternel drame de la

..gence" to refer, not to a drama of diligence, but to the recurrently ..thralling stagecoach game played by imaginative children. Diligence, ..owever, is named in the same breath. *La diligence* is what Michael Riffaterre in *Semiotics of Poetry* calls a "dual sign"—"an equivocal word situated at the point where two sequences of semantic or formal associations intersect."[6] One set of associations comes from the sign's immediate context, its syntactical position. The other set of associations comes from a wider context, from themes active in the text as a whole, or, as Riffaterre puts it, from "another text" in the text. In the dual sign, a semiotic text located at the level of paradigms intrudes upon a mimetic text located at the level of syntax. But in this case, I would claim, the "semiotic text" within "Morale du joujou" is not the only other text to intrude upon the syntax of Baudelaire's paragraph. The other "other text" that intrudes is another dual sign that *diligence* translates. The "syntactical ungrammaticality" of Baudelaire's dual sign functions as a rigorously abusive translation of another such abuse in another text, Rousseau's *Neuvième Promenade*.

The abuse that occurs in the *Neuvième Promenade* is the defacement of a word's most resonant meaning. The word is *oublie*, which means waffle or wafer: cylindrical or cone-shaped wafers that could be gotten by buying chances from a vendor equipped with a sort of numbered wheel or turntable. These wafers figure as one of various fragile edible souvenirs of an encounter with Rousseau (like the apples bought for the little Savoyards in another episode recounted in the *Promenade*). Rousseau recalls presiding over the distribution of such oublies to a class of schoolgirls at the edge of the Bois de Boulogne.[7] That occasion, he tells us, is one of his fondest memories. Rousseau tells us he is remembering—and tells us of engaging an *oublieur*. Like *diligence*, *oublie* is a dual sign with directly opposite sets of associations. Baudelaire celebrates play and writes a word that suggests work. Rousseau celebrates a memory and writes a word that sounds like forgetting. The reader is forced to forget the meaning of the word's sound in order to follow its function in the syntax of the anecdote. What the reader is forced to forget is forgetting. At the same time the dual sign forces forgetting on the reader: *e* or no *e, oubli(e)* forces forgetting down our throat. Baudelaire's dual sign, too, forces forgetting on the reader. *Diligence* translates *oublie:* the translation's rigor lies in its reenactment of Rousseau's imposition on the reader. Rousseau's wording forces something down, and Baudelaire's reading forces that out. Baudelaire's *diligence*, like Rousseau's *oublie*, designates a thing—a game, a toy—with a word that also names an abstraction, a concept, and a concept *opposed* to the pleasure the same word designates.

Why is it *this* moment in the *Neuvième Promenade* that "Morale du joujou" repeats? Why does Baudelaire translate, and why this word? Baudelaire's dual sign repeating Rousseau's requires us to analyze the peculiarly inassimilable or compelling quality of oublies.

The prominence of oublies in a passage about a memory calls attention to the word's etymology and permits an archaeology of the sign. *Oublie* is a word whose meaning in the so-called semiotic text located at the level of themes or paradigms *names* the effacement, or oubli, of the etymology of its meaning in the mimetic text located at the level of syntax. For *oublie* derives from *oblata,* the Latin word for the consecrated host, the wafer consumed *in memory* of the sacrifice of the Word made Flesh. The forgetting of the "origin" of *oublie* — its etymology, its figural status, commemorating the disfiguration of "Flesh" fixed on a cross—leaves waffles, edible souvenirs to be consumed forgetfully. Thus the dual sign *oublie* at once reveals and defaces the effaced disfiguration that produces literal language, language that can be taken into the mouth without a special act of remembering. The etymology of *oublie* recapitulates the account in Rousseau's *Essai sur l'origine des langues,* where the postulate "Que le premier language dut être figuré" is illustrated in a parable tracing the origin of the word *homme* from a forgetting of a figure for fear (initially the word *géant*).[8] Compacted in *oublies* is Rousseau's history of language as disfiguration. Such a sign might well prove indigestible.

The rest of Rousseau's *rêverie* may be absorbed, diffused, by Baudelaire's essay; only the toy food and dual sign comes up as if he cannot keep it down. Rousseau's oublies may be hard to keep down because of the way he distributes them. The game of getting a wafer—buying a chance, watching the vendor spin his wheel—becomes part of a business of ensuring equal desserts. The little girls are made to line up, take turns, share, and plead their differences at what Rousseau gaily calls his *tribunal de justice.* Taking pleasure in giving pleasure takes the form, here, of meting out justice. A kind of game gets an ethical framework; playing is bound up with ethical scheming.

Rousseau cites the scene with the *oublieur* as the kind of thing that induces the *contentement* he is concerned to analyze in the rest of this text. Contentment is a crucial category in the *Neuvième Promenade.* Rousseau distinguishes it from a more fleeting and less readable condition he calls *bonheur* and identifies it, explicitly, with reading: "le contentement se lit dans les yeux."[9]

Rousseau goes on to identify contentment as the condition inspired in him by the visible signs of other people's contentment. He makes two claims for this condition. It is, he insists, a physical pleasure in visible signs, a *plaisir de sensation*. But he also insists that it has a *cause morale;* he has to know that the signs he reads signify other people's contentment in others' contentment, not in their suffering: "Quoique ce ne soit là qu'un plaisir de sensation, il a certainement une cause morale et la preuve en est que ce même aspect, au lieu de me flater, de me plaire peut me déchirer de douleur et d'indignation quand je sais que ces signes de douleur et de joye sur les visages des méchans ne sont que des marques que leur malignité est satisfaite."[10]

Rousseau thus locates contentment in the two modes of activity that are excluded from aesthetic pleasure by Kant: enjoyment of sensation, and moral reflection. Since *contentement* designates the activity of reading signs, Rousseau situates *reading* remote by definition from aesthetic activity or aesthetic pleasure.

That implication is one that the reader of literature must find it virtually impossible to assimilate, for both the practice of reading and the theory of literature need to invoke the realm of aesthetics to articulate the continuity between signifying procedures and significance, between poetics and hermeneutics. However, Rousseau insists: insists that he feels good when he feels *good*. This is as much as to insist that we do the same: the enjoyment is urged on us with the claim that it is caused by the signs' moral significance, and the moral interpretation is urged on us with the claim that it is a source of pleasure. We feel *forced* to enjoy.

Kant's comments on this special effect in paragraph 48 of the Third Critique, "Of the Relation of Genius to Taste":

> Denn, weil in dieser sonderbaren, auf lauter Einbildung beruhenden Empfindung der Gegenstand gleichsam, als ob er sich zum Genusse *aufdränge,* wider den wir doch mit Gewalt streben, vorgestellt wird: so wird die künstliche Vorstellung des Gegenstandes von der Natur dieses Gegenstandes selbst in unserer Empfindung nicht mehr unterschieden, und jene kann alsdann unmöglich für schön gehalten werden.[11]

> [For in this peculiar sensation, which rests on mere imagination, the object is represented as it were obtruding itself for our enjoyment while we strive against it. . . . And the artistic representation is no longer distinguished from the nature of the object itself in our sensation, and thus it is impossible that it can be regarded as beautiful.][12]

Certainly Rousseau's contentment cannot be regarded as beautiful; but it is precisely not a matter of taste. Rousseau demands not that one exercise taste but that one take something in. He exacts an act of reading

about the activity of reading signs. Rousseau situates that activity ⌐
the two instances that Kant excludes from the aesthetic, and he
forces them together and insists on their coincidence. He urges his
reader to swallow the notion of *moral gratification.*

A notion that would force one to enjoy in this way exceeds the
limits of taste to produce the "peculiar sensation" analyzed by Kant
and identified as (not distaste but) disgust. *Ekel:* the word is Kant's
for that "peculiar sensation" excited by what cannot become an object of aesthetic judgment. Here Derrida intervenes. "Il faut s'assurer
que le mot *dégout* (*Ekel*) ne désigne pas le répugnant ou le négatif en
général. Il s'agit bien de ce qui donne *envie de vomir*" ("One must be
assured that the word *disgust* [*Ekel*] does not designate the repugnant
or the negative in general. It is indeed a matter of that which makes
one *want to vomit*").[13] Forced to swallow Rousseau's moral gratification, forced to enjoy his contentment, a person wants, then, rigorously
speaking, to throw up. As Baudelaire does: he throws up Rousseau's
plaisirs, Rousseau's *oublies,* as a recognizably similar sign—*la diligence.*

But why throw up Rousseau's *oublies* rather than some other item
on the menu of moral gratification? The reasons must lie in the context of that peculiar word, in the dimensions of that dual sign, *oubli(e).*
The more insistent *aural* sense of *oubli* comes into the sentences that
describe Rousseau's gratification at seeing the schoolgirls take pleasure
in their equal desserts. "La gentillesse de quelques-unes," remarks
Rousseau, "faisait oublier leur laideur."[14] I was not gloating over pretty
little girls, he tells us. But the sentence says something else. It cites
forgetting as the connection between a moral quality and an aesthetic
one. Response to a moral quality *precludes* response to an aesthetic
one; they are separated by a moment of forgetfulness, of *oubli.* Kant
sets the same terms in a similar relation. We recall the so-called "First
Moment of the Judgement of Taste": "the satisfaction which deter-
mines the judgement of taste is disinterested," whereas "the satisfaction in the good is bound up with interest." Hence a pure judgment of
taste involves a momentary forgetting of the moral qualities of the
object. Rousseau claims, instead, a momentary forgetting of the object's aesthetic inadequacy, thanks to its moral qualities. Rousseau's
formulation calls attention to what he does not claim: disinterested
aesthetic pleasure, pleasure without interest. Forget that, the sentence
says; forget the forgetting entailed in making a judgment of taste: *this*
oubli forgets and forgoes that forgetting. In the situation Rousseau
imposes on us, the condition of the possibility of beauty, the condition of aesthetic judgment, must be gone without.

What does Rousseau forgo forgetting? The *purpose* of the scene he

ontemplates, the *end* of the process he presides over: just enjoyment
of equal desserts. The *Neuvième Promenade* is a revery about the kind
of satisfaction available to man in the contemplation of man ("a man,
a woman, or a child," says Kant; or a schoolgirl, says Rousseau): sole
object, says Kant, to have an unforgettable end in itself, a purpose:
humanity. (Man alone can be the subject of a work of "ideal" beauty,
which is not "free" beauty, constituted by aesthetic detachment, by a
forgetting of one's interest in the subject represented, but rather a
gratification of our "Reason's" interest, our ethical interest in the subject. So Kant writes in par. 17 of the Third Critique, "Of the Ideal of
Beauty.")[15] Thus the end is reached when the humanity of the oublies'
recipients emerges in such a way that the matter of their beauty is put
in brackets. What is put in brackets, then, is a certain bracketing. For
beauty, free beauty, has this condition: that the purpose of the object
be bracketed, be momentarily forgotten. The condition of beauty is
purposiveness without purpose. The condition of Rousseau's contentment is purposiveness *without* the condition of being without purpose.

What "contents" Rousseau is an inversion, or negation, of purposiveness without purpose: not the contemplation of purpose, but
the *suspension* of purposiveness without purpose. This is not simply
because his object is the paragon, man, who has his purpose of his
existence in himself, who therefore is alone capable of ideal beauty—
and *not* capable of free beauty, not allowing the forgetfulness of its
purpose that allows an object to be freely beautiful. It is, rather, because Rousseau formulates his contentment in terms that determine
it as the deprivation of an exclusion.

Furthermore, the very idea of the paragon turns out itself to be
determined in this way. For man, in his ideal beauty, turns out to be
determined by a framework around a frame, the frame that separates
the beautiful object from its purpose.

The integrity of Kant's critical system defining man's faculties
depends upon the faculty analyzed in the Third Critique: "Judgement, which in the order of our cognitive faculties forms a mediating
link between Understanding and Reason."[16] It turns out, furthermore,
that Judgment must be analyzed as aesthetic judgment, for it is "mainly
in those judgements that we call aesthetical, which concern the Beautiful and the Sublime," that it is possible to discover a cognitive process
that neither contributes to the knowledge of the object nor confuses
attendant feelings of pleasure or pain with the subject's will or motives
(with what Kant refers to as "the faculty of desire, which has its
principles a priori in concepts of reason").[17] Only aesthetic judgment,
that is, may be sufficiently distinguished from the workings of the

Understanding and the Reason to enable the identification of an independent faculty mediating between them.

The frame that separates the object from its purpose constitutes an object as aesthetic. From the "First Moment of the Judgement of Taste," aesthetic judgment is defined as a certain bracketing, as the posing of a frame, the frame that presents an object as a figure, separated from purpose and so susceptible of being judged freely beautiful. Aesthetic judgment, taste, is then examined, in the "Analytic of the Beautiful," according to quality, quantity, relation to purposes, and modality, a categorial frame imported from the analysis of concepts in the First Critique. Judgment of the freely beautiful thereby becomes subordinated, finally, to the conception of an ideal of beauty. In the Third Critique, then, as Derrida puts it, the question of the frame is framed. It is set within a critical framework that sets it up as the link between man's understanding and his reason, the link that establishes his special status. That status is established by framing the free beauty that can never be man's: by presenting it as a matter of a frame, as a question of a "without," as a purposiveness-without-purpose forever less *ideal* than ideal beauty. The special status of man depends on the framing—the frame-up—of a frame.[18] The "man" of Kant's Third Critique originates as does the word *man* analyzed in Rousseau's *Essai:* as an initial act of framing becomes obscured. What is a frame? It may be an ornament, or an essential support, or an accessory, or a frame-up. What is a parergon? It is, for instance, a frame, writes Kant, writes Derrida. (Derrida is reading Kant's par. 14, "Elucidation by Means of Examples"; see "Parergon," *La Vérité en peinture.*)[19] We may translate: the paragon is determined as the parergon of a parergon or the envelope of an hors d'oeuvre. In Derrida's rendering, the Third Critique mixes not only with Rousseau's *Essai* but also with his *Neuvième Promenade.*

The *Promenade* connects with the passage in which Kant affirms man's ability to conceive an ideal of beauty (par. 17). As Derrida translates it, the condition of beauty, in the Third Critique, is *finalité-sans-fin.* "C'est la finalité-sans-fin qui est *dite* belle." "It's purposiveness-without-purpose which is *said* to be beautiful. . . . It's the *without* that counts, then, for beauty, neither the purposiveness nor the purpose . . . , but the *without* of purposiveness without purpose."[20] "C'est donc le *sans* qui compte pour la beauté": the *sans,* not the *sens;* the "without," not the "sense"; not a sense to be enjoyed, not a sense to be understood, but rather a *sans,* a "without." Derrida's "*sans*" is a dual sign, resonant with the "meaning" it is "without." It translates the *ohne* of "Zweckmässigkeit ohne Zweck" in a way that displaces and reinscribes an abuse in the Kantian text, an abuse of the frame. "Ce *sans*-là, est-il traduisible?" And is it useable?—for instance, to translate what in Rousseau is translated by Baudelaire? The slide in the sense of "translation" here may be a matter for disgust. But sense itself is not without such sliding.

"It's the 'without' that counts, for beauty." Why then does *man* count so? "Il est seul capable d'un idéal de beauté. . . . Il [en] est capable . . . parce qu'il est doué de raison, ce qui veut dire, en langage kantien, apte à se fixer ses propres fins. [C'est le] Seul être dans la nature à se donner ses propres fins, à lever en lui le *sans*" ("He alone is capable of an ideal of beauty. He is capable [of it] because he is endowed with reason, which means, in Kantian terms, apt at determining his own ends. [He is] the only being in nature to give himself his own ends, to suspend in himself the 'without'").[21] Kant's paragon, in Derrida's "Parergon," is "the only being to *suspend* in himself the 'without'"—to do without being without. It's the additional "without" that counts for man's status as paragon.

That "without" is also the sum of Rousseau's contentment. For concurrent claims to take pleasure in a sensation and to exercise ethical judgment cancel each other, and by the end of the *Neuvième Promenade,* Rousseau is calling up moments of physical discomfort and moral confusion. But what, exactly, does he go without? Going in for reading, Rousseau goes without aesthetic judgment, without beauty, without purposiveness without purpose. Yet he claims not one but both of the two modes of experience that the aesthetic excludes, moral judgment and sensual pleasure, which cannot as such condition each other. The double claim cancels itself out; what remains? Going without being without has to be gone without, too. It turns out, reading Rousseau, that one cannot have freedom *from* aesthetic activity any more than one can have aesthetic activity, freedom from moral and sensual responses.

In the process of writing, *oubli(e)* has a tendency to become forgoing forgetting, and "being without" to become "doing without being without," and "without" to become "without without," or *sans* "*sans* sans." "Ils jouent," writes Baudelaire, "sans joujoux."[22] How did this reiteration of negative syllables ever begin? Rousseau tells a story of how it began with a promise, his promise to the *oublieur.* "Faites tirer . . . et je vous paierai le tout."[23] He says that he will pay for the oublies; not that he will eat them. He guarantees vicarious consumption of oubli(es). Rousseau makes promises; but it is Baudelaire who eats Rousseau's words.

They cannot be kept down, they have to be thrown up. That

proliferating sign, that sliding *sans,* disgusts us and eludes our comprehension; it makes one want to throw up. "Comment avoir *envie* de vomir?" presses Derrida. How could someone *want* to throw up? One wants to throw up to reverse the process, to draw the line, and "mettre la chose à la bouche." [24] So Baudelaire throws up—*la diligence.*

A dual sign, like *oublie, diligence* requires the reader to reread. Even as it designates a supremely autonomous kind of play, it names a quality valuable for purposeful work. Baudelaire's dual sign engages us in construing the relevance of diligence in this ostensible celebration of play. We reread to create a context in which, to use Riffaterre's words, "the dual sign's second (or syntactically unacceptable) semantic allegiance can be *vindicated.*" [25] *La diligence* engages us in understanding that a name for a game, for a particular kind of play, also inscribes a conceptual framework that valorizes purposeful activity. Kant's "Critique of the Aesthetical Judgement" engages us along the same lines. Taste is conceived as a connection between man's purposeful activity (understanding as a means of knowledge) and his purpose (his reason). In inviting us to imagine a similar situation to warrant the senses of his dual sign, Baudelaire's inscription of *la diligence* would be truly Kantian. We are induced to conceive a framework that vindicates the sense of diligence; we are lured into complicity with a complicity between purposefulness and play.

Or are we lured into drawing a line between them? We are made to feel that the two senses of *la diligence* conflict; that in the immediate mimetic context the word means play free of purpose, whereas in the vaster semiotic context it means almost the reverse: commitment to purposeful activity. One meaning of the word points to something done without a purpose (the stagecoach game). Another meaning points to something done with a purpose (with diligence). The sharp opposition between the two senses of *la diligence* would seem to reinstall, then, the distinction eroded by the sense of *oublie*—to reestablish the difference between forgoing playfulness and forgetting purposefulness. For Rousseau's "doing without being without" (or going without doing without being without), Baudelaire substitutes either doing without or else doing with a purpose.

Except how are we made to draw the line, to think that either/or? We are made to construe the framework in which *diligence* as diligence makes sense, in which the line is drawn between work and play, by bracketing, momentarily, the first appropriate sense. To make sense of the other sense, we have to do without the stagecoach game. We have to do without that play without purpose to get at the opposition between purposeful work and purposeless play. To draw the line, we have to do without the sense of doing without. Drawing the line, then, is a matter of adding *another* "without" to distinguish from "with" a "without" that was already there. Baudelaire reenacts the proliferation of *sans* of Rousseau's text in the very line he draws against it.

So it will come up again; it cannot be thrown up once and for all. It comes up again when Baudelaire introduces a distinction between his prose poem and his prose *prose,* where he substitutes one group of words for another in rewriting two paragraphs of "Morale du joujou" as the prose poem *Le joujou du pauvre.* The prose poem follows the essay almost word for word except at one point. Where the essay describes the poor child as "one of those urchins who," and so forth, the prose poem introduces an analogy. Baudelaire compares the eye it takes to discover the child's beauty beneath the "patina of miserable poverty" with the eye it takes to divine "une peinture idéale sous un vernis de carrossier": an ideally beautiful painting obscured by coachmaker's varnish. Cheap varnish is the idea. But "coachmaker" points back to the stagecoach name, *carrossier,* to *diligence.* When Baudelaire rewrites his prose as prose poem, one of the words he writes recalls the word with which he translates Rousseau. *Carrossier* points back to *diligence,* and *diligence* translates *oublie:* where Baudelaire rewrites, he reinscribes a translation of Rousseau.

So the oublie comes up again, not just as the toy food, the *cadeau-morceau* contemplated by the catlike children, but in the words that name the film that can fill the frame of the ideal painting. "Vernis de carrossier"; *vernis de diligence?* We sense a frame in that reference to "une peinture idéale sous un vernis de carrossier." Isn't the film of varnish a sort of frame effect, a sign of an excessive diligence in desiring that the painting be thoroughly framed? Baudelaire's image tempts us to take it as a reading of Kant and Rousseau.

To read is to make the sign come to rest in a meaning, to let it be understood. In Baudelaire's text something else is under way. The word *carrossier*—pointing to *diligence*—marks this moment of rewriting as a repetition not of reading but of translation, Baudelaire's translation of Rousseau's *oublie. Carrossier* repeats and remarks that gesture replacing one signifier-and-signified with another, one sign with another whose *relations* must be homologous. What does the rewritten version repeat or replace? It replaces Baudelaire's essay with a prose poem— making the essay prose prose (another sort of "without without"). It also replaces a passage in the essay that describes a function that could be regarded as not unlike the way in which Baudelaire repeats Rousseau. This passage describes not vomiting but snot. Where the prose poem describes the child's patina of poverty analogically, the essay describes it literally: the child is "one of those urchins upon whom *snot* slowly makes a pathway in the dirt and dust" ("un de ces marmots sur lesquels *la morve se fraye lentement un chemin* dans la crasse et la poussière").[26]

We would hesitate, perhaps, to say that this is a moment of disgust. Baudelaire describes a snotty urchin. Something other than disgust, other, in other words, than the desire to throw up, makes this passage represent the way Baudelaire repeats Rousseau. The passage draws a line between negligibly different elements, marking the trace of "la morve . . . dans la crasse et la poussière" and locating the snotty child "sur la route, entre les chardons et les orties" ("between the thistles and the nettles"). This drawing of lines between minimally different conditions characterizes the process by which Baudelaire translates Rousseau: a process of distinguishing *doing* without from doing *without* being without; of distinguishing one *sans,* and one *oubli(e),* from another. But the sense of this image of snot making a line is that the line itself is one of those slippery *sans.* Instead of drawing a line against what disgusts, Baudelaire's repetition of his process of translation draws a slightly disgusting line.

Rousseau's *oublie* does not just come up again as *diligence; diligence* glides into "vernis de carrossier," and "vernis de diligence" slides into *morve. La morve* would seem to be a variant of *le vomi,* that is, of what Baudelaire throws up in the process of drawing a line between his text and Rousseau's. But snot can't be thrown up. It oozes down. Not just snot, perhaps, but its variants. What we sense in Baudelaire's text, and in Rousseau's, is the variance. We can point to certain words, we can locate some substitutions. But if that localization seems other than sheerly arbitrary, it is only because the peculiar tendency shared by these dual signs (and their repetitions) is to shift locale and to evoke locations that are no more than multiplying localizations, places for drawing the line against drawing the line. What we sense in Baudelaire's text, and in Rousseau's, is not lines that disgust, and not the place of disgust, but rather the vicariousness of disgust. Baudelaire's repetition of Rousseau's dual sign does not exhaust disgust; it does not satisfy the desire to throw up. The reason could be that there lies, in Rousseau's text, what is "worse than the literally disgusting." I translate Derrida near the end of "Economimesis," beginning at "il y a pire que le dégoutant littéral": "There is worse than the literally disgusting. And if there's worse it's because the literally disgusting is maintained, for security's sake, in the place of the worse. If not of something worse, at least of an 'in place of'; in place of a replacement without a proper place, without a trajectory, without economic and circular return. In place of prosthesis."[27]

Prosthesis, then—an adding of artificial parts that remarks and perpetuates a disfiguration—characterizes Rousseau's text. For in Baudelaire's text it produces not only signs of satisfied disgust, but traces of vicariousness. But can prosthesis be said to *characterize* Rousseau's text, when the word evokes the fungibility of organic characteristics—the fungibility, say, of organic parts of Baudelaire's text and organic parts of Rousseau's?

We are reminded that another name can be attached to the practice of inserting prosthetic devices, of adding artificial organs to supply a deficiency. That is the process, for instance, of translation, of the surgically intrusive, rigorously abusive translation that replaces one device with another. A translation will be deficient in the force of the translated text: deficient at least in the forcings peculiar to it, such as the duality of its dual signs. But a translation may supply—not deny— that deficiency, in allowing other forcings to appear in place of those: not in their places, but in *other* places in the translation. These devices, these abuses, both signal and defend against what the translation must ward off: not the peculiar force of the translated text but its translatability.[28] Baudelaire's "Morale du joujou" responds to the intolerable translatability of Rousseau's *Neuvième Promenade*.

Notes

Introduction

1. See, for example, Jacques Derrida, "La loi du genre," in *Glyph 7: Textual Studies* (Baltimore: Johns Hopkins University Press, 1980), pp. 176–201; Philippe Lacoue-Labarthe and Jean-Luc Nancy, *L'Absolu littéraire* (Paris: Seuil, 1978); and Paul de Man, "Autobiography as De-facement" and "Anthropomorphism and Trope in the Lyric," in *The Rhetoric of Romanticism* (New York: Columbia University Press, 1984).

2. See de Man, *Allegories of Reading: Figural Language in Rousseau, Nietzsche, Rilke and Proust* (New Haven: Yale University Press, 1979); Derrida, *Dissemination* (Chicago: University of Chicago Press, 1982) and *Margins of Philosophy* (Chicago: University of Chicago Press, 1983); Sarah Kofman, *Nietzsche et la métaphore* (Paris: Payot, 1972; Galilée, 1983) and *Nietzsche et la scène philosophique* (Paris: Union générale d'éditions, 1979); Bernard Pautrat, *Versions du soleil: Figures et système de Nietzsche* (Paris: Seuil, 1971); and Andrzej Warminski, *Readings in Interpretation: Hegel, Heidegger, Hölderlin* (Minneapolis: University of Minnesota Press, 1986).

3. De Man, *Allegories of Reading*.

4. Ibid., p. 82.

5. See Lacoue-Labarthe, *Le Sujet de la philosophie* (Paris: Flammarion, 1979).

6. De Man, *Allegories of Reading*, p. 245.

7. Lacoue-Labarthe, *Le Sujet de la philosophie*, p. 61.

8. This term was first made significant by Barbara Johnson in *Défigurations du langage poétique: La seconde révolution baudelairienne* (Paris: Flammarion, 1979).

9. George Eliot, *Daniel Deronda* (Harmondsworth: Penguin, 1967), p. 527.

10. De Man, *Allegories of Reading*, p. 121–22.

11. J. L. Austin, *How to Do Things with Words* (Cambridge: Harvard University Press, 1975), p. 147.

Chapter 1 The Accidents of Disfiguration

1. Quotations are from the Norton Critical Edition, *The Prelude 1799, 1805, 1850*, ed. Jonathan Wordsworth, M. H. Abrams, and Stephen Gill (New York: Norton, 1979).

2. Slightly barer than the text of 1805 is the 1798–99 wording of these lines, which reads: "A heap of garments, as if left by one / Who there was bathing" (1798–99, first part, ll. 269–70). Here, literalization restricts the significance of "as if": instead of initiating a metaphor, it merely extends a description.

3. Cf. Paul de Man, *The Rhetoric of Romanticism* (New York: Columbia University Press, 1984), pp. 53–54:

> There is a hidden but indubitable connection between the loss of the sense of correspondence and the experience of death. The boy's surprise at standing perplexed before the sudden silence of nature was an anticipatory announcement of his death, a movement of his consciousness passing beyond the deceptive constancy of a world of correspondences into a world in which our mind knows itself to be in an endlessly precarious state of suspension: above an earth, the stability of which it cannot participate in, and beneath a heaven that has rejected it. The only hope is that the precariousness will be fully and wholly understood through the mediation of poetic language, and that thereby the fall into death will be every bit as gentle as that of the 'uncertain Heaven, receiv'd / Into the bosom of the steady Lake.'

4. *The Prose Works of William Wordsworth,* ed. W. J. B. Owen and Jane Worthington Smyser (Oxford: Clarendon Press, 1974), 3:31.

5. The recurrence is described by Geoffrey Hartman in *Wordsworth's Poetry, 1787–1814* (New Haven: Yale University Press, 1971), p. 232.

6. Ibid., p. xvii.

7. Ibid., p. 232.

8. The unresolved conditional in this sentence suggests "I might advert, but I choose not to," as Peter Manning writes in "Reading Wordsworth's Revisions: Othello and the Drowned Man" (*Studies in Romanticism* 22 [Spring 1983]). Manning's essay interprets "Wordsworth's act of evoking but occluding what he evokes"; what Wordsworth evokes and occludes in this passage is "the connection between story and death," resonant in these lines as they echo Othello's description of his wooing of Desdemona: "Wherein I spake of most disastrous chances, / Of moving accidents by flood and field" (Manning, p. 4). Desdemona and Othello, as the quarry and the Moor, reappear in Wordsworth's landscape:

> I might advert
> To numerous accidents in flood or field,
> *Quarry* or *moor,* or 'mid the winter snows,
> Distresses and disasters. . . .

The submerged pun figures the text's concern with the danger of "moving accidents," of narrating.

9. Lines 285–87 can be read not as a denial or denegation but as a description of Wordsworth's figural language, language resistant to the sublation implicit in metaphor. A dead metaphor (Hegel's example is *begreifen,* to "grasp" a concept) is a word transported (*übertragen: meta-phorein*) from the sensory into the spiritual order (*"auf Geistiges"*). The effacement or decay of the metaphorical status of a word, as it loses its sensory proper meaning and acquires a nonsensory proper meaning, coincides with a gain in value, for the passage from sensory to nonsensory signification is a movement of idealisation. (Cf. Jacques Derrida, "White Mythology: Metaphor in the Text of Philosophy," *Margins of Philosophy* [Chicago: University of Chicago Press, 1982], pp. 225–26). That

gain in value through the wearing down, the *usure,* the usury of figures, belongs to the "usury of time" denounced by Wordsworth in the passage decrying "Sages, who in their prescience would control / All accidents"—

> the tutors of our youth,
> The guides, the wardens of our faculties
> And stewards of our labour, watchful men
> And skilful in the usury of time.
>
> *(The Prelude* 5. 376–80)

10. See Jacques Lacan, *Le Séminaire XI: Les quatre concepts fondamentaux de la psychanalyse* (Paris: Seuil, 1973), p. 54: "That which is repeated, in fact, is always something produced—the very expression reveals its relation to *tuché—as if by chance.* . . . The function of *tuché,* of the real as encounter [*rencontre*]—an encounter insofar as it can be missed, and that it is in essence an encounter which is missed [*rencontre manquée*]—first appeared in the history of psychoanalysis in a form which in itself is enough to awaken our attention—as trauma."

11. The terms *literal* and *figurative* are stretched beyond their limits here, disqualified by Wordsworth's figural language—which cannot rightly be called literal, or about the literal, except insofar as these terms are understood to name a language that resists and exceeds division into "figurative" and "literal" and suspends the movement of metaphorisation. In this sense Wordsworth's figural language is always already disfiguration, and any narrative account of that suspension—such as this reading's description of disfiguration as a process taking place between the opening of book 5 and the drowned man episode—must misrepresent it. The "garments" that are "books," celebrated in the opening lines of the book ("Tremblings of the heart / It gives, to think that the immortal being / No more shall need such garments"), are already the "unclaimed garments" of a dead body, the garments of garments, as Andrzej Warminski writes, due to the system of figures *soul: body: garments* that links garments to body as body to soul. This is the claim made in de Man, "Autobiography as Defacement," *The Rhetoric of Romanticism,* pp. 79–80. The reading of this system of figures is carried out in Andrzej Warminski, "Missed Crossing: Wordsworth's Apocalypses," *MLN* 99 (December 1984), 917–35, a rigorously rhetorical interpretation of book 5 true to the non-narrative problematic of disfiguration in Wordsworth.

12. The Norton edition notes: "James Jackson, schoolmaster at the neighboring village of Sawrey, was drowned on June 18, 1779, while bathing in Esthwaite Water."

Chapter 2 The Ring of Gyges and the Coat of Darkness

1. Jean-Jacques Rousseau, *Les Rêveries du promeneur solitaire,* in *Oeuvres complètes,* vol. 1: *Les Confessions, autres textes autobiographiques,* ed. Bernard Gagnebin and Marcel Raymond (Paris: Gallimard, 1959), pp. 1057–58. References within the text to the *Rêveries* and the *Confessions* are to this edition. For translation of the former I have used, substantially modified, *Reveries of the Solitary Walker,* trans. Peter France (New York: Penguin, 1979).

2. The immediate context of Rousseau's reference to a ring of Gyges—the

question of the character of his actions were he to be protected by the power of invisibility—closely resembles the context in which Glaucon relates the tale of "the ancestor of Gyges, the Lydian" in book 2 of *The Republic*. As part of his argument that men act justly only when their power to act unjustly in their own interest is restrained, Glaucon recalls that the possessor of the magic ring used his power to commit adultery with the king's wife, kill the king, and become the new ruler. Rousseau reappropriates the reference to the ring in an argument that is the inverse of Glaucon's: a man (or Rousseau himself, at any rate) acts unjustly only when his power to act is restrained. Rousseau's claim is made all the more emphatic by performing this inversion of the traditional moral of the story. At the end of the passage, however, Rousseau reintroduces the suspicion that the gift of invisibility must induce some kind of disaster.

3. William Wordsworth, *The Prelude* (1805), in *The Prelude: 1799, 1805, 1850*, ed. Jonathan Wordsworth, M. H. Abrams, and Stephen Gill (New York: Norton, 1979), 7:297–310. (Further references to this edition are given parenthetically in the text.) Lines 306-7 quote *Samson Agonistes*, replacing Milton's *silent* ("silent as the moon / Hid in her vacant interlunar cave") with the word *safe*. The 1850 version of the passage revises out that revealing replacement; it reads

> He dons his coat of darkness; on the stage
> Walks, and achieves his wonders from the eye
> Of living Mortal covert, as the moon
> Hid in her "vacant interlunar cave."

> (1850, 7.281–84)

The 1850 text alters a line that is perhaps slightly awkward ("safe as is") but that reveals the stakes of the figure: the possibility of being "safe" rather than "silent" through the operation of a trope. See below, p. 71 ff.

4. Wordsworth, *Essays upon Epitaphs*, in *The Prose Works of William Wordsworth*, ed. W. J. B. Owen and Jane Worthington Smyser (Oxford: Clarendon Press, 1974), 2:53.

5. Like Rousseau's statements about "*le coeur*," his critique of motivation concerns not just desire, in a psychological sense, but the production of meaning, generated by positing motives—or intentions—for signs. Cf. Juliet Flower Mac-Cannell, "Nature and Self-Love: A Reinterpretation of Rousseau's 'Passion primitive,'" *PMLA* 92 (1977): 890-902.

6. Paul de Man's *Blindness and Insight: Essays in the Rhetoric of Contemporary Criticism* (New York: Oxford University Press, 1971) theorizes the power of the fictional text to analyze its critical interpretations. Interpreting the critical accounts by means of the fictional text they claim to interpret is a strategy that has informed many highly productive readings, among them Shoshana Felman, "Turning the Screw of Interpretation," pp. 94–207 in *Literature and Psychoanalysis: The Question of Reading: Otherwise*, ed. Shoshana Felman (Baltimore: Johns Hopkins University Press, 1982), a reprint edition of *Yale French Studies* 55/56 (1977) and "Woman and Madness: The Critical Phallacy" (*Diacritics* 5 [1975]: 2-10) and Barbara Johnson, *The Critical Difference* (Baltimore: Johns Hopkins University Press, 1980).

7. *La Nouvelle Héloise* portrays the complete sequence of interpretive moves that are possible in reconstruing a figurative system, as Paul de Man argues in

"Allegory (Julie)," in *Allegories of Reading: Figural Language in Rousseau, Nietzsche, Rilke, and Proust* (New Haven: Yale University Press, 1979).

8. Rousseau's text may be said to elaborate the consequences of what Geoffrey Hartman has called "the matter of perceptibility" of literary language: that "there is a conventional rather than inherent relation between linguistic features and their marked/unmarked status" ("The Unremarkable Wordsworth," in *On Signs*, ed. Marshall Blonsky [Baltimore: Johns Hopkins University Press, 1985], p. 321). The literary is language we presume to be disinterested but meant—motivated in the sense of being marked, and hence re-markable; Hartman writes, "It is the literary intervention which moves the commonplace from indeterminate to determinate and meaningful status" (327). Rousseau evokes the violent potential of this movement of figuring. Wordsworth, for Hartman, makes of it an interposition that checks violent passage past perceptible signs: "The act of description, in Wordsworth, tends to 'compose' a precarious relation between signs and sensibility, between what befalls—accidents, incidents—and imaginative character—the active and prophetic mind, and perhaps the poetical character as such" (329). In the magisterial description in this essay, Wordsworth for Hartman is not unlike Rousseau for Hölderlin in "The Image of Rousseau in the Poetry of Hölderlin" (de Man, *The Rhetoric of Romanticism* [New York: Columbia University Press, 1984], pp. 19–46).

9. Rousseau, "Lettre à M. d'Alembert sur son article 'Genève' dans le septième volume de l'*Encyclopédie*, et particulièrement sur le projet d'établir un théâtre de comédie en cette ville," in *Du Contrat social et autres oeuvres politiques* (Paris: Garnier, 1962), pp. 140–41.

10. My discussion of this passage in book 2 of Rousseau's *Confessions* repeats de Man's reading in the last chapter of *Allegories of Reading* (New Haven: Yale University Press, 1979).

11. Leslie Brisman, *Milton's Poetry of Choice and Its Romantic Heirs* (Ithaca: Cornell University Press, 1973), p. x.

12. Wordsworth, *Lines composed a few miles above Tintern Abbey*, in *The Poetical Works of William Wordsworth* (Oxford: Clarendon Press, 1952), 2: 260, ll. 23–25.

13. Wordsworth, *The Excursion*, in *Poetical Works*, 5:4, ll. 35–41.

14. For another account of the irreducible element of chance or arbitrariness evoked in the lines on the blind beggar, see Neil Hertz, *The End of the Line* (New York: Columbia University Press, 1985), pp. 233–39, on the "feeling of arbitrariness that always clings to the irreducible": "the almost meaningless (but meaning-producing) difference between a 'face' and a written 'label.'" The feeling of arbitrariness is associated with an irreducible difference that can be assimilated to the arbitrary nature of the sign, and it "prompts," Hertz writes, "Wordsworth's figure of material recalcitrance, the 'stone of native rock' . . . rewritten as the stolid, assiduous old woman," the "old dame" with her huckster's wares in book 2 of *The Prelude* (1805, 2.36–47). Hertz's reading demonstrates how Wordsworth's texts lay out the mutual implication of the materiality and the figurality of language ("the irreducible" and "the arbitrary"). Cf. chap. 4, below, pp. 123–29.

15. John Milton, *Samson Agonistes*, in *Complete Shorter Poems*, ed. John Carey (London: Longman, 1968), ll. 1605–6, 1629–30, 1635–56.

16. De Man, *The Rhetoric of Romanticism*, p. 73.

17. See Mary Jacobus, "Wordsworth and the Language of the Dream," *ELH* 46 (1979): 629–30, on how "spectral saves spectacle for the imagination," in books 7 and 8 of *The Prelude*.

18. Milton, *Paradise Lost,* ed. Alastair Fowler (London: Longman, 1971), 7: 21–27; my italics.

19. Wordsworth, *Essays upon Epitaphs,* p. 53.

20. The following account of the muteness of language derives from de Man's interpretation in "Autobiography as De-facement," in *The Rhetoric of Romanticism.*

21. Milton, *On Shakespeare,* in *Complete Shorter Poems,* p. 123.

22. See, for example, Frances Ferguson, *Wordsworth: Language as Counterspirit* (New Haven: Yale University Press, 1977), pp. xv–xvii, and de Man, "Autobiography as De-facement," p. 929.

23. Wordsworth, *Essays upon Epitaphs,* pp. 84–85.

24. De Man, "Autobiography as De-facement," p. 80.

25. Wordsworth has recourse throughout the *Essays* to the metaphors of "garment" and "body," maintained in an opposition to each other which as such is tenuous and breaks down when further specifying terms are added, such as "incarnation" (Wordsworth's word here) or "skeleton." The evocation of the deaf-mute also evokes the vulnerability to accident that is constitutive of the body, an arbitrariness in "the incarnation of the thought." Like Samson's complaint that the sun is silent, the Dalesman's predicament in possessing sight "silent as a picture" entails an ironic generalization about the subversive weakness of sight in its very site and provokes a reflection on what it means to be "sighted." Being sighted, for Wordsworth and for Milton, is a privative mode of being blind, a blindness taking the form of silence.

26. Shelley, "The Triumph of Life," in *Shelley's Poetry and Prose,* ed. Donald Reiman and Sharon Powers (New York: Norton, 1977), p. 460.

27. De Man, "Literary History and Literary Modernity," in *Blindness and Insight,* p. 165.

Chapter 3 Viewless Wings

1. Morris Dickstein makes this point in *Keats and His Poetry: A Study in Development* (Chicago: University of Chicago Press, 1971), p. 208. Keats's poems are quoted from *The Poems of John Keats,* ed. Jack Stillinger (Cambridge: Harvard University Press, 1978).

2. Earl Wasserman, *The Finer Tone: Keats' Major Poems* (Baltimore: Johns Hopkins University Press, 1953), pp. 192–93.

3. Leslie Brisman, *Romantic Origins* (Ithaca: Cornell University Press, 1978), p. 83.

4. Jack Stillinger, *The Hoodwinking of Madeline and Other Essays on Keats's Poems* (Urbana: University of Illinois Press, 1971), p. 102.

5. Ibid., p. 100.

6. Jonathan Culler, *The Pursuit of Signs* (Ithaca: Cornell University Press, 1981), p. 138.

7. Paul de Man, "Hypogram and Inscription: Michael Riffaterre's Poetics of Reading," *Diacritics* 11 (Winter 1981):32.

8. Culler, *The Pursuit of Signs,* p. 140.

9. Giambattista Vico, *The New Science* (New York: Doubleday, 1961), p. 87.

10. Dickstein, *Keats and His Poetry,* p. 219.

11. Milton's poetry is quoted from the Longman editions: *Complete Shorter Poems* (1968), ed. John Carey, and *Paradise Lost* (1971), ed. Alastair Fowler (London: Longman).

12. Cf. de Man, *The Rhetoric of Romanticism* (New York: Columbia University Press, 1984), p. 78.

13. John Hollander, *The Figure of Echo: A Mode of Allusion in Milton and After* (Berkeley: University of California Press, 1981), p. 90. I owe to conversation with Margaret Ferguson the connection between this nightingale singing in darkness and the "self-begotten bird" of *Samson Agonistes,* discussed below.

14. Eamon Grennan, "Keats's Contemptus Mundi: A Shakespearian Influence on 'Ode to a Nightingale,'" *MLQ* 36 (1975):272–92.

15. Brisman, *Romantic Origins,* p. 83.

16. *The Poetical Works of William Wordsworth,* ed. E. de Selincourt (Oxford: Clarendon Press, 1965), 2:216.

17. Cf. de Man, "The Rhetoric of Temporality," in *Blindness and Insight* (Minneapolis: University of Minnesota Press, 1983), p. 223–24.

18. On Keats's identifying the "blushful" with the "true," see Christopher Ricks, *Keats and Embarrassment* (London: Oxford University Press, 1974), pp. 201–2.

19. Hollander, *The Figure of Echo,* pp. 36–37.

20. On the deictic function and on pointing to examples *(Beispiel)* in chap. 1 of the *Phenomenology of the Spirit,* see Paul de Man, "Hypogram and Inscription," pp. 27–30; and Andrzej Warminski, "Reading for Example: 'Sense Certainty' in Hegel's *Phenomenology of Spirit,*" *Diacritics* 11 (Summer 1981): 83–94.

21. John Keats, *Selected Poems and Letters,* ed. Douglas Bush (Boston: Houghton Mifflin, 1959), p. 292.

Chapter 4 Giving a Face to a Name

1. Paul de Man, *The Rhetoric of Romanticism* (New York: Columbia University Press, 1984), pp. 80–81. References to this work are identified hereafter in the text as *RR.*

2. De Man, "Hypogram and Inscription: Michael Riffaterre's Poetics of Reading," *Diacritics* 11 (Winter 1981): 30.

3. William Wordsworth, *The Prelude 1799, 1805, 1850,* ed. Jonathan Wordsworth, M. H. Abrams, and Stephen Gill (New York: Norton, 1979). All references to *The Prelude* are to this edition.

4. For a more extensive interpretation of the Blest Babe passage, and a careful rhetorical reading of the story of "props" and propping in Wordsworth and in Freud, see Catherine Caruth, "Past Recognition: Narrative Origins in Wordsworth and Freud," *MLN* 100 (Dec. 1985).

5. *The Prose Works of William Wordsworth,* ed. W. J. B. Owen and Jane Worthington Smyser (Oxford: Clarendon Press, 1974), 2:84–85.

6. Ibid., p. 96.

7. De Man, "Sign and Symbol in Hegel's *Aesthetics,*" *Critical Inquiry* 8 (Summer 1982):768.

8. De Man, *Allegories of Reading* (New Haven: Yale University Press, 1979), pp. 121–22. References to this work are identified hereafter in the text as *AR*.

9. G. W. F. Hegel, *Phänomenologie des Geistes,* ed. Johannes Hoffmeister (Hamburg: Felix Meiner, 1952), pp. 50–51; and *The Phenomenology of Mind,* trans. J. B. Baillie (New York: Harper and Row, 1967), pp. 119–20.

10. Andrzej Warminski, "Reading for Example: 'Sense Certainty' in Hegel's *Phenomenology of Spirit,*" *Diacritics* 11 (Summer 1981): 83–94; and *Readings in Interpretation: Hegel, Heidegger, Hölderlin* (Minneapolis: University of Minnesota Press, forthcoming). With the word *soll,* Hegel's description of speculative thought approaches Nietzsche's analysis of the identity principle, quoted by de Man: "Either it asserts something about actual entities as if one already knew this from some other source; namely that opposite attributes *cannot* be ascribed to them (*können*). Or the proposition means: opposite attributes *should* not be ascribed to it (*sollen*). In that case, logic would be an imperative, *not* to know the time (*erkennen*), but to posit (*setzen*) and arrange a world that *should be there for us.*" (*AR,* 120)

11. De Man, "Sign and Symbol in Hegel's *Aesthetics,*" p. 775.

12. See Andrzej Warminski, "Reading for Example," particularly p. 86.

13. Hegel, *Phenomenology,* p. 152.

14. De Man, "Hypogram and Inscription," p. 28.

15. Idem.

16. Hegel, *Phenomenology,* p. 158.

17. Warminski, "Reading for Example," quoting Hegel, *Phänomenologie des Geistes,* pp. 88–89; *Phenomenology,* p. 160.

18. Hegel, *Phenomenology,* p. 152.

19. Warminski, "Reading for Example," p. 89.

20. De Man, "Sign and Symbol in Hegel's *Aesthetics,*" p. 769.

21. Idem.

22. Ibid., p. 767.

23. Idem.

24. Ibid., p. 768.

25. Ibid., p. 770.

26. G. W. F. Hegel, *Aesthetics: Lectures on Fine Art,* trans. T. M. Knox (Oxford: Clarendon Press, 1975), 2: sec. 1.2.

27. De Man, "Shelley Disfigured," in *The Rhetoric of Romanticism,* p. 117.

28. Hegel, *Aesthetics,* p. 364.

29. De Man, "Hegel on the Sublime," in *Displacement: Derrida and After,* ed. Mark Krupnick (Bloomington: Indiana University Press, 1982), p. 146.

30. Ibid., p. 148.

31. Ibid., p. 149.

32. Ibid., p. 151.

33. De Man, "Sign and Symbol in Hegel's *Aesthetics,*" p. 775.

34. Ibid., p. 769.

35. Martin Heidegger, *Being and Time* (New York: Harper & Row, 1962), p. 27.

36. This statement would dispute, in particular, Heidegger's interpretation of

predication in *Was Heisst Denken?*, or would disqualify a reading of that text in which its insistent thematization and performance of the question were construed as a value. (Among other resonances, the quotation from Hölderlin's "Patmos" appearing at this moment in the argument of "Shelley Disfigured" alerts one to the engagement with Heidegger; the same lines are invoked in the opening pages of *Was Heisst Denken?*)

37. De Man, "Hypogram and Inscription," p. 31.

38. Jean Starobinski, *Les mots sous les mots: Les anagrammes de Ferdinand de Saussure* (Paris: Gallimard, 1971), p. 31 and note.

39. De Man, "Hypogram and Inscription," p. 24.

40. See especially Starobinski, *Les mots sous les mots,* p. 132.

41. De Man, "Hypogram and Inscription," p. 34.

42. Ibid., p. 24.

43. De Man, "Hegel on the Sublime," p. 150.

44. Starobinski, *Les mots sous les mots,* pp. 30–31.

45. See de Man, *Allegories of Reading,* pp. 200–201 and 288–93.

46. Sylvère Lotringer, "The Game of the Name," *Diacritics* 3 (Summer 1973): 8–16.

47. See de Man, "Hypogram and Inscription," p. 25.

48. Ibid., p. 28.

49. Warminski, "Reading for Example," p. 90.

50. For a strongly stated differentiation between the phenomenal and the material "This piece of paper," see Andrzej Warminski, "Dreadful Reading: Blanchot on Hegel," *Yale French Studies* 69 (1985).

51. De Man, "Hypogram and Inscription," p. 33.

52. Starobinski, *Les mots sous les mots,* p. 152.

53. Lotringer, "The Game of the Name," p. 9.

54. De Man, introduction to Hans Robert Jauss, *Toward an Aesthetic of Reception,* trans. Timothy Bahti (Minneapolis: University of Minnesota Press, 1982), p. xx.

55. De Man's focus on the moment of reading in which the second kind of poetic figure (functioning not like recollection but like memorization) displaces the first (a figure and an instance of the poetic figure as recollection) belongs to his critique of Jauss's conception of the poetic text as *Erinnerung,* or recollection (for which see, in particular, "Sketch of a Theory and History of Aesthetic Experience," in *Aesthetic Experience and Literary Hermeneutics* (Minneapolis: University of Minnesota Press, 1982), pp. 3–151. On figure, or "the external manifestation of the idea," as *Gedächtnis* rather than *Erinnerung,* see my chap. 5, and "Sign and Symbol in Hegel's *Aesthetics,*" pp. 771–73.

56. De Man, introduction to Jauss, p. xxi.

57. Idem.

58. Ibid., p. xxiii.

59. De Man, "Sign and Symbol in Hegel's *Aesthetics,*" p. 775, quoting Hegel.

60. De Man, introduction to Jauss, p. 190, note 26. On the demolition of the Vendôme column in 1871 during the Paris Commune and the threat to aesthetic, psychological, and economic values this exemplified, see Neil Hertz, "Medusa's Head: Male Hysteria Under Political Pressure," in *The End of the Line* (New York: Columbia University Press, 1985).

61. *The Standard Edition of the Complete Psychological Works of Sigmund Freud,* trans. James Strachey (London: Hogarth Press, 1957), 14: 257; *Gesammelte Werke* 10: 445.
62. Larousse, *Grand Dictionnaire Universel du dix-neuvième siècle.*
63. Idem.

Chapter 5 Getting Versed

1. William Wordsworth, *The Prelude 1799, 1805, 1850,* ed. Jonathan Wordsworth, M. H. Abrams, and Stephen Gill (New York: Norton, 1979), p. 217.
2. Immanuel Kant, *The Critique of Judgment,* trans. J. C. Meredith (Oxford: Clarendon Press, 1952), pp. 111–12; *Kritik der Urteilskraft* Werkausgabe 10 (Frankfurt am Main: Suhrkamp, 1979): 186.
3. Paul de Man, *The Rhetoric of Romanticism* (New York: Columbia University Press, 1984), p. 239.
4. G. W. F. Hegel, *Enzyclopädie der philosophischen Wissenschaften* (Leipzig: Georg Lasson, 1905). Numbers after quotations from Hegel refer to sections ("paragraphs") and pages in this edition. Part three of the *Encyclopedia* is entitled in English *The Philosophy of Mind,* trans. William Wallace, to which is added the *Zusätze* of Ludwig Boumann's 1845 text, trans. A. V. Miller (Oxford: Oxford University Press, 1971). Quotations in English followed by page numbers are from this translation.
5. *Zusatz* to par. 445 (Wallace, p. 192).
6. On how Kant's own elaboration of the analogy describes the power to generate signs and, specifically, commodities, see Richard Klein, "Kant's Sunshine," *Diacritics* 11 (Summer 1981): 26–41.
7. Wordsworth envisions such a figure in "London," *The Prelude* (1805), 7:422.
8. Walter Benjamin, "Zur Kritik der Gewalt," in *Gesammelte Schriften,* Werkausgabe (Frankfurt am Main: Suhrkamp, 1980), 2.1:179–203. Trans. in W. Benjamin, *Reflections: Essays, Aphorisms, Autobiographical Writings* (New York: Harcourt Brace, 1978).
9. *The Prose Works of William Wordsworth,* ed. W. J. B. Owen and Jane Worthington Smyser (Oxford: Clarendon Press, 1974), 2:88.
10. Benjamin, *Reflections,* pp. 296–97, *Gesammelte Schriften* 2.1:199.
11. Charles Baudelaire, *Oeuvres complètes* (Paris: Gallimard, 1961), p. 79.
12. Ibid., p. 232.
13. Benjamin, "Über einige Motive bei Baudelaire," in *Gesammelte Schriften* 1.2:605–55, trans. as "On Some Motifs in Baudelaire," in Benjamin, *Illuminations* (New York: Schocken, 1969), pp. 155–200. Benjamin's reference to the opening stanza of *Le Soleil* follows a section of his essay that sets out from Freud's dictum in *Beyond the Pleasure Principle* that within the same system memory and consciousness are incompatible, to distinguish two different modes of disjunction between them: Proust's *mémoire involontaire,* a kind of recollection possible only of what has not been consciously experienced, and Baudelaire's shock-defense, a mode of consciousness which prevents an impression's penetration into the memory as trauma. The involuntary character of Proustian memory—not a process the subject can deliberately activate, nor a dependable compensation for the failure of conscious appropriation—differentiates it de-

cisively from Hegel's *Erinnerung*. The preeminence of consciousness instead of memory, which Benjamin ascribes to Baudelaire, in crucial respects resembles Hegel's *Gedächtnis*—both when it fails (and what takes effect is shock) and when it succeeds: that achievement, writes Benjamin, entails "assigning to an incident a precise point in time in consciousness at the cost of the integrity of its contents" (*Illuminations*, p. 163; *Gesammelte Schriften* 1.2:615).

14. Cf. Benjamin on "the special achievement of shock defense," quoted in note. 13.

15. Benjamin's account of *Le Soleil* seemingly calls attention to its representational and autobiographical aspect: "In solch phantastischem Gefecht begriffen, hat Baudelaire sich selbst in der Anfangsstrophe des Gedichts 'Le soleil' porträtiert; und dass ist wohl die einzige Stelle der 'Fleurs du mal,' die ihn bei der poetischen Arbeit zeigt" (*Gesammelte Schriften* 1.2:616). This portraiture is not pictorial but, rather (in all senses), graphic: it depicts not the scene of Baudelaire's walks through the city but the "Intermittenzen zwischen Bild und Idee, Wort und Sache, in denen die poetische Erregung bei Baudelaire ihren eigentlichen Sitz vorfinde" (*Gesammelte Schriften* 1.2:617; *Illuminations*, p. 164). Baudelaire's graphic depiction of the experience of shock (as a "combat"—"ma fantasque escrime") registers, for Benjamin, his contact with the crowd; the crowd, a part of Baudelaire's experience, is significant precisely insofar as it neither appears nor means itself, as such, in Baudelaire's writing: "Diese Menge, deren Dasein Baudelaire nie vergisst, hat ihm zu keinem seiner Werke Modell gestanden. Sie ist aber seinem Schaffen als verborgene Figur eingeprägt . . . Das Bild des Fechters lässt sich aus ihr entziffern; die Stösse, welche er austeilt, sind bestimmt, ihm durch die Menge den Weg zu bahnen. Freilich sind die faubourgs, durch die der Dichter des 'Soleil' sich hindurchschlägt, menschenleer. Aber die geheime Konstellation (in ihr wird die Schönheit der Strophe bis auf den Grund durchsichtig) ist wohl so zu fassen: es ist die Geistermenge der Worte, der Fragmente, der Versanfänge, mit denen der Dichter in den verlassenen Strassenzügen den Kampf um die poetische Beute ausficht" (*Gesammelte Schriften* 1.2:618; *Illuminations*, p. 165).

16. Benjamin, *Reflections*, p. 295; *Gesammelte Schriften* 2.1:199.

17. Benjamin, *Reflections*, pp. 295-96.

18. Cf. in Baudelaire's *Petits poèmes en prose*, the poor child and the rich child of *Le joujou du pauvre*, who "se riaient fraternellement, avec des dents d'une *égale* blancheur," on either side of the grill dividing the château from the thoroughfare; and the "*légitime propriétaire*" and the "*usurpateur*" of "*Le Gâteau*" equal in their hunger and ferocity (*Oeuvres Complètes*, pp. 256, 250).

19. Benjamin, "Die Aufgabe des Übersetzers," in *Gesammelte Schriften* 4.1:12.

20. Ibid., p. 11.

21. Baudelaire, *Oeuvres complètes*, pp. 69-70.

22. For this reading of *oublié sur la carte* as "left off the map," see Paul de Man, introduction to Hans Robert Jauss, *Toward an Aesthetic of Reception* (Minneapolis: University of Minnesota Press, 1982), p. xxv.

23. Friedrich Hölderlin, *Werke und Briefe* (Frankfurt: Insel, 1969) 1:117. See de Man, "The Intentional Structure of the Romantic Image," in *The Rhetoric of Romanticism*, p. 2.

24. Friedrich Nietzsche, *Werke* (Munich: Musarion, 1922) 3:239.

25. Kant, *Kritik der Urteilskraft,* p. 155.
26. The expression is de Man's, *The Rhetoric of Romanticism,* p. 6.
27. Baudelaire, *Oeuvres complètes,* p. 11.
28. De Man, *The Rhetoric of Romanticism,* p. 250.
29. Baudelaire, *Les Fleurs du Mal,* ed. Jacques Crepet and Georges Blin (Paris: Corti, 1942), p. 453.
30. Ibid., p. 500.
31. Geoffrey Hartman plays on the proximity of *fit* and *fiat* in Harold Bloom et al., *Deconstruction and Criticism* (New York: Seabury Press, 1979), pp. 199–200.

Chapter 6 Mechanical Doll, Exploding Machine

1. Heinrich von Kleist, "Über das Marionettentheater" and "Unwahrscheinliche Wahrhaftigkeiten," in *Werke in einem Band* (Munich: Carl Hanser, 1966). The translation of "Unwahrscheinliche Wahrhaftigkeiten" quoted here is Carol Jacobs's, "Improbable Veracities," *Diacritics* 9 (Winter 1979): 45–47. Translations of "Über das Marionettentheater" have appeared in the *Times Literary Supplement* (October 20, 1978) by Idris Parry; and *Salmagundi* (Spring-Summer 1976) by Beryl de Zoete (from Beryl de Zoete, *The Thunder and the Freshness,* [New York: Theater Arts, 1963], pp. 64–71).
2. See Paul de Man, "Aesthetic Formalization: Kleist's 'Über das Marionettentheater,'" in *The Rhetoric of Romanticism* (New York: Columbia University Press, 1984).
3. One might also note that the purity of the aesthetic model is made questionable from the start in this story of an encounter in a public bath, in which the boy's grace might be expected to elicit not only aesthetic pleasure but also desire.
4. The exchange is as follows:

> "Glauben Sie diese Geschichte?
> Vollkommen! rief ich, mit freudigem Beifall; jedwedem
> Fremden, so wahrscheinlich ist sie; um wie viel mehr Ihnen!"
>
> (Kleist, *Werke.* 807)

5. Cf. Carol Jacobs, "The Style of Kleist," *Diacritics* 9 (Winter 1979): 47–62. My interpretation of "Improbable Veracities" owes a great deal to Carol Jacobs's essay. Cf. also the responses to her essay: Cynthia Chase, "Telling Truths," and Andrzej Warminski, "A Question of an Other Order: Deflections of the Straight Man," *Diacritics* 9 (Winter 1979): 62–69 and 70–78.
6. The close reading of these two expressions is carried out by Carol Jacobs. Jacobs also analyzes a phrase in another detail of "Improbable Veracities": the officer says that when tools fail to dislodge the gigantic blocks of stone in the quarry at Königstein, the workmen throw small wedge-shaped objects like pipe-stems into the fisure in order to sunder a block from the cliff. Jacobs points out that the word *keilförmig* also means "cuneiform," so that the peculiar force that displaces the blocks of stone is named, like the other forces in the stories, in such a way as to mark it as a force of language—or more specifically, in this instance, of writing.

7. Cf. Walter Benjamin's "Critique of Violence," ("Zur Kritik der Gewalt") discussed in chap. 5.

8. Friedrich von Schiller, *Geschichte des Abfalls der vereinigten Niederlande* (Leipzig: Freidrich Christian Wilhelm Vogel, 1809). Cf. Carol Jacobs's discussion of the role of this account in Kleist's text, "The Style of Kleist," pp. 52–59.

9. De Man, *Allegories of Reading* (New Haven: Yale University Press, 1979), p. 300.

10. De Man, foreword to Carol Jacobs, *The Dissimulating Harmony* (Baltimore: Johns Hopkins University Press, 1978), p. xi.

11. Idem.

12. Cf. the disruption of the model connection between performative and cognitive rhetoric by the machine of Rousseau's confessional narrative, discussed by Paul de Man in the last chapter of *Allegories of Reading*. Rousseau's narrative, like Kleist's, first thrusts the connection between performative and cognitive upon the reader and then ruptures it. Kleist offers us the case of telling unbelievable facts, ineffectual truths that may give truth a bad reputation. Rousseau proposes the case (in the *Quatrième Promenade* of *Les Rêveries du promeneur solitaire*) of withholding useless facts, "*faits oiseux*," and telling harmless nonfacts, "fictions," instead. This can occur simply as the automatic effect of pressure to talk in a social situation, and in the absence of any intention on the part of the speaker—far from being a rhetorical manipulation (whether of speech-act effects or of the constative cognitive effect of speech). Yet at the end of the *Promenade* it is this very "*effet machinal*" that is said to disfigure truth and is found to be inexcusable: a performance to which no performative function could match up (not even the powerful energy of Rousseau's excuses), and which is also, to Rousseau, ethically "inexcusable."

Chapter 7   The Decomposition of the Elephants

1. George Eliot, *Daniel Deronda* (Harmondsworth: Penguin, 1967), p. 704 (bk. 7, chap. 52). All page references are to this edition of the novel.

2. In this rereading of Eliot's last novel, I follow the hint of Henry James's Theodora, that in *Daniel Deronda* the "mass is for the detail and each detail is for the mass," and ask the question of whether, and how, the detail and the mass are "for" each other in this text. Theodora defends the novel in James's "*Daniel Deronda*: A Conversation," originally published in the *Atlantic Monthly* in 1876 and republished in Gordon Haight's valuable collection, *A Century of George Eliot Criticism* (Boston: Houghton Mifflin, 1965). I am indebted to previous critics of *Deronda* for analyzing the meanings of the novel enforced by its narrator and pointing out the contradictions and insufficiencies of this narration. Important studies include David Kaufmann, *George Eliot and Judaism* (New York: Haskell, 1970); F. R. Leavis, *The Great Tradition* (London: Chatto and Windus, 1948) and his introduction to the edition of the novel (New York: Harper, 1961); Barbara Hardy, *The Novels of George Eliot: A Study in Form* (London: Athlone, 1959) and her introduction to the Penguin edition (cited in n.1); and W. J. Harvey, *The Art of George Eliot* (New York: Oxford University Press, 1961). Felicia Bonaparte, *Will and Destiny: Morality and Tragedy in*

George Eliot's Novels (New York: New York University Press, 1975), has a pertinent chapter on "loose threads in the causal web."

In "The Apocalypse of the Old Testament: *Daniel Deronda* and the Interpretation of Interpretation" (*PMLA* 99 [January 1984]:56–71), which appeared after the first publication of this essay, Mary Wilson Carpenter argues that George Eliot devised the novel's two narrative strands to reflect her viewpoint in contemporary controversy concerning the Book of Daniel and the philosophy of history. The novel is designed to embody Eliot's conception of "how prophetic vision functions in a scientific age to end the individual's exile from history and the Christian's exile from Judaism" (p. 64). For Carpenter, the notion of history or narrative as "the present causes of past effects" is not a problem but an expression of the philosophy of history George Eliot affirms, and affirms to have regenerative value: "the formation of history through poetic vision" (p. 65), history as "the product of human interpretation" (p. 67).

3. These other notes or letters are Deronda's note to Gwendolen, accompanying her redeemed necklace; Lush's message to Gwendolen; Gwendolen's note summoning Herr Klesmer; the notes exchanged between Grandcourt and Gwendolen during their second courtship; Lydia Glasher's letter to Gwendolen, accompanying the poisoned diamonds; the Princess Halm-Eberstein's summons to Deronda; and Gwendolen's final missive to Deronda on his wedding day. In contrast with these decisive missives, the gratuitous, purposeless character of Meyrick's letter stands out sharply. The gratuitous character of order is also one of its explicit topics.

4. The distinction between two plots is a sort of fiction that begs a great many questions. Actually, to distinguish "narrative modes" in the novel, with the intention of relating them to the separate plots, would be a complicated task, if not impossible. Nevertheless, this broad division has been registered almost unanimously by readers of the novel who, preferring the "English part," have deplored its subordination to the "Jewish part." There is more in this than a mere objection to what have been described as the novel's occasional sentimentalities or moralisms; there is more also than Victorian readers' anti-Semitic objections to the glorification of Jewishness. As I shall argue, the supremacy of the "Jewish part" challenges fundamental tenets of belief about the structure and validity of language.

5. Meyrick practices not just a narrative mode alien to the narrator's but a nonnarrative art: he is a painter. Deronda's imaginative sympathy with the histories of the novel's heroines contrasts with Meyrick's enthusiasm for their appearance as paintings—Gwendolen as a "Van Dyke duchess," Mirah as a Berenice (see chap. 37). Both the rivalry between language and painting and the conflict between different narrative modes appear also in *Middlemarch*. Will Ladislaw speaks up for the "fuller image" of language, the "true seeing [which] is within," in objection to the painted images of Dorothea as a "perfect young Madonna" enthusiastically composed by his friend Adolf Naumann, a German painter (chap. 19). However, Ladislaw's easy and playful use of language resembles Meyrick's and contrasts with that of Casaubon, who searches for origins and cause, tracing the history of myths. Both Meyrick and Deronda, then, are revisions of the ambivalent and incompletely realized figure of Ladislaw. The different distribution of allegiances and values among these characters in *Mid-*

dlemarch and in *Daniel Deronda* could be the starting point for a study of the distinctive ways that these two texts exploit the functions of narrative.

6. The discrediting of Meyrick's letter is only one instance among many in which this strategy is employed; see, for example, the beginning of chap. 41 (p. 568), which portrays Deronda's rehearsal to himself of the commonsensical view of his encounter with Mordecai. This is identified as "the answer Sir Hugo would have given," an observation that partially discredits it, since Sir Hugo's limited judgment has been documented. In the novel's larger scheme, the English side as a whole comes to occupy this role. Since "English" characters' judgments are portrayed ironically, their criticism of, or disbelief in, the Deronda plot implicitly ratifies that plot's implausibilities.

7. Henry James, "*Daniel Deronda:* A Conversation," in Haight, *A Century of George Eliot Criticism.* See also J. Hillis Miller on flowing water as one of the recurrent metaphors that tend to appear in expressions of the classic assumptions about narrative and history ("Narrative and History," *ELH* 41 [1974]: 460).

8. Meyrick's next sentence continues the satire of formal critical discourse, with its pretensions to neutrality and exactness: "My own idea that a murrain will shortly break out in the commercial class, and that the cause will subsequently disclose itself in the ready sale of all rejected pictures, has been called an unsound use of analogy" (704). The critical mind responds to Meyrick's nonsensical and mischievous fantasy by decrying merely his "unsound use of analogy"—an incongruous understatement parodying the whitened diction distinctive of philosophy and criticism (and deconstructive criticism).

9. The narrative is a series of "unwarranted substitutions leading to ontological claims based on misinterpreted systems of relationship"; see Paul de Man, *Allegories of Reading* (New Haven: Yale University Press, 1979), p. 123.

10. De Man, *Allegories of Reading,* pp. 121–22.

11. J. L. Austin, *Philosophical Papers* (Oxford: Oxford University Press, 1961), p. 223. Austin introduces a distinction between the constative, or descriptive, function of language and another, "performative" function. In its ordinary usage, language includes, in addition to statements, such performative utterances as "I apologize" or "I name this ship the *Queen Elizabeth,*" assertions in which "in saying what I do, I actually perform that action." Another example would be the act of baptizing, which confers a name and a religious identification on the person baptized. Conversion to Christianity can be effected by such a performative utterance. Mordecai's talks with Deronda partly function in this way, but they cannot confer Jewish identity.

12. The narrator stresses Mirah's "transformation" after her fairy-tale rescue and her adoption by the Meyricks (see chap. 32).

13. Deronda did not go to live with Sir Hugo Mallinger until he was two years old.

14. Stephen Marcus, *Representations: Essays on Literature and Society* (New York: Random, 1976), p. 212, note: "It is only when he is a grown man, having been to Eton and Cambridge, that he discovers that he is a Jew. What this has to mean—given the conventions of medical practice at the time—is that he never looked down. In order for the plot of *Daniel Deronda* to work, Deronda's circumcised penis must be invisible, or non-existent—which is one more demonstration in detail of why the plot does not in fact work."

Mary Wilson Carpenter (see my n. 2) argues persuasively that the plot is in fact richly informed by Eliot's use of contemporary theological interpretation of the Feast of the Circumcision: a day bringing together Hebrew and Christian prophecy, and a rite interpreted, by Keble and others, as symbolizing the redemptive suffering inaugural of a union of the old and new "churches"—like the penitence urged on Gwendolen by Deronda at their encounter on the Feast of the Circumcision, New Year's Day.

15. Discovery of identity generally does involve both physical lineage and a spiritual, cultural, even financial patrimony, and the importance of one or the other factor may vary from case to case, but neither is so extreme or decisive as both are in *Daniel Deronda.*

16. De Man, *Allegories of Reading,* p. 129.

17. In book 2, chap. 1 of *The Mill on the Floss,* the narrator criticizes the delusory effects of metaphor (see J. Hillis Miller, "Optic and Semiotic in *Middlemarch,*" in *The Worlds of Victorian Fiction,* ed. Jerome H. Buckley [Cambridge: Harvard University Press, 1975]). It is interesting that the passage aims at delusory metaphors as the basis of our sense of control or authority: the narrator is satirizing, specifically, the school authorities' control over Tom Tulliver. In *Daniel Deronda,* Meyrick's letter resists the narrator's authority to impose metaphors. The letter closes with a satirical citation literalizing a biblical metaphor: "But while her brother's life lasts I suspect she would not listen to a lover, even one whose 'hair is like a flock of goats on Mt. Gilead'—and I flatter myself that few heads would bear that trying comparison better than mine."

18. The relation between the aphorism and the novel, that is, may be construed as an example of how metaphorical structure is deconstructed by narrative structure, or vice versa (since the conspicuous rhetoricity of the aphorism evokes a deconstruction of the narrative's rhetorical premises).

19. De Man, *Allegories of Reading,* p. 140: "The self which was at first the center of the language as its empirical referent now becomes the language of the center as fiction, as metaphor of the self. What was originally a simply referential text now becomes the text of a text, the figure." This narrative of the metamorphosis of the text should not be understood any more literally than the personification of two kinds of text.

20. See Meyrick's letter, p. 708: "Excuse the brevity of this letter. You are not used to more from me than a bare statement of facts without comment or digression. One fact I have omitted. . . ."

Chapter 8 Oedipal Textuality

1. See André Green, *Un Oeil en trop: Le complexe d'Oedipe dans la tragédie* (Paris: Minuit, 1969), and Philippe Lacoue-Labarthe, "Theatrum Analyticum," in *Glyph 2: Johns Hopkins Textual Studies* (Baltimore: Johns Hopkins University Press, 1977).

2. Sigmund Freud, *The Interpretation of Dreams* (New York: Avon Books, 1965), p. 295. Quotations from *The Interpretation of Dreams,* henceforth cited as *ID,* are from this edition unless otherwise indicated.

3. Freud, *The Origins of Psychoanalysis: Letters to Wilhelm Fliess,* trans. E. Mosbacher and J. Strachey (New York: Basic Books, 1954), p. 322: "Do you

suppose that some day a marble tablet will be placed on the house, inscribed with these words: 'In this house on July 24, 1895, the Secret of Dreams was revealed to Dr. Sigmund Freud'?"

4. Freud, *Project for a Scientific Psychology, Complete Psychological Works,* ed. J. Strachey (London: Hogarth Press, 1966), 1:352.

5. See Jean Laplanche, *Life and Death in Psychoanalysis,* trans. Jeffrey Mehlman (Baltimore: Johns Hopkins University Press, 1976), chap. 2, especially p. 30ff. This book, together with Thomas Gould, *Oedipus the King, A Translation with Commentary* (Englewood Cliffs, N.J.: Prentice Hall, 1970), generates the ideas of the present essay. Quotations from *Oedipus the King* are taken from Gould's translation.

6. Freud, *Gesammelte Werke* (London: Imago Press, 1941) 2/3:269.

7. Laplanche, *Life and Death,* p. 40, and p. 43 where he quotes Freud: "The retardation of puberty makes possible the occurrence of posthumous primary process."

8. Freud, *Project,* 1:410.

9. Jacques Lacan, *Le Séminaire XI: Les quatre concepts fondamentaux de la psychanalyse,* (Paris: Seuil, 1973), p. 54.

10. Cf. Shoshana Felman's Lacanian-Freudian critique of "psychoanalysis"—of a psychoanalytic interpretation setting itself in opposition to literature—in "Turning the Screw of Intepretation," *Yale French Studies* 55/56 (1977). See pp. 197–98 on the symptom as interpretation.

11. Sandor Goodhart, "Oedipus and Laius's Many Murderers," *Diacritics* 8 (Spring 1978).

12. It would seem that one could distinguish between the two oracles in terms of the difference between anxiety and fear, or in terms of Freud's conception of the threat of anxiety as an endemic hazard like free-floating libido, or alternatively, as a specific hazard like castration. Cf. Jeffrey Mehlman, *Revolution and Repetition* (Berkeley and Los Angeles: University of California Press, 1977), pp. 96–97.

13. Jonathan Culler, "Semiotic Consequences," paper presented at the Semiotics Forum, Modern Language Association of America Convention, Chicago, December 1977.

14. Sandor Goodhart, *Who Killed Laius?,* Ph.D. diss., State University of New York at Buffalo, 1977, pp. 186, 183.

15. René Girard, *Violence and the Sacred* (Baltimore: Johns Hopkins University Press, 1977).

16. For a detailed analysis of Girard's exemplary interpretive predicament, see Philippe Lacoue-Labarthe, "Typographie," in S. Agacinski et al., *Mimesis: Des articulations* (Paris: Flammarion, 1975), especially pp. 235–44.

17. See John Brenkman, "The Other and the One: Psychoanalysis, Reading, *The Symposium.*" *Yale French Studies* 55/56 (1977), especially pp. 438–43, for a lucid explanation of Lacan's concept of the signifier and of castration.

18. Gould, *Oedipus the King,* p. 63. Gould also points out that the messenger who recounts Oedipus's blinding speaks of his piercing of his ball-joints, arthra, in "an unparalleled use of this word." With this catachresis naming eyes as feet, Sophocles calls attention to Oedipus's completion of his first maiming (and naming). We are also brought to "see" the two acts as putative and deliberate castrations.

19. Jean-Pierre Vernant, "Ambiguity and Reversal: On the Enigmatic Structure of *Oedipus Rex,*" *New Literary History* 9 (1978):474.

20. See Jacques Derrida, "Fors," *The Georgia Review* 21:2 (1977).

21. Laplanche, *Life and Death,* p. 45.

22. "Nom-du-Père"; the concept is Lacan's. See *Ecrits* (Paris: Gallimard, 1966), p. 583.

23. Gould, *Oedipus the King,* p. 19.

24. In *Three Essays on the Theory of Sexuality,* in re-editions in 1910, 1915, 1920, and 1924–25, *Complete Psychological Works* 7:125–243. See Laplanche, *Life and Death,* chap. 1, especially pp. 18–22.

25. Cf. Shoshana Felman, "Turning the Screw," p. 200: "The fact that literature has no outside, that there is no safe spot assuredly outside of madness, from which one might demystify and judge it, locate it in the Other without oneself participating in it, was indeed ceaselessly affirmed by Freud in the most revealing moments of his text (and in spite of the constant opposite temptation— the mastery temptation—to which he at other times inevitably succumbed)."

26. Jacques Lacan, *Le Séminaire I: Les Ecrits techniques de Freud* (Paris: Seuil, 1975).

27. Freud, *Complete Psychological Works* 5:530. Retranslated by Samuel Weber, *The Legend of Freud* (Minneapolis: University of Minnesota Press, 1982), p. 75.

28. Weber, *The Legend of Freud,* p. 81.

29. Freud, *Complete Psychological Works,* 8:99–101, 144–45. Weber goes on to evoke a special case described by Freud, the bad joke in which the only joke is that there is no joke, and the expectation of the listener is thwarted. This is another instance of that marginal logic whereby the exception comes to appear more exemplary than the norm, for Freud's theory of jokes depends on his being able to refer to this joke of the joke. Weber is suggesting that Freud's text operates as a bad joke or no-joke of this kind. *The Legend of Freud,* pp. 108–15.

30. Green, *Un Oeil en trop,* p. 167n.

31. Laplanche, *Life and Death,* chap. 1.

32. Girard, *Violence and the Sacred,* p. 201.

33. Freud, *Totem and Taboo* (New York: Norton, 1950), p. 161. For a compelling interpretation of how event is constituted by structure in Freud's account of the primal patricide, see Jonathan Culler, *Ferdinand de Saussure* (New York: Penguin, 1977), pp. 78–79.

34. For a persuasive account of the logic of a certain kind of "secondary revision" in Freud's writing, see Jeffrey Mehlman's summary of Laplanche on anxiety in *Revolution and Repetition,* pp. 96–101. Laplanche identifies the "castration anxiety" version of the Oedipus complex as a phobic symptom predictable in terms of the earlier, "naive" theory of anxiety as "a free-floating form of affect" that Freud called a "poison."

35. Laplanche, *Life and Death,* p. 34.

36. Karl Rheinhardt, *Sophokles* (Frankfurt am Main: Klosterman, 1949), p. 127.

37. Freud is quoting the last lines of "Die beiden Gulden," Strachey's note tells us, which is "a version by Rückert of one of the Maqâmât of al-Hairiri," quoting "Die Schrift". *Beyond the Pleasure Principle, Complete Psychological Works* 18:64. Cf. Friedrich Rückert, *Die Verwandlungen des Abu Said von Serug oder die Makamen des Hariri,* in *Gesammelte Poetische Werke* (Frankfurt am Main: J. D. Sauerländer, 1869) 11: 239.

Chapter 9 Paragon, Parergon

1. Charles Baudelaire, "De l'essence du rire et généralement du comique dans les arts plastiques," in *Oeuvres complètes* (Paris: Gallimard, 1961), pp. 975–93; first published in 1855. "Morale du joujou" was first published in 1853. Baudelaire transformed pars. 12 through 14 of this essay into a prose poem *Le joujou du pauvre* (19 in *Le Spleen de Paris*), first published in 1862.
2. Baudelaire, *Le joujou du pauvre*, in *Oeuvres complètes*, p. 255.
3. Walter Benjamin, "Die Aufgabe des Übersetzers,' in *Gesammelte Schriften* 4:1 (Frankfurt am Main: Suhrkamp, 1972): pp. 7–21. Benjamin wrote this essay as an introduction to his translation of *Les Fleurs du Mal*. Paul de Man, introduction to Hans Robert Jauss, *Toward an Aesthetic of Reception* (Minneapolis: University of Minnesota Press, 1982), p. xvi.
4. Philip Lewis, "Vers la traduction abusive," in *Les Fins de l'homme: A partir du travail de Jacques Derrida* (Paris: Galilée, 1981), pp. 253–61.
5. Ibid., pp. 255–56.
6. Michael Riffaterre, *Semiotics of Poetry* (Bloomington: Indiana University Press, 1978), p. 86.
7. See *Les Rêveries du promeneur solitaire*, in *Oeuvres complètes de Jean-Jacques Rousseau*, ed. Bernard Gagnebin and Marcel Raymond, (Paris: Gallimard, 1959), 1:1090–91.
8. Rousseau, *Essai sur l'origine des langues* (Bordeaux: Ducros, 1970), pp. 45–47. Cf. de Man, *Allegories of Reading* (New Haven: Yale University Press, 1979), pp. 149–155.
9. Rousseau, *Oeuvres complètes* 1:1085.
10. Ibid., 1:1094.
11. Immanuel Kant, *Kritik der Urteilskraft* (Frankfurt am Main: Suhrkamp, 1979), p. 248.
12. *Kant's Critique of Judgement*, trans. J. H. Bernard (London: Macmillan, 1931), p. 195.
13. Jacques Derrida, "Economimesis," in S. Agacinski et al., *Mimesis: Des articulations* (Paris: Flammarion, 1975), p. 91.
14. Rousseau, *Oeuvres complètes* 1:1091.
15. Kant, *Kritik der Urteilskraft*, pp. 149–54.
16. *Kant's Critique of Judgement*, Bernard, p. 2.
17. Ibid., p. 4.
18. On the frame as frame-up, see also Barbara Johnson, "The Frame of Reference: Poe, Lacan, Derrida," in *The Critical Difference: Essays in the Contemporary Rhetoric of Reading* (Baltimore: Johns Hopkins University Press, 1980), particularly pt. 4, pp. 126–38, which opens with the following epigraph (from Mallarmé's *Sonnet en x*):

> Elle, défunte *nue* en le miroir, encor
> Que, *dans l'oubli fermé par le cadre,* se fixe
> De scintillations sitôt le septuor.

(Johnson's italics)

Johnson's essay detects the framing of Lacan in Derrida's reading of Lacan's reading of Poe, in "Le facteur de la vérité," *La Carte postale: De Socrate à Freud et au-delà* (Paris: Flammarion, 1980).

19. Derrida, *La Vérité en peinture* (Paris: Flammarion, 1978), pp. 66–89.

20. Ibid., p. 101.

21. Idem.

22. Baudelaire, *Oeuvres complètes,* p. 525.

23. Rousseau, *Oeuvres complètes,* 1:1091.

24. Derrida, "Economimesis," pp. 91, 93.

25. Riffaterre, *Semiotics of Poetry,* p. 91.

26. Baudelaire, *Oeuvres complètes,* p. 527.

27. Derrida, "Economimesis," p. 93.

28. Walter Benjamin writes at the end of "Die Aufgabe des Übersetzers" ("The Task of the Translator") of the sense in which the text is *schlechthin übersetzbar*—utterly translatable—in such a way that it radically endangers the translator. Benjamin's suggestion that such translatability is intolerable is reinforced in Maurice de Gandillac's translation of this essay (in *Mythe et violence,* Paris: Denoel, 1971) by a revealing mistranslation, or felicitous *coquille,* noticed by Irving Wohlfarth in a seminar of Derrida's that was using both the French and the German texts of Benjamin's essay: for *schlechthin übersetzbar,* the French reads "purement et simplement *in*traduisible."

Index

Works are indexed under their authors.

The Johns Hopkins University Press

Decomposing Figures

This book was set in Aldine text and Bembo display type by
A. W. Bennett, Inc., from a design by Ann Walston. It was printed
on 50-lb. Sebago Eggshell Cream paper and bound in GSB cloth
by BookCrafters.